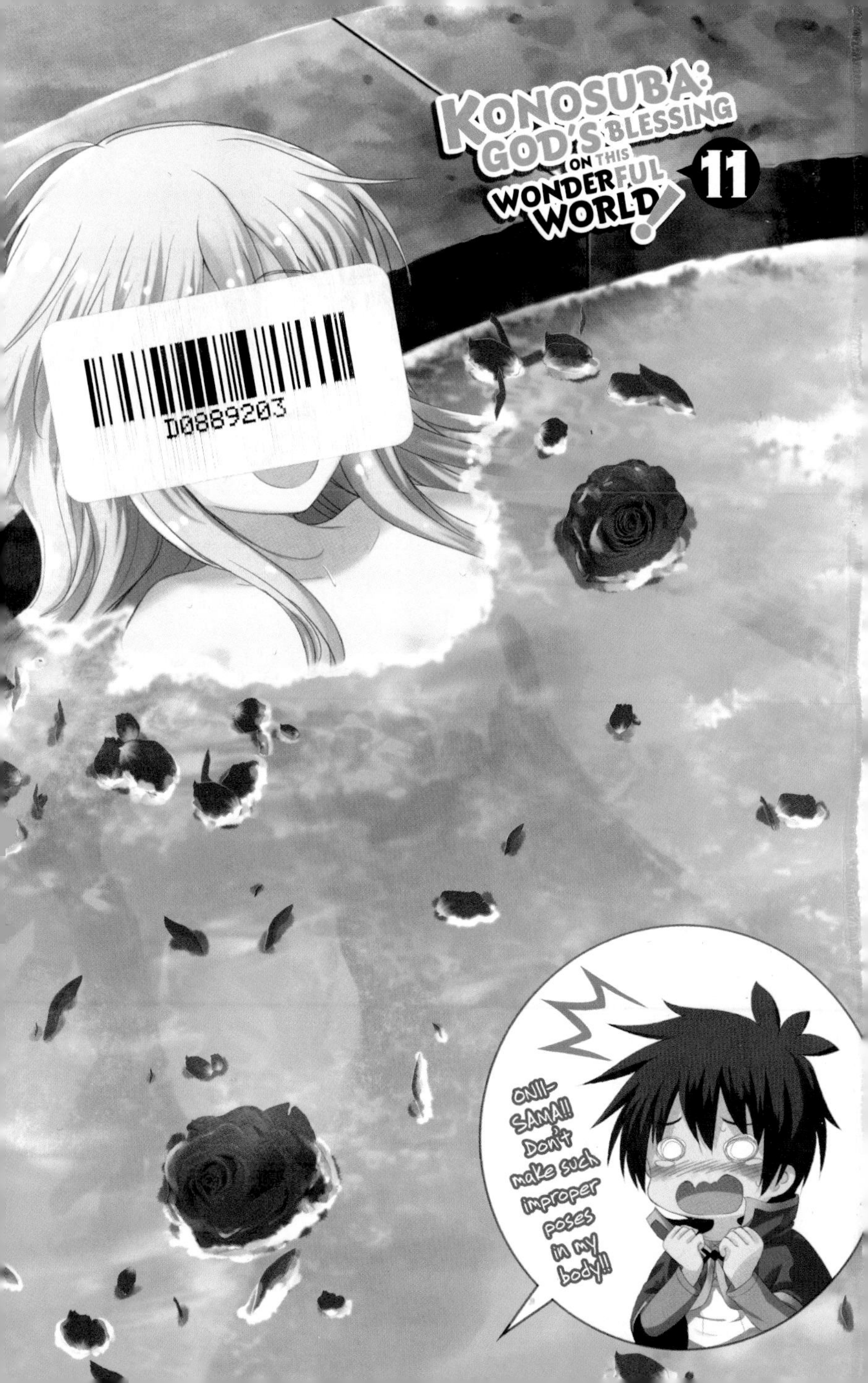
KONOSUBA: GOD'S BLESSING ON THIS WONDERFUL WORLD!
11
ONII-SAMA!! Don't make such improper poses in my body!!

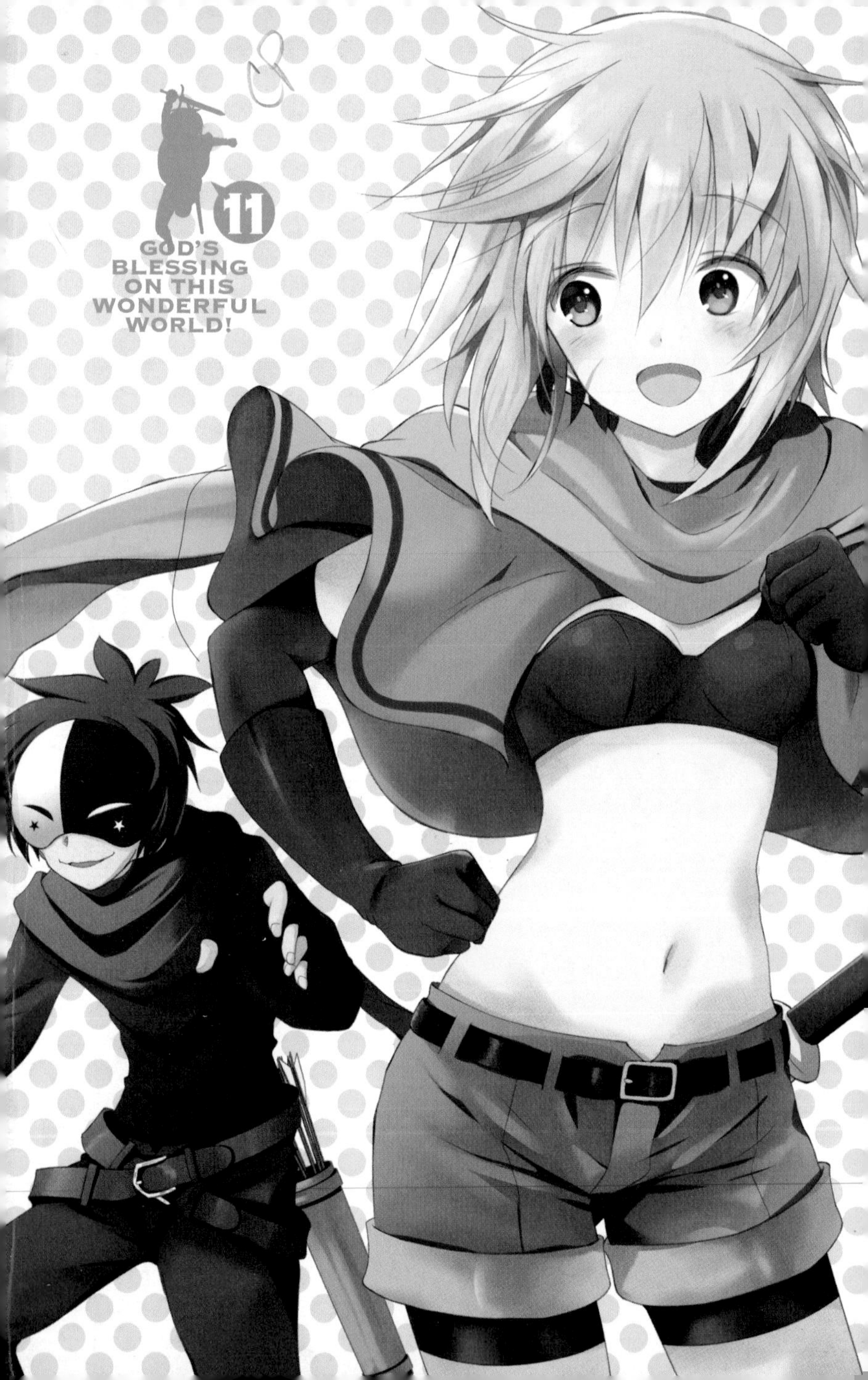
11
GOD'S BLESSING ON THIS WONDERFUL WORLD!

11

KONOSUBA:
GOD'S BLESSING ON THIS WONDERFUL WORLD!

 ART **Masahito Watari**

Natsume Akatsuki

Kurone Mishima

GOD'S BLESSING ON THIS WONDERFUL WORLD!
CONTENTS

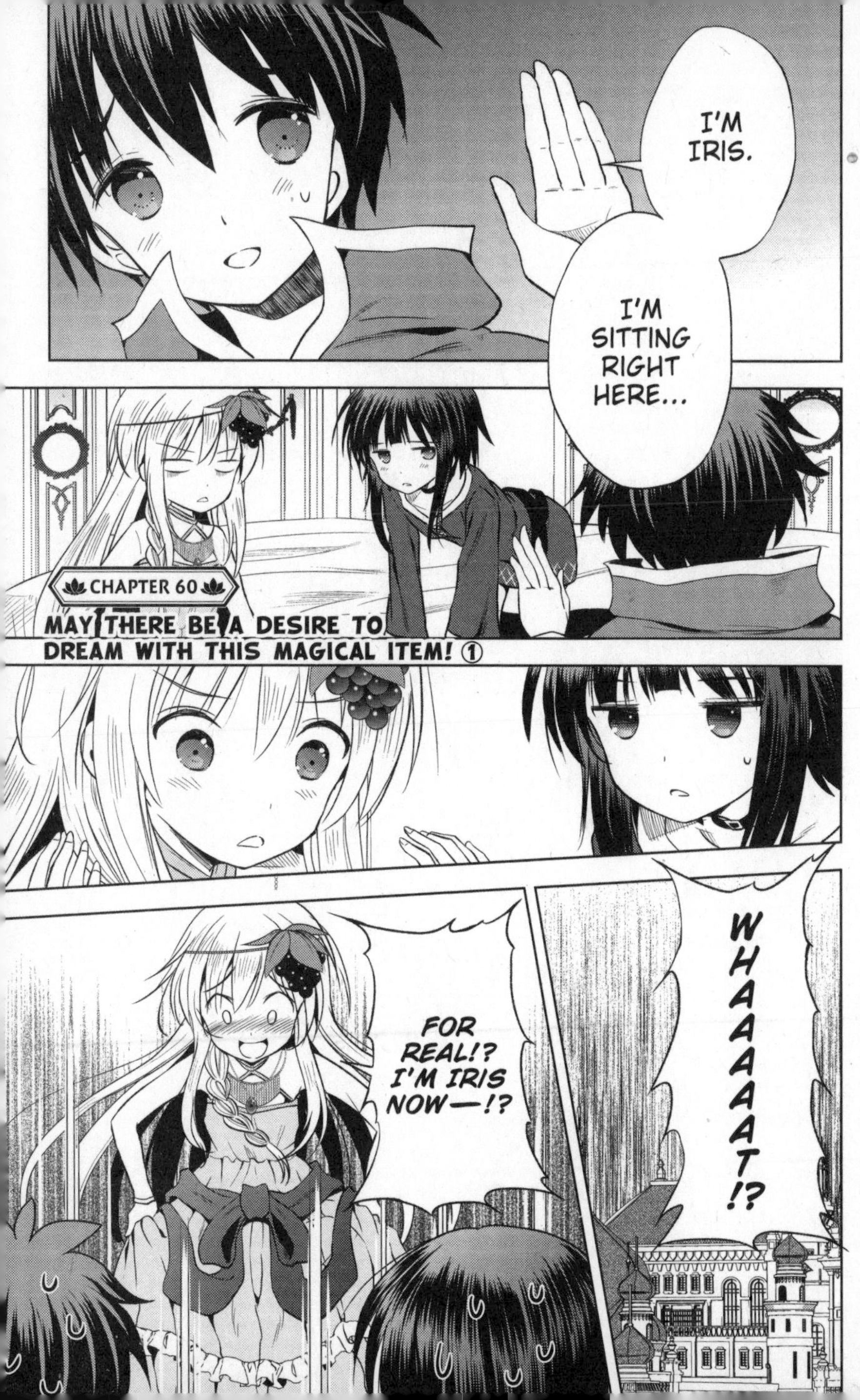
I'M IRIS.
I'M SITTING RIGHT HERE...
CHAPTER 60
MAY THERE BE A DESIRE TO DREAM WITH THIS MAGICAL ITEM! ①
WHAAAAAAT!?
FOR REAL!? I'M IRIS NOW—!?

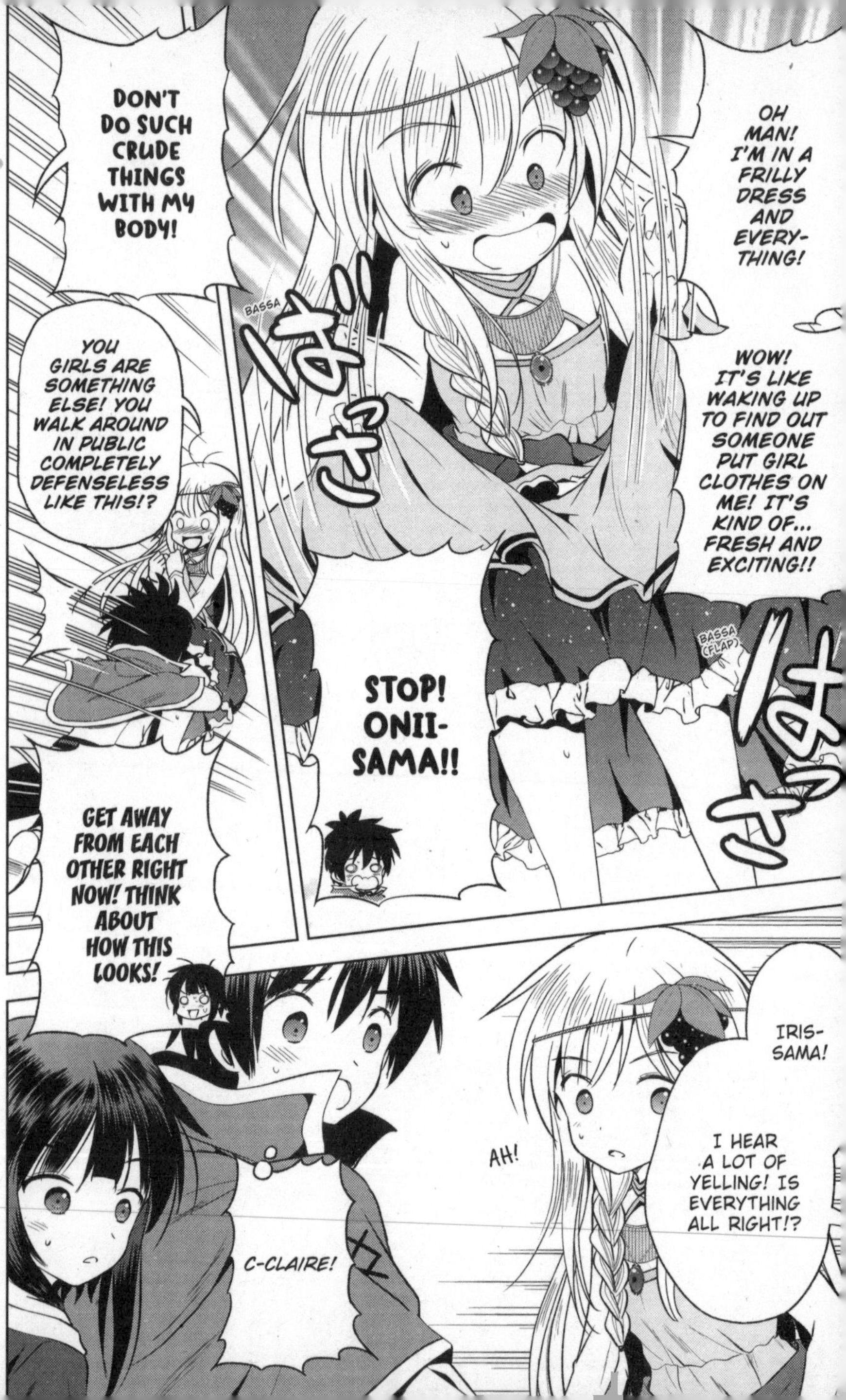
OH MAN! I'M IN A FRILLY DRESS AND EVERY-THING!
WOW! IT'S LIKE WAKING UP TO FIND OUT SOMEONE PUT GIRL CLOTHES ON ME! IT'S KIND OF... FRESH AND EXCITING!!
BASSA (FLAP)
BASSA
STOP! ONII-SAMA!!
DON'T DO SUCH CRUDE THINGS WITH MY BODY!
YOU GIRLS ARE SOMETHING ELSE! YOU WALK AROUND IN PUBLIC COMPLETELY DEFENSELESS LIKE THIS!?
GET AWAY FROM EACH OTHER RIGHT NOW! THINK ABOUT HOW THIS LOOKS!
IRIS-SAMA!
I HEAR A LOT OF YELLING! IS EVERYTHING ALL RIGHT!?
AH!
C-CLAIRE!

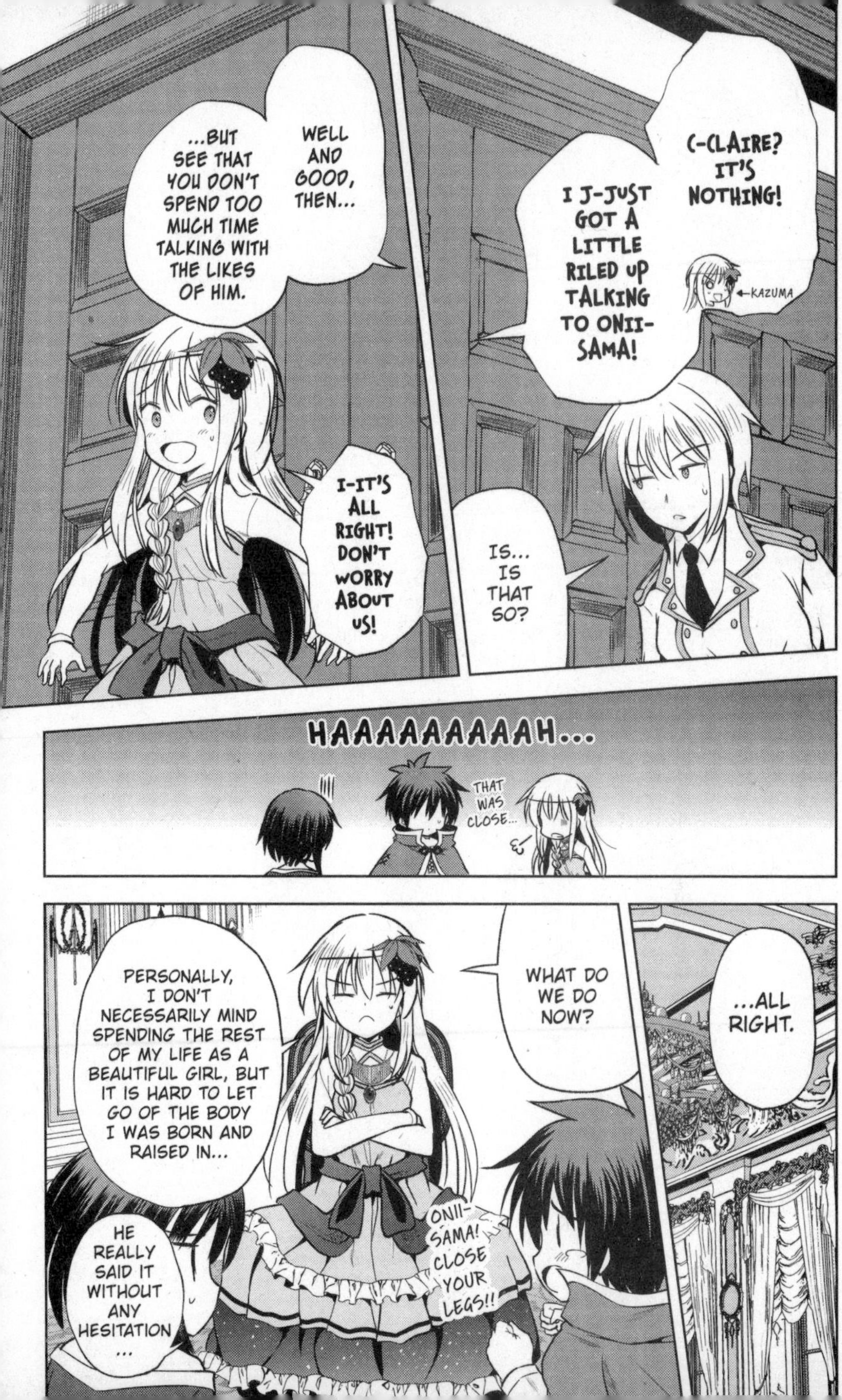
C-CLAIRE? IT'S NOTHING!
I J-JUST GOT A LITTLE RILED UP TALKING TO ONII-SAMA!
←KAZUMA
IS... IS THAT SO?
WELL AND GOOD, THEN...
...BUT SEE THAT YOU DON'T SPEND TOO MUCH TIME TALKING WITH THE LIKES OF HIM.
I-IT'S ALL RIGHT! DON'T WORRY ABOUT US!
HAAAAAAAAAH...
THAT WAS CLOSE...
...ALL RIGHT.
WHAT DO WE DO NOW?
PERSONALLY, I DON'T NECESSARILY MIND SPENDING THE REST OF MY LIFE AS A BEAUTIFUL GIRL, BUT IT IS HARD TO LET GO OF THE BODY I WAS BORN AND RAISED IN...
ONII-SAMA! CLOSE YOUR LEGS!!
HE REALLY SAID IT WITHOUT ANY HESITATION ...

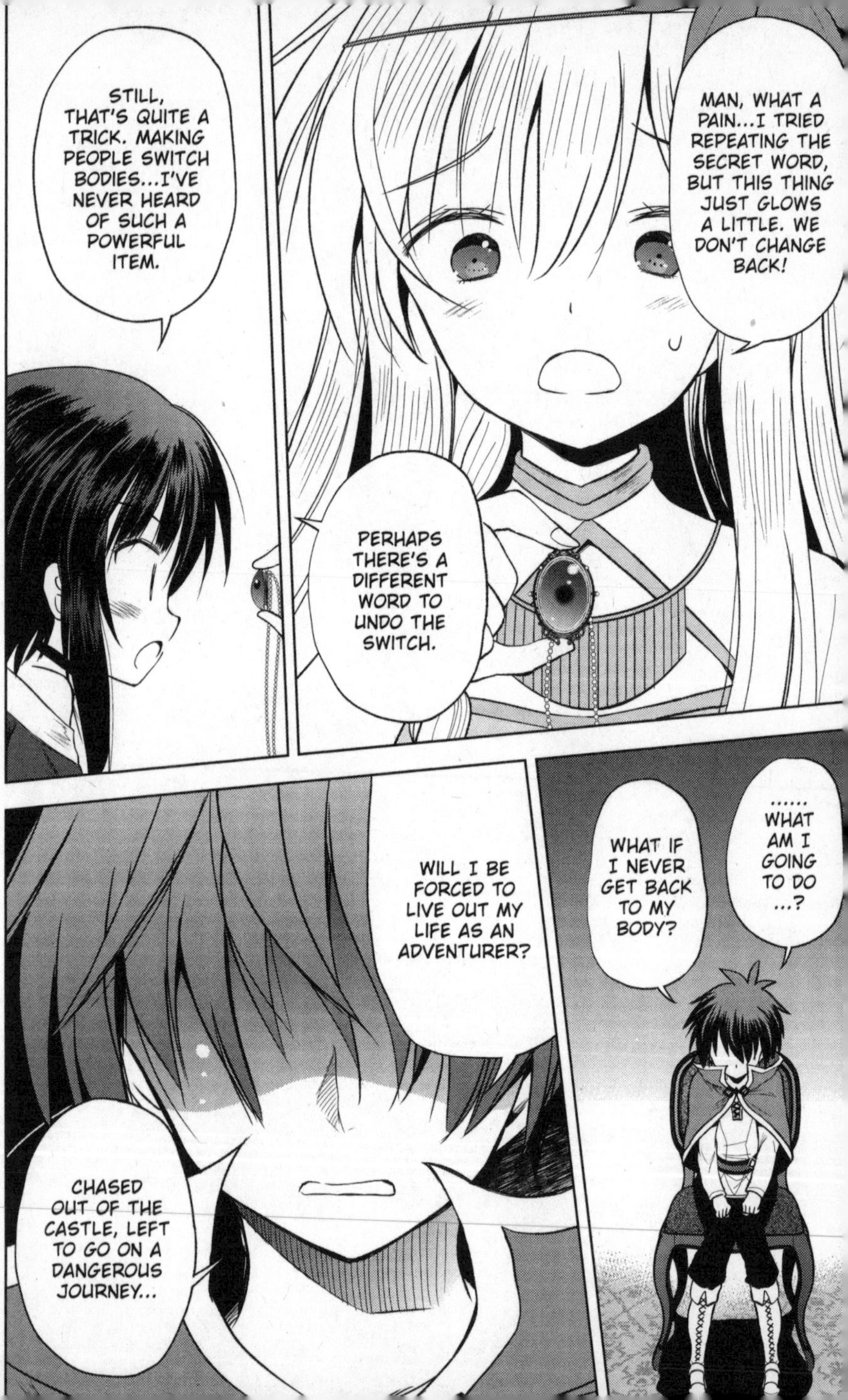
MAN, WHAT A PAIN...I TRIED REPEATING THE SECRET WORD, BUT THIS THING JUST GLOWS A LITTLE. WE DON'T CHANGE BACK!
PERHAPS THERE'S A DIFFERENT WORD TO UNDO THE SWITCH.
STILL, THAT'S QUITE A TRICK. MAKING PEOPLE SWITCH BODIES...I'VE NEVER HEARD OF SUCH A POWERFUL ITEM.
......WHAT AM I GOING TO DO ...?
WHAT IF I NEVER GET BACK TO MY BODY?
WILL I BE FORCED TO LIVE OUT MY LIFE AS AN ADVENTURER?
CHASED OUT OF THE CASTLE, LEFT TO GO ON A DANGEROUS JOURNEY...

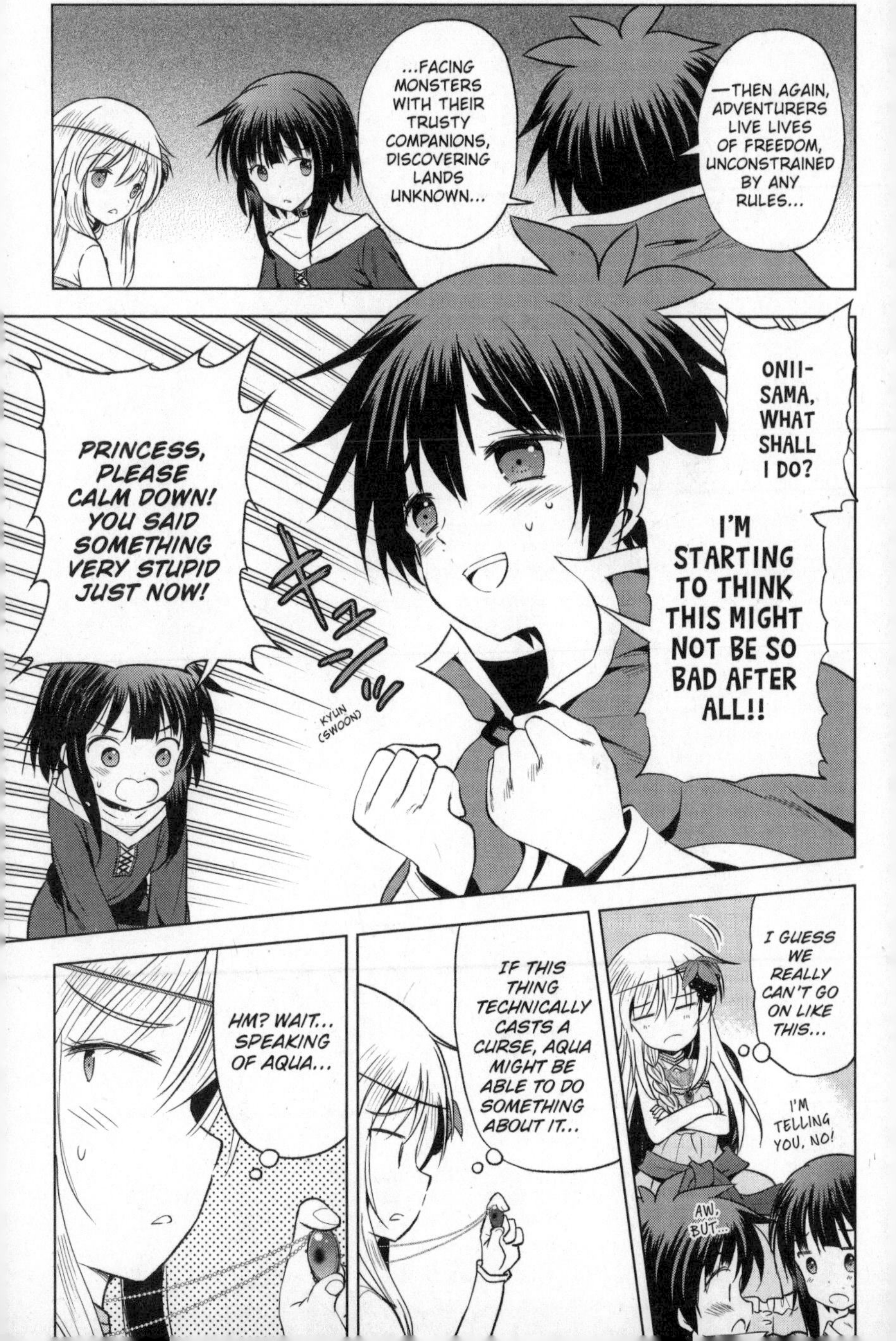
—THEN AGAIN, ADVENTURERS LIVE LIVES OF FREEDOM, UNCONSTRAINED BY ANY RULES...
...FACING MONSTERS WITH THEIR TRUSTY COMPANIONS, DISCOVERING LANDS UNKNOWN...
ONII-SAMA, WHAT SHALL I DO?
I'M STARTING TO THINK THIS MIGHT NOT BE SO BAD AFTER ALL!!
キューンッ
KYUN (SWOON)
PRINCESS, PLEASE CALM DOWN! YOU SAID SOMETHING VERY STUPID JUST NOW!
I GUESS WE REALLY CAN'T GO ON LIKE THIS...
I'M TELLING YOU, NO!
AW, BUT...
IF THIS THING TECHNICALLY CASTS A CURSE, AQUA MIGHT BE ABLE TO DO SOMETHING ABOUT IT...
HM? WAIT... SPEAKING OF AQUA...

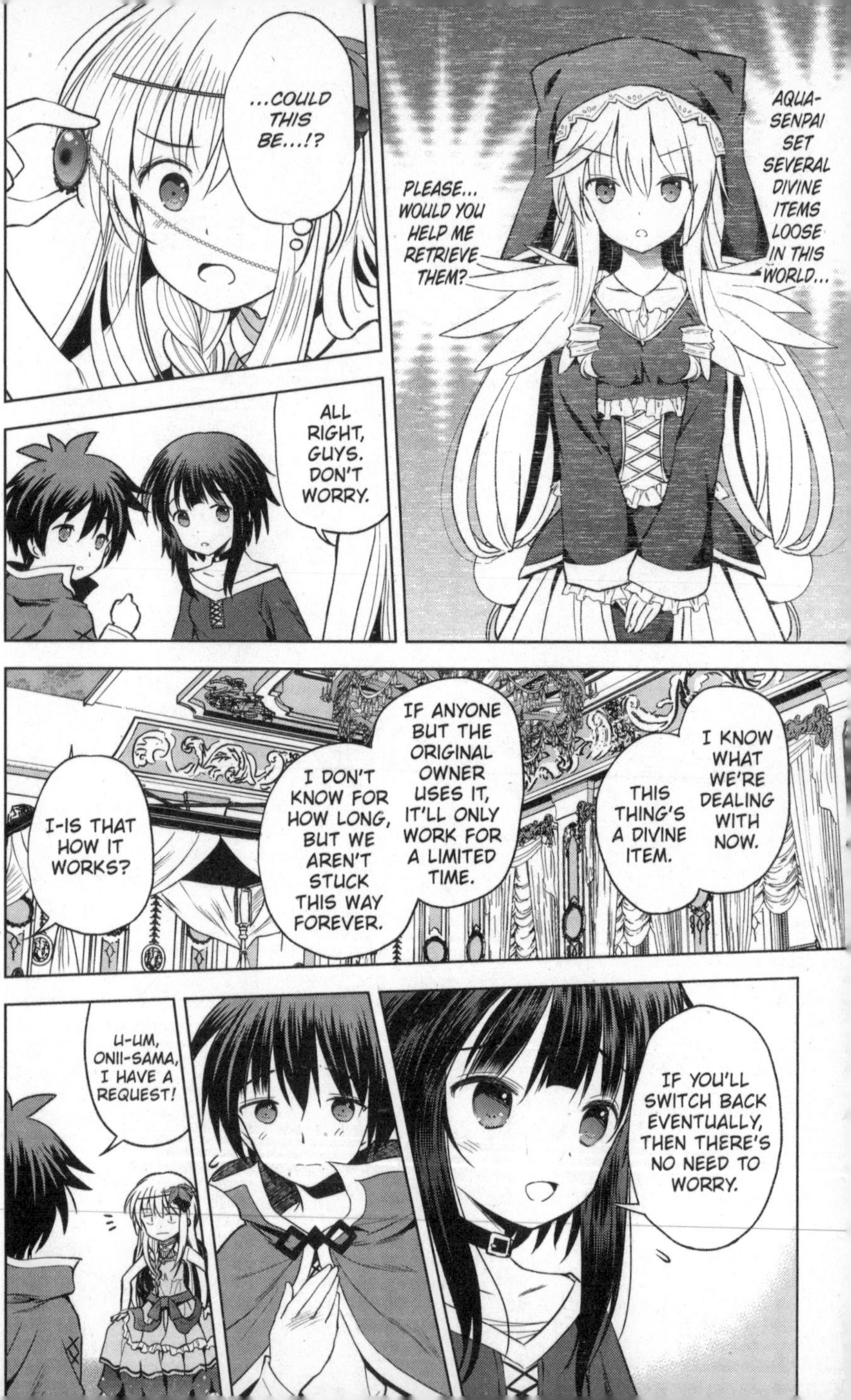
AQUA-SENPAI SET SEVERAL DIVINE ITEMS LOOSE IN THIS WORLD...
PLEASE... WOULD YOU HELP ME RETRIEVE THEM?
...COULD THIS BE...!?
ALL RIGHT, GUYS. DON'T WORRY.
I KNOW WHAT WE'RE DEALING WITH NOW.
THIS THING'S A DIVINE ITEM.
IF ANYONE BUT THE ORIGINAL OWNER USES IT, IT'LL ONLY WORK FOR A LIMITED TIME.
I DON'T KNOW FOR HOW LONG, BUT WE AREN'T STUCK THIS WAY FOREVER.
I-IS THAT HOW IT WORKS?
IF YOU'LL SWITCH BACK EVENTUALLY, THEN THERE'S NO NEED TO WORRY.
U-UM, ONII-SAMA, I HAVE A REQUEST!

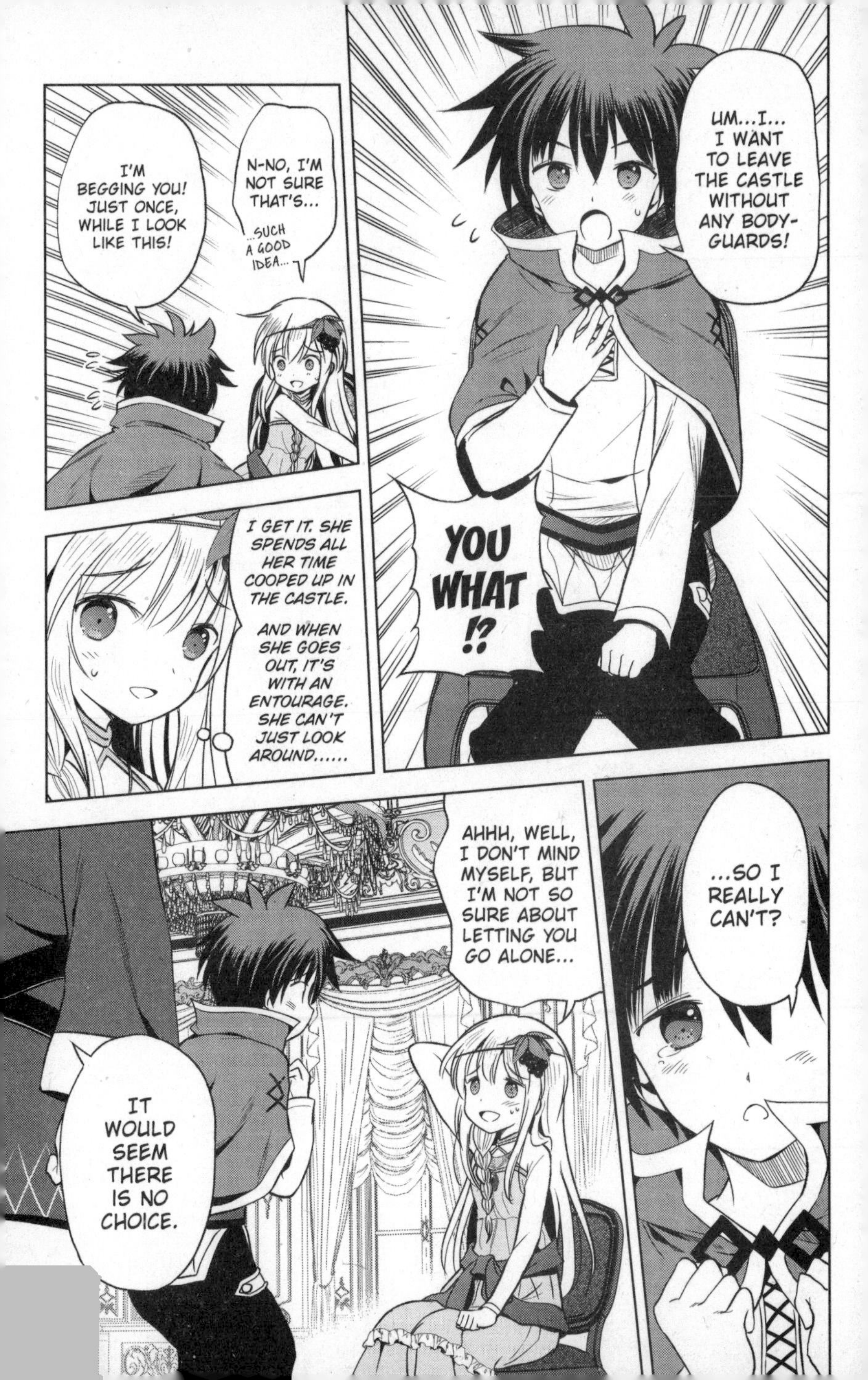
UM...I... I WANT TO LEAVE THE CASTLE WITHOUT ANY BODY-GUARDS!
YOU WHAT!?
N-NO, I'M NOT SURE THAT'S...
...SUCH A GOOD IDEA...
I'M BEGGING YOU! JUST ONCE, WHILE I LOOK LIKE THIS!
I GET IT. SHE SPENDS ALL HER TIME COOPED UP IN THE CASTLE.
AND WHEN SHE GOES OUT, IT'S WITH AN ENTOURAGE. SHE CAN'T JUST LOOK AROUND......
...SO I REALLY CAN'T?
AHHH, WELL, I DON'T MIND MYSELF, BUT I'M NOT SO SURE ABOUT LETTING YOU GO ALONE...
IT WOULD SEEM THERE IS NO CHOICE.

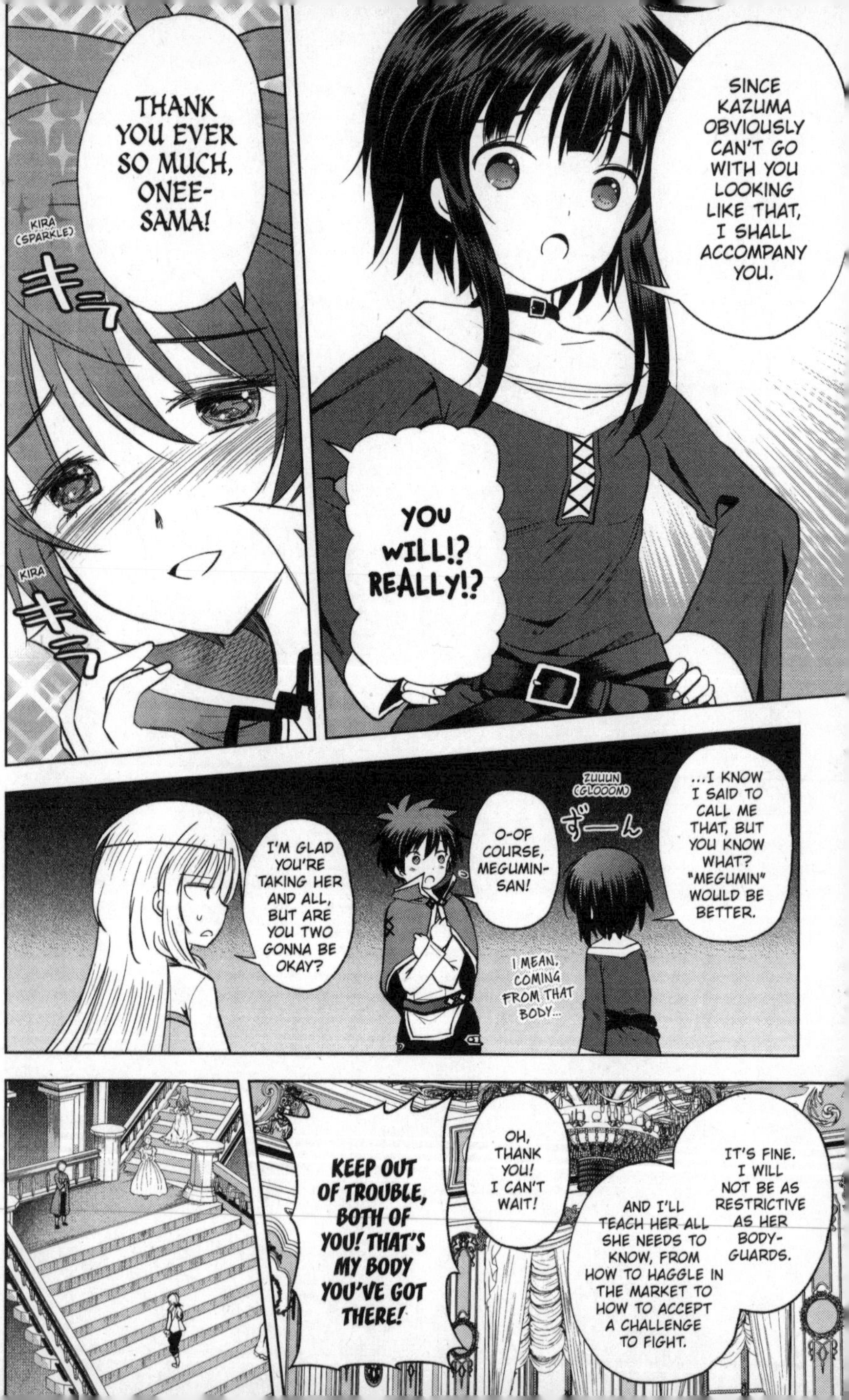
SINCE KAZUMA OBVIOUSLY CAN'T GO WITH YOU LOOKING LIKE THAT, I SHALL ACCOMPANY YOU.
YOU WILL!? REALLY!?
THANK YOU EVER SO MUCH, ONEE-SAMA!
KIRA (SPARKLE)
キラ
KIRA
キラ
...I KNOW I SAID TO CALL ME THAT, BUT YOU KNOW WHAT? "MEGUMIN" WOULD BE BETTER.
ZUUUN (GLOOOM)
ずーん
O-OF COURSE, MEGUMIN-SAN!
I MEAN, COMING FROM THAT BODY...
I'M GLAD YOU'RE TAKING HER AND ALL, BUT ARE YOU TWO GONNA BE OKAY?
IT'S FINE. I WILL NOT BE AS RESTRICTIVE AS HER BODY-GUARDS.
AND I'LL TEACH HER ALL SHE NEEDS TO KNOW, FROM HOW TO HAGGLE IN THE MARKET TO HOW TO ACCEPT A CHALLENGE TO FIGHT.
OH, THANK YOU! I CAN'T WAIT!
KEEP OUT OF TROUBLE, BOTH OF YOU! THAT'S MY BODY YOU'VE GOT THERE!

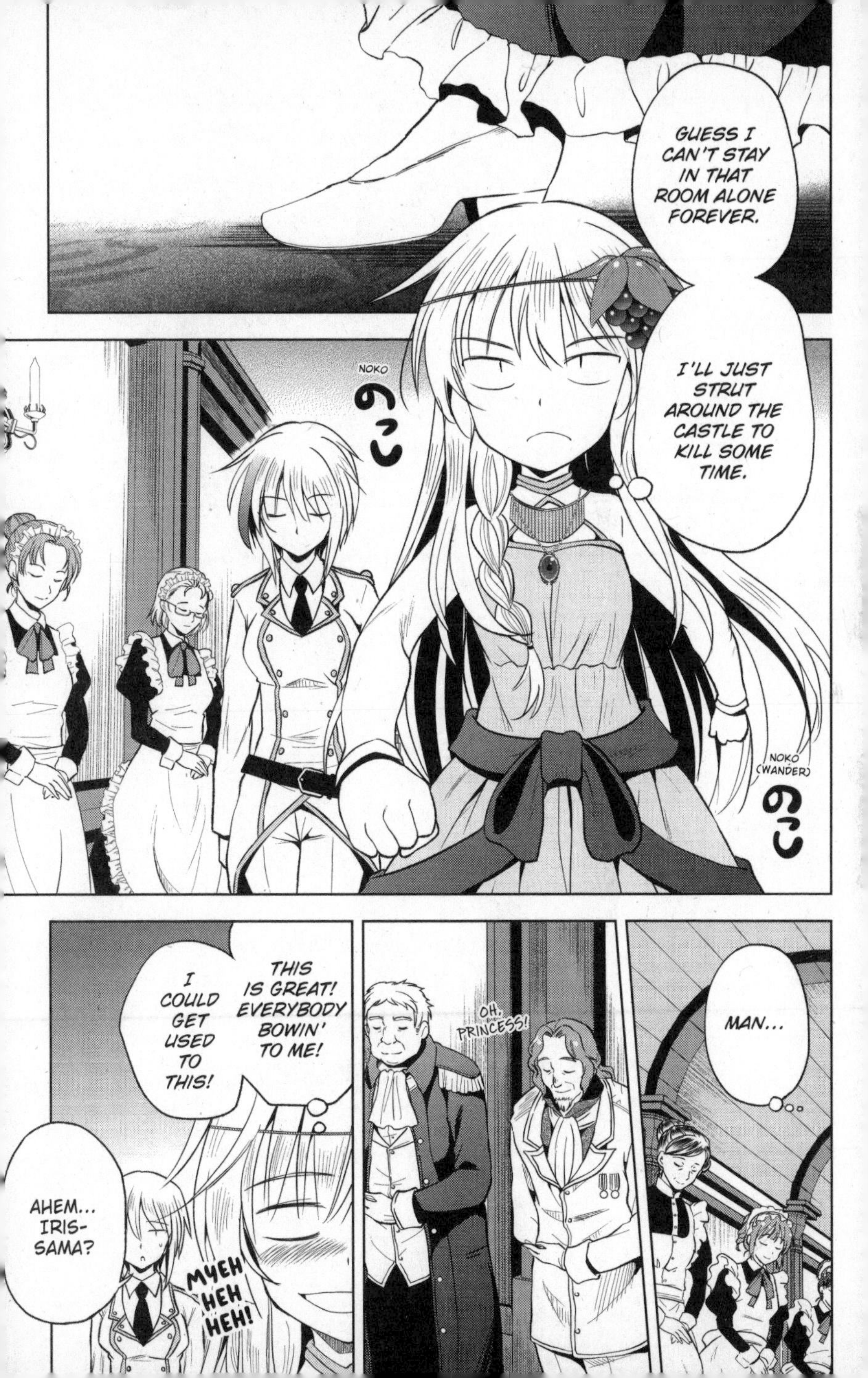
GUESS I CAN'T STAY IN THAT ROOM ALONE FOREVER.
I'LL JUST STRUT AROUND THE CASTLE TO KILL SOME TIME.
NOKO
のこ
NOKO (WANDER)
のこ
MAN...
OH, PRINCESS!
THIS IS GREAT! EVERYBODY BOWIN' TO ME!
I COULD GET USED TO THIS!
AHEM... IRIS-SAMA?
MYEH HEH HEH!

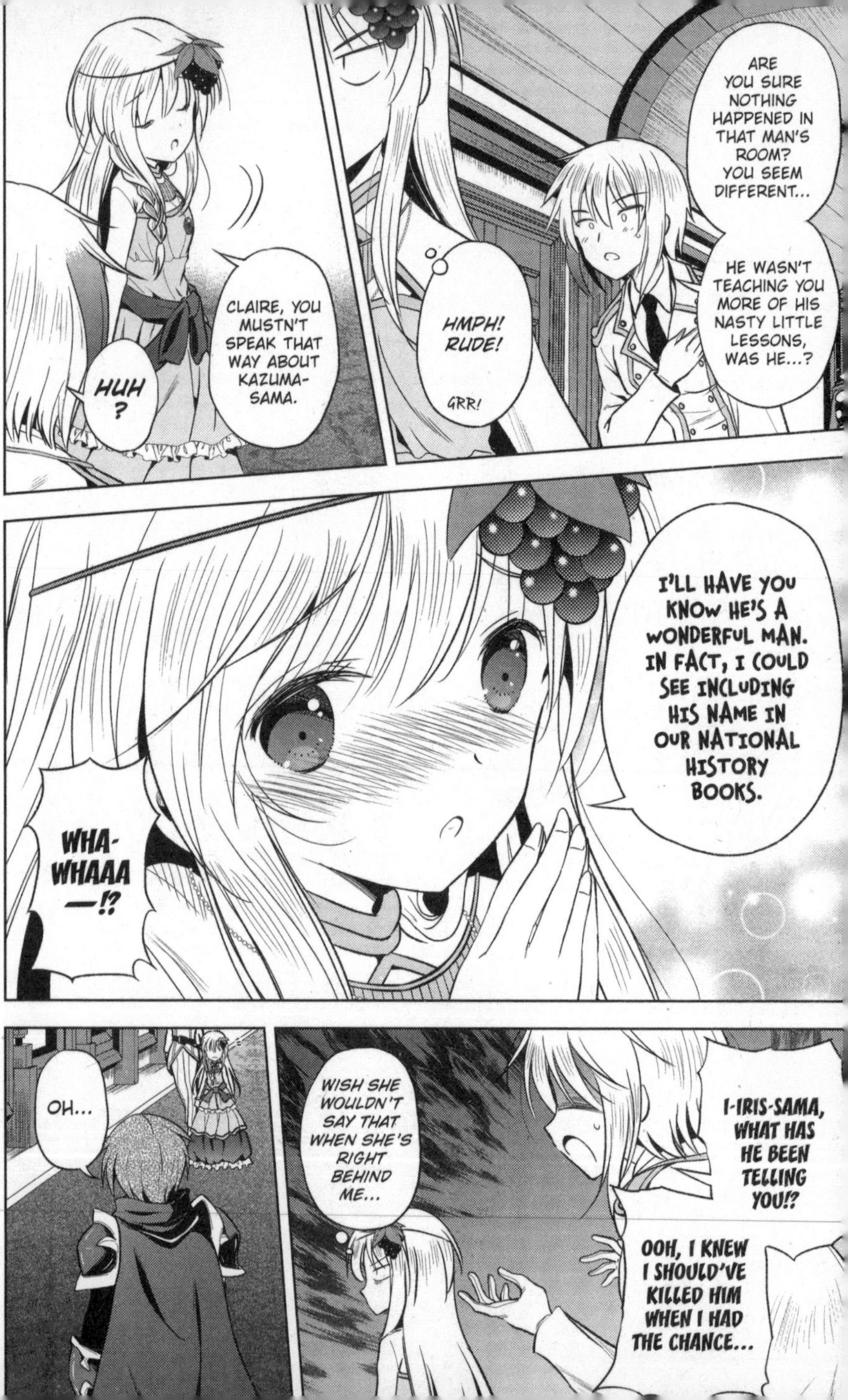
ARE YOU SURE NOTHING HAPPENED IN THAT MAN'S ROOM? YOU SEEM DIFFERENT...
HE WASN'T TEACHING YOU MORE OF HIS NASTY LITTLE LESSONS, WAS HE...?
HMPH! RUDE!
GRR!
CLAIRE, YOU MUSTN'T SPEAK THAT WAY ABOUT KAZUMA-SAMA.
HUH?
I'LL HAVE YOU KNOW HE'S A WONDERFUL MAN. IN FACT, I COULD SEE INCLUDING HIS NAME IN OUR NATIONAL HISTORY BOOKS.
WHA-WHAAA—!?
I-IRIS-SAMA, WHAT HAS HE BEEN TELLING YOU!?
OOH, I KNEW I SHOULD'VE KILLED HIM WHEN I HAD THE CHANCE...
WISH SHE WOULDN'T SAY THAT WHEN SHE'S RIGHT BEHIND ME...
OH...

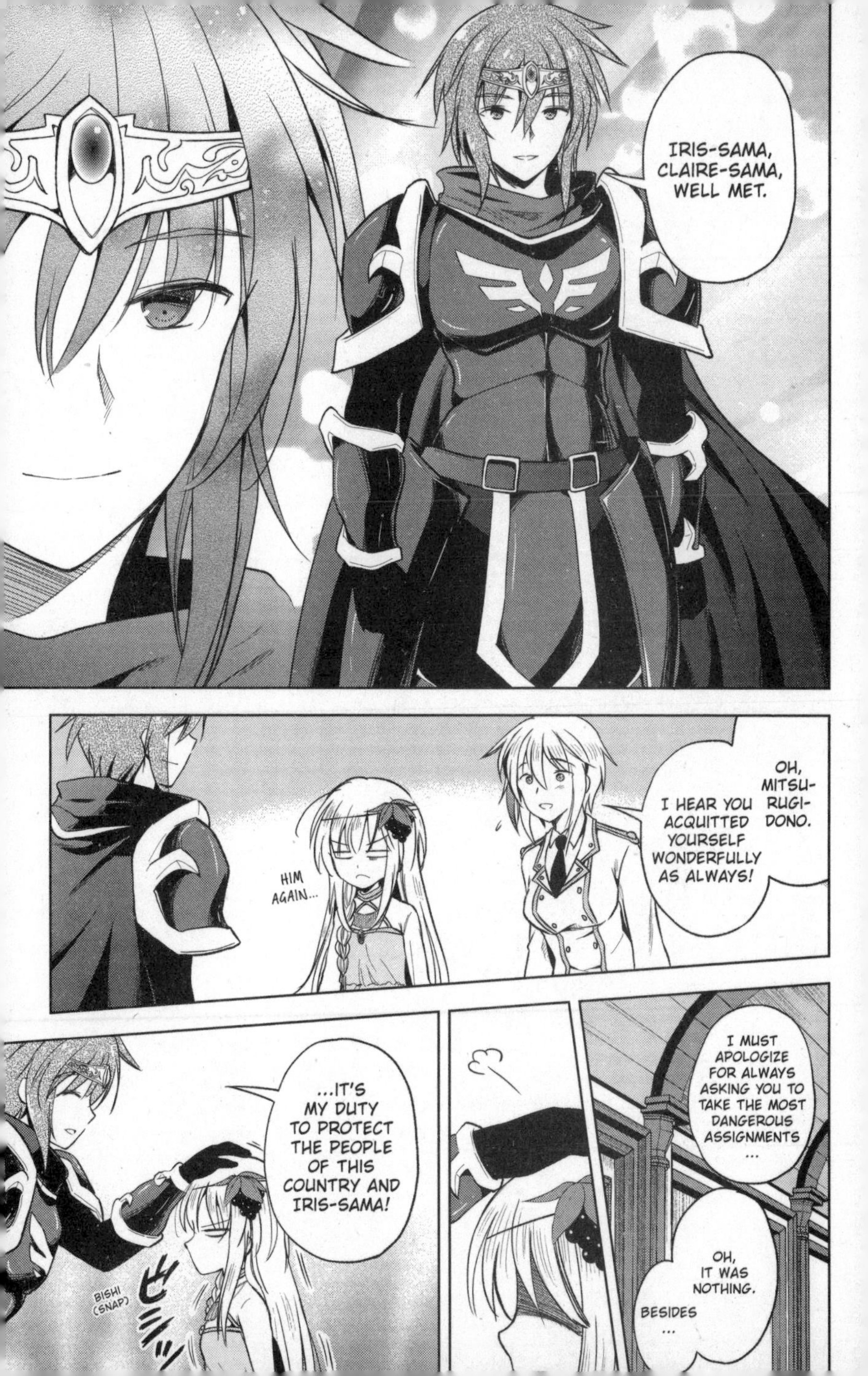
IRIS-SAMA, CLAIRE-SAMA, WELL MET.
OH, MITSURUGI-DONO.
I HEAR YOU ACQUITTED YOURSELF WONDERFULLY AS ALWAYS!
HIM AGAIN...
I MUST APOLOGIZE FOR ALWAYS ASKING YOU TO TAKE THE MOST DANGEROUS ASSIGNMENTS ...
OH, IT WAS NOTHING.
BESIDES ...
...IT'S MY DUTY TO PROTECT THE PEOPLE OF THIS COUNTRY AND IRIS-SAMA!
BISHI (SNAP)

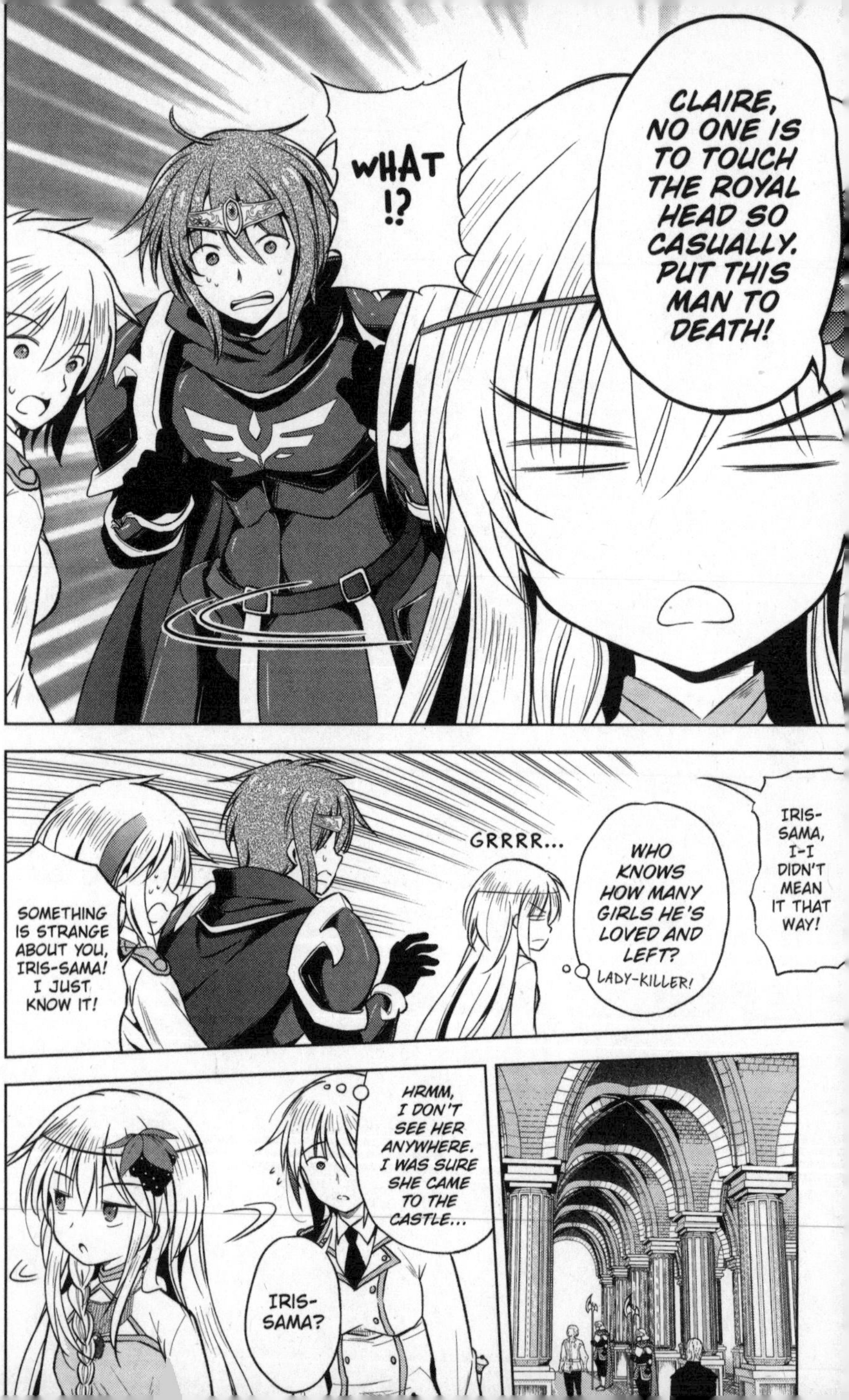
CLAIRE, NO ONE IS TO TOUCH THE ROYAL HEAD SO CASUALLY. PUT THIS MAN TO DEATH!
WHAT !?
IRIS-SAMA, I-I DIDN'T MEAN IT THAT WAY!
WHO KNOWS HOW MANY GIRLS HE'S LOVED AND LEFT?
LADY-KILLER!
GRRRR...
SOMETHING IS STRANGE ABOUT YOU, IRIS-SAMA! I JUST KNOW IT!
HRMM, I DON'T SEE HER ANYWHERE. I WAS SURE SHE CAME TO THE CASTLE...
IRIS-SAMA?

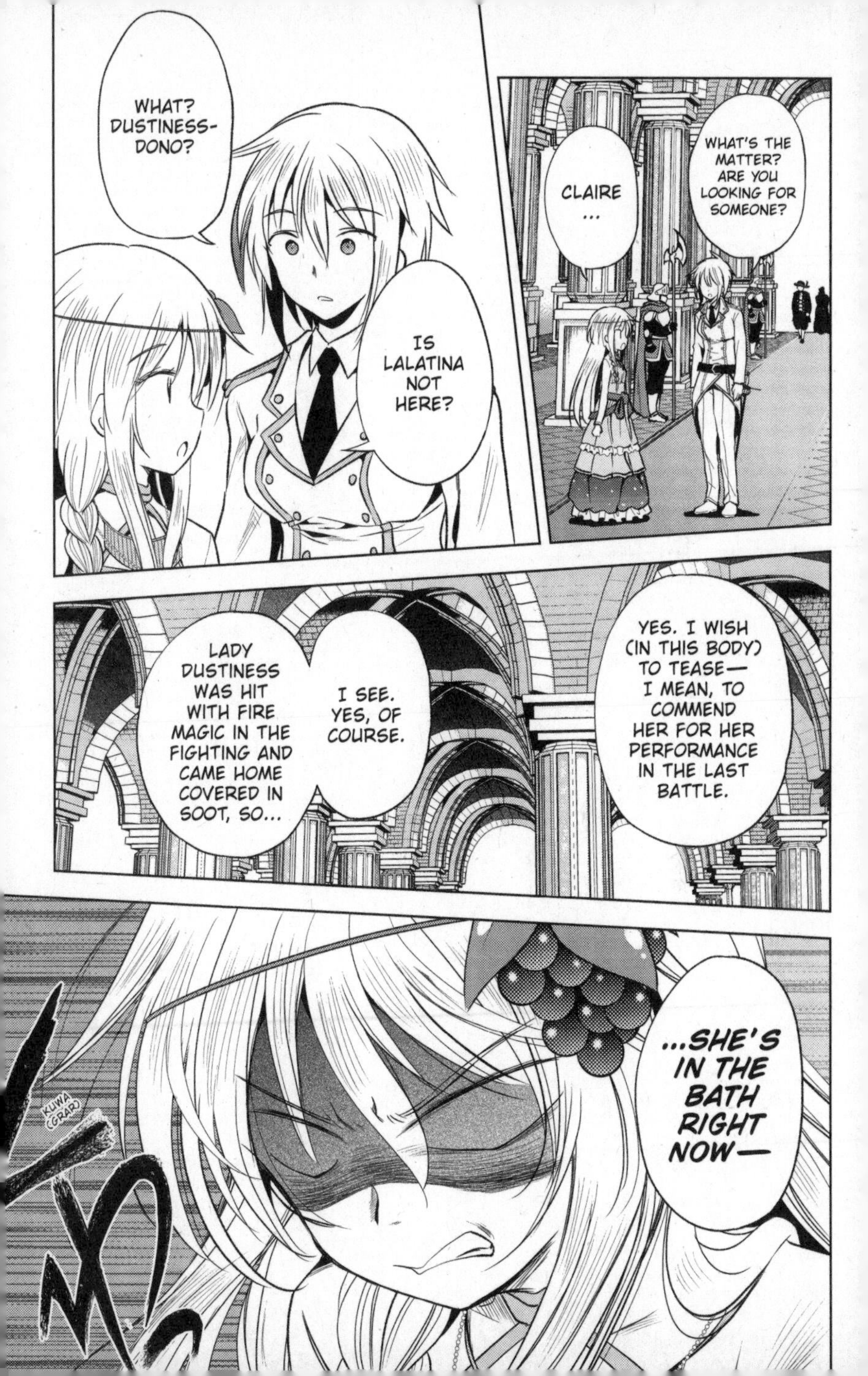
WHAT'S THE MATTER? ARE YOU LOOKING FOR SOMEONE?
CLAIRE ...
IS LALATINA NOT HERE?
WHAT? DUSTINESS-DONO?
YES. I WISH (IN THIS BODY) TO TEASE— I MEAN, TO COMMEND HER FOR HER PERFORMANCE IN THE LAST BATTLE.
LADY DUSTINESS WAS HIT WITH FIRE MAGIC IN THE FIGHTING AND CAME HOME COVERED IN SOOT, SO...
I SEE. YES, OF COURSE.
...SHE'S IN THE BATH RIGHT NOW—
KUWA (GRAR)

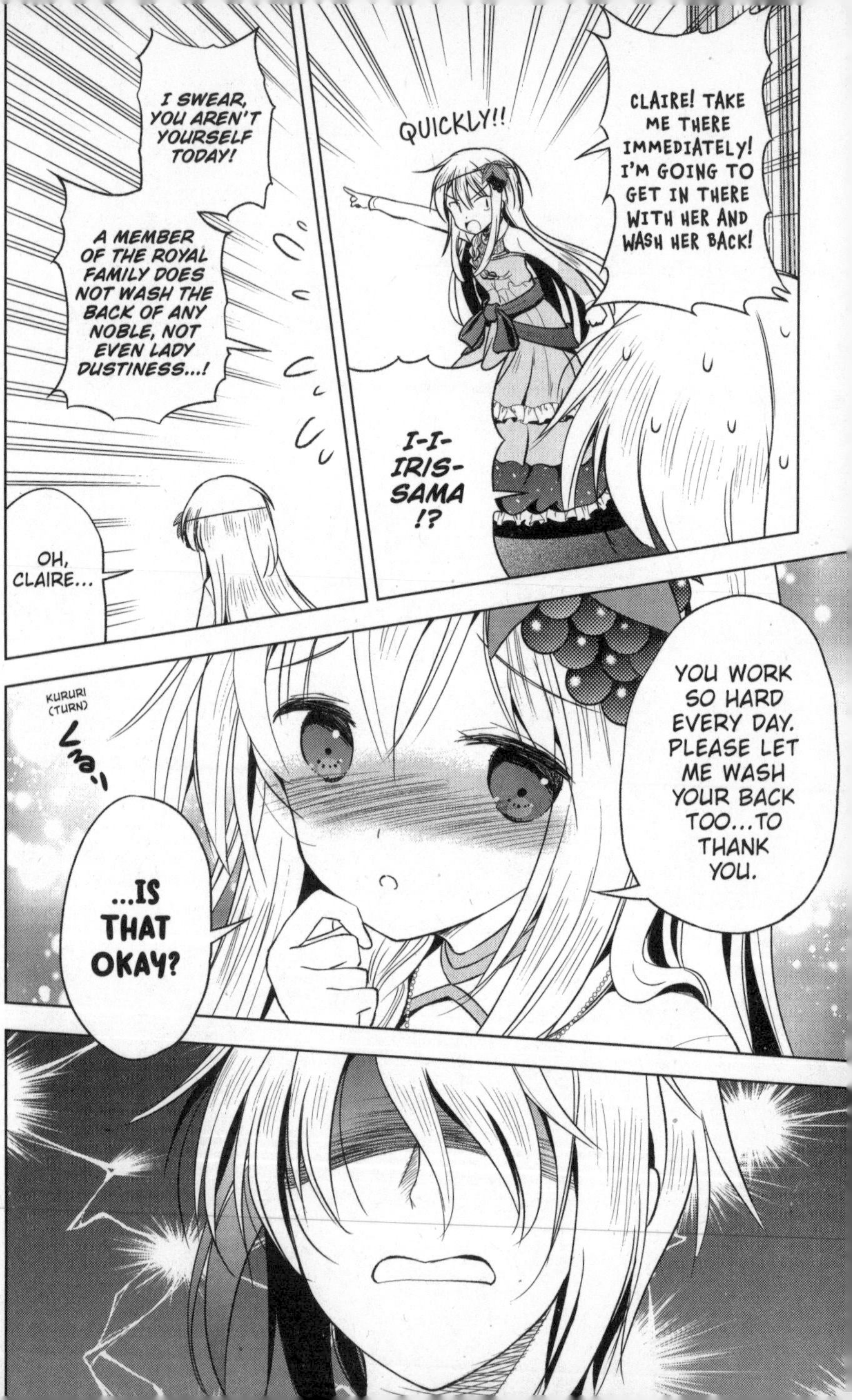
CLAIRE! TAKE ME THERE IMMEDIATELY! I'M GOING TO GET IN THERE WITH HER AND WASH HER BACK!
QUICKLY!!
I-I-IRIS-SAMA!?
I SWEAR, YOU AREN'T YOURSELF TODAY!
A MEMBER OF THE ROYAL FAMILY DOES NOT WASH THE BACK OF ANY NOBLE, NOT EVEN LADY DUSTINESS...!
OH, CLAIRE...
YOU WORK SO HARD EVERY DAY. PLEASE LET ME WASH YOUR BACK TOO...TO THANK YOU.
KURURI (TURN)
...IS THAT OKAY?

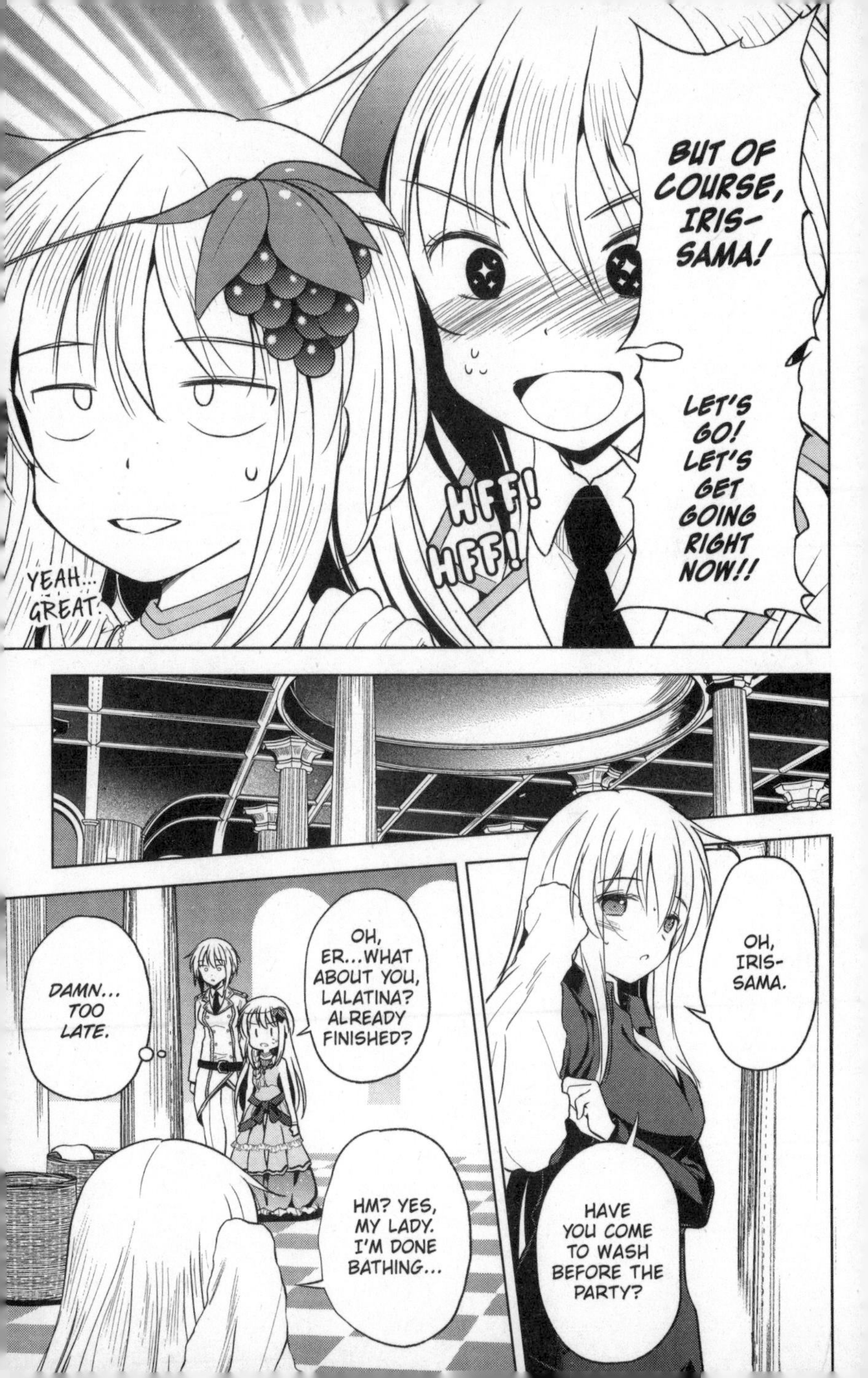
BUT OF COURSE, IRIS-SAMA!
LET'S GO! LET'S GET GOING RIGHT NOW!!
HFF! HFF!
YEAH... GREAT.
OH, IRIS-SAMA.
HAVE YOU COME TO WASH BEFORE THE PARTY?
OH, ER...WHAT ABOUT YOU, LALATINA? ALREADY FINISHED?
HM? YES, MY LADY. I'M DONE BATHING...
DAMN... TOO LATE.

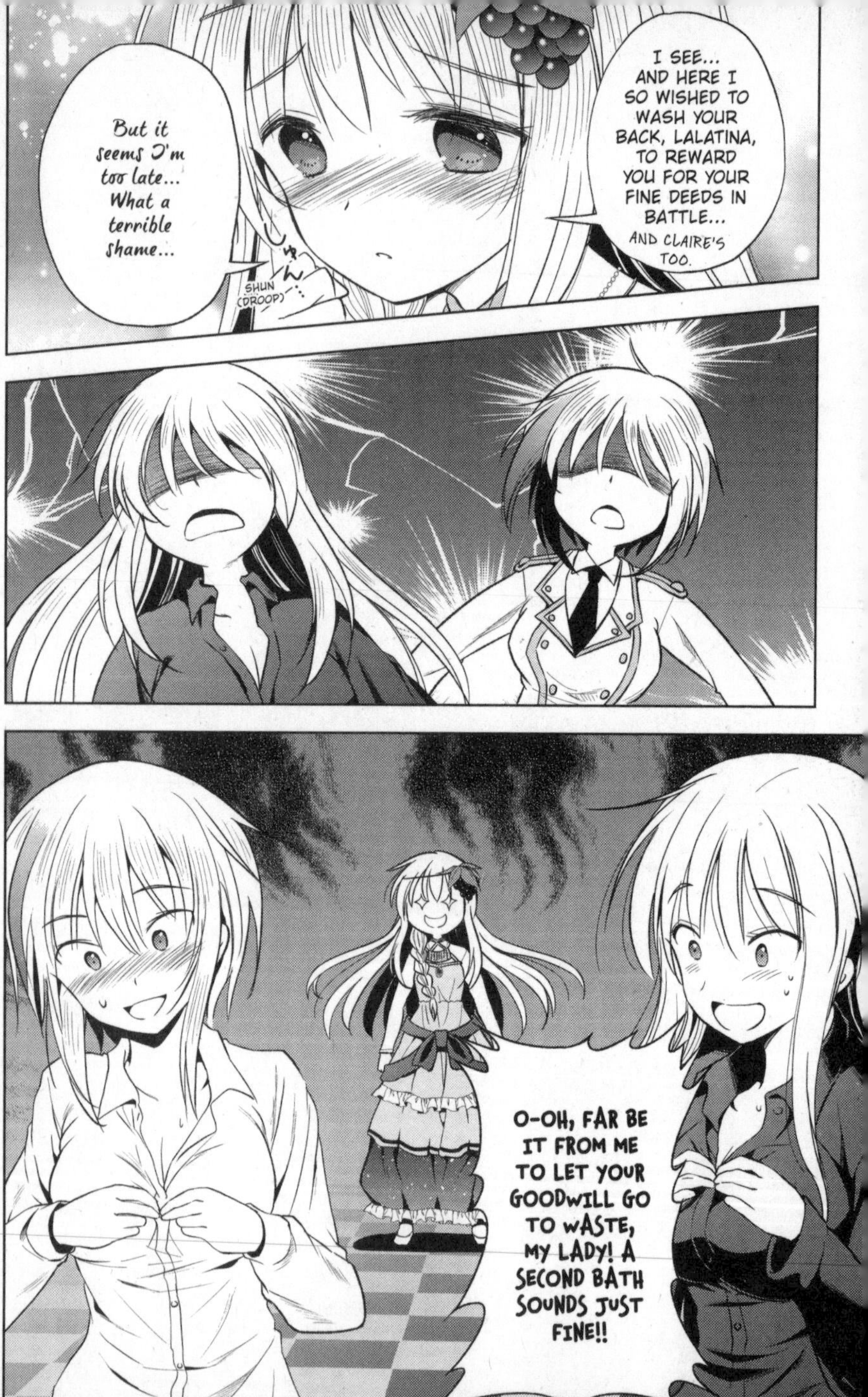
I SEE... AND HERE I SO WISHED TO WASH YOUR BACK, LALATINA, TO REWARD YOU FOR YOUR FINE DEEDS IN BATTLE...
AND CLAIRE'S TOO.
SHUN (DROOP)
But it seems I'm too late... What a terrible shame...
O-OH, FAR BE IT FROM ME TO LET YOUR GOODWILL GO TO WASTE, MY LADY! A SECOND BATH SOUNDS JUST FINE!!

GOD'S
BLESSING
ON THIS
WONDERFUL
WORLD!

11

11

GOD'S
BLESSING
ON THIS
WONDERFUL
WORLD!

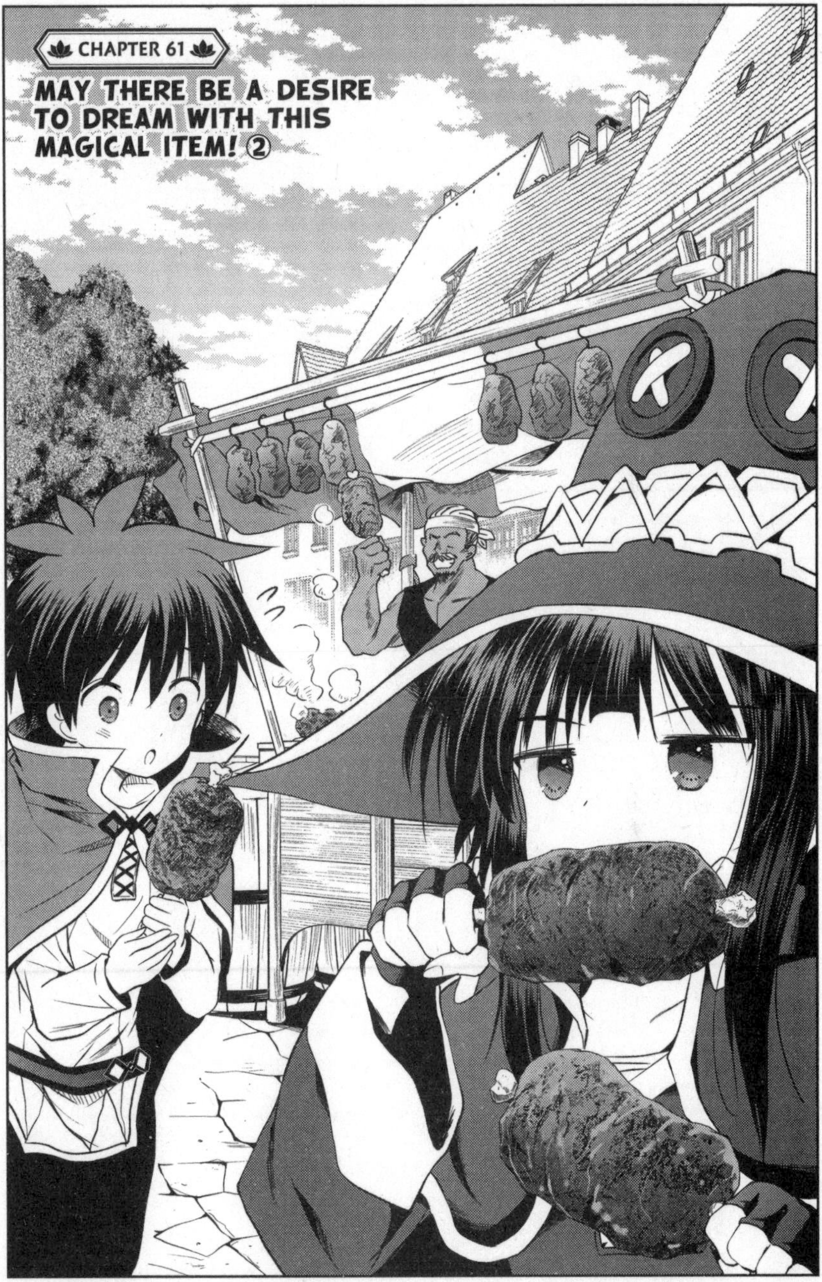
CHAPTER 61
MAY THERE BE A DESIRE TO DREAM WITH THIS MAGICAL ITEM! ②

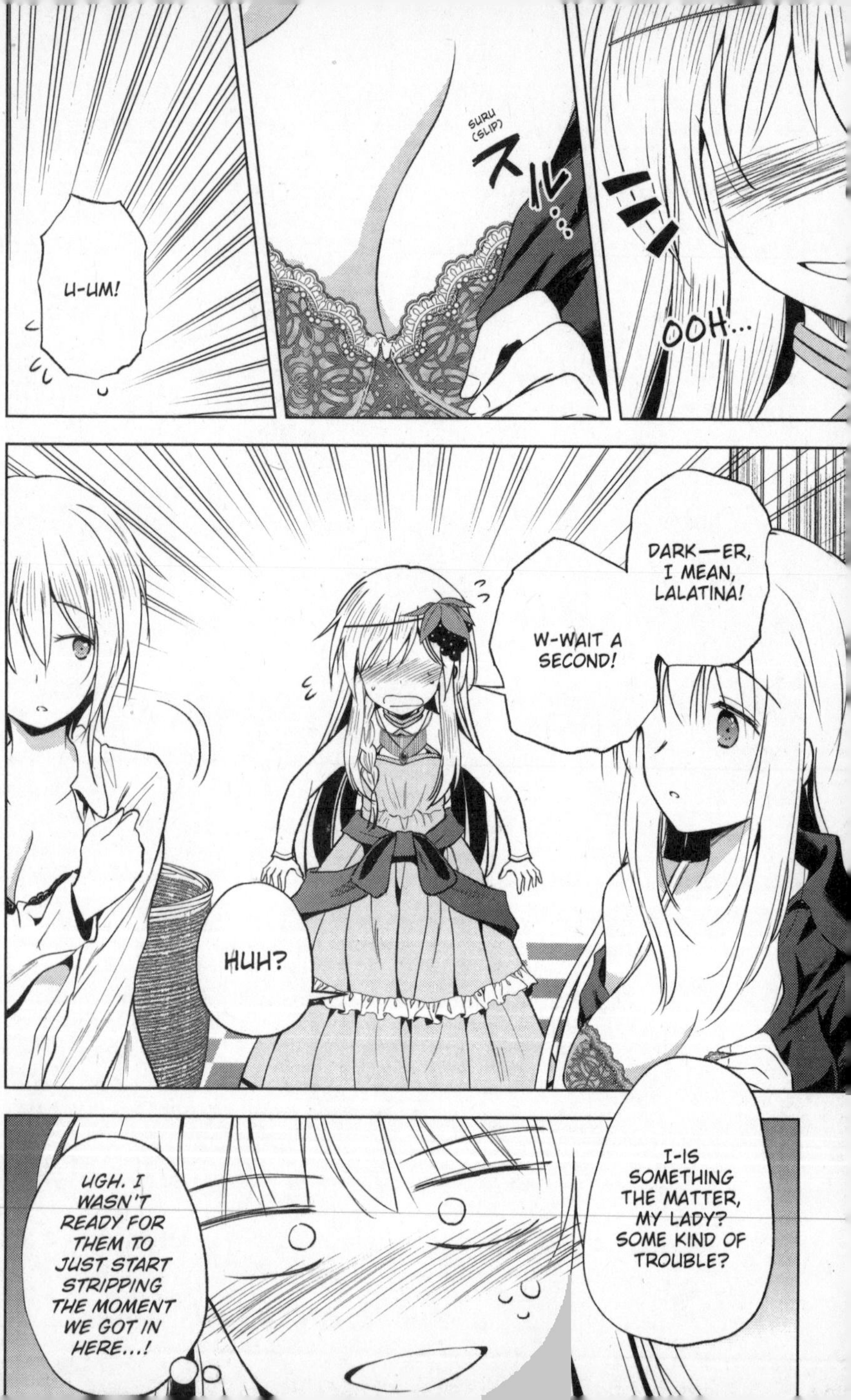
OOH...
SURU (SLIP)
スル
U-UM!
DARK—ER, I MEAN, LALATINA!
W-WAIT A SECOND!
HUH?
I-IS SOMETHING THE MATTER, MY LADY? SOME KIND OF TROUBLE?
UGH. I WASN'T READY FOR THEM TO JUST START STRIPPING THE MOMENT WE GOT IN HERE...!

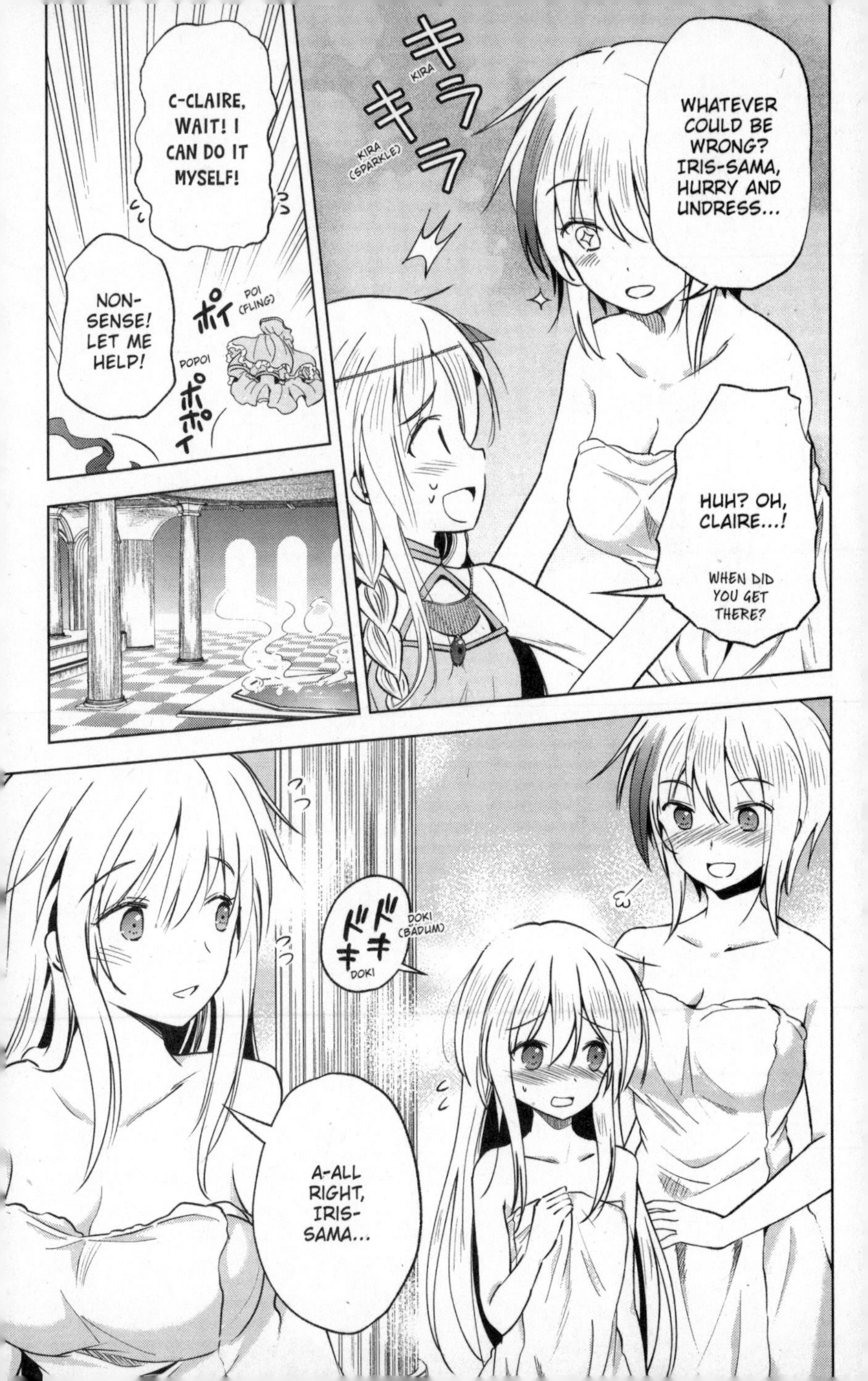
キラキラ
KIRA
KIRA (SPARKLE)
WHATEVER COULD BE WRONG? IRIS-SAMA, HURRY AND UNDRESS...
HUH? OH, CLAIRE...!
WHEN DID YOU GET THERE?
C-CLAIRE, WAIT! I CAN DO IT MYSELF!
NON-SENSE! LET ME HELP!
ポイ
POI (FLING)
POPOI
ポポイ
ドキドキ
DOKI (BADUM)
DOKI
A-ALL RIGHT, IRIS-SAMA...

A-ahem... Let us start washing one another's backs, then...

>MUMBLE<
>MUMBLE<

AH... NOW I SEE.

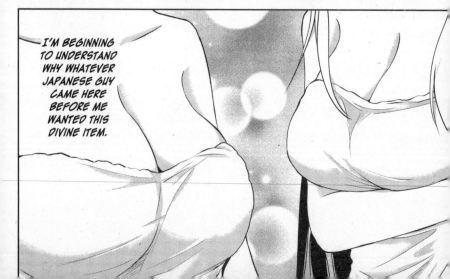

I'M BEGINNING TO UNDERSTAND WHY WHATEVER JAPANESE GUY CAME HERE BEFORE ME WANTED THIS DIVINE ITEM.

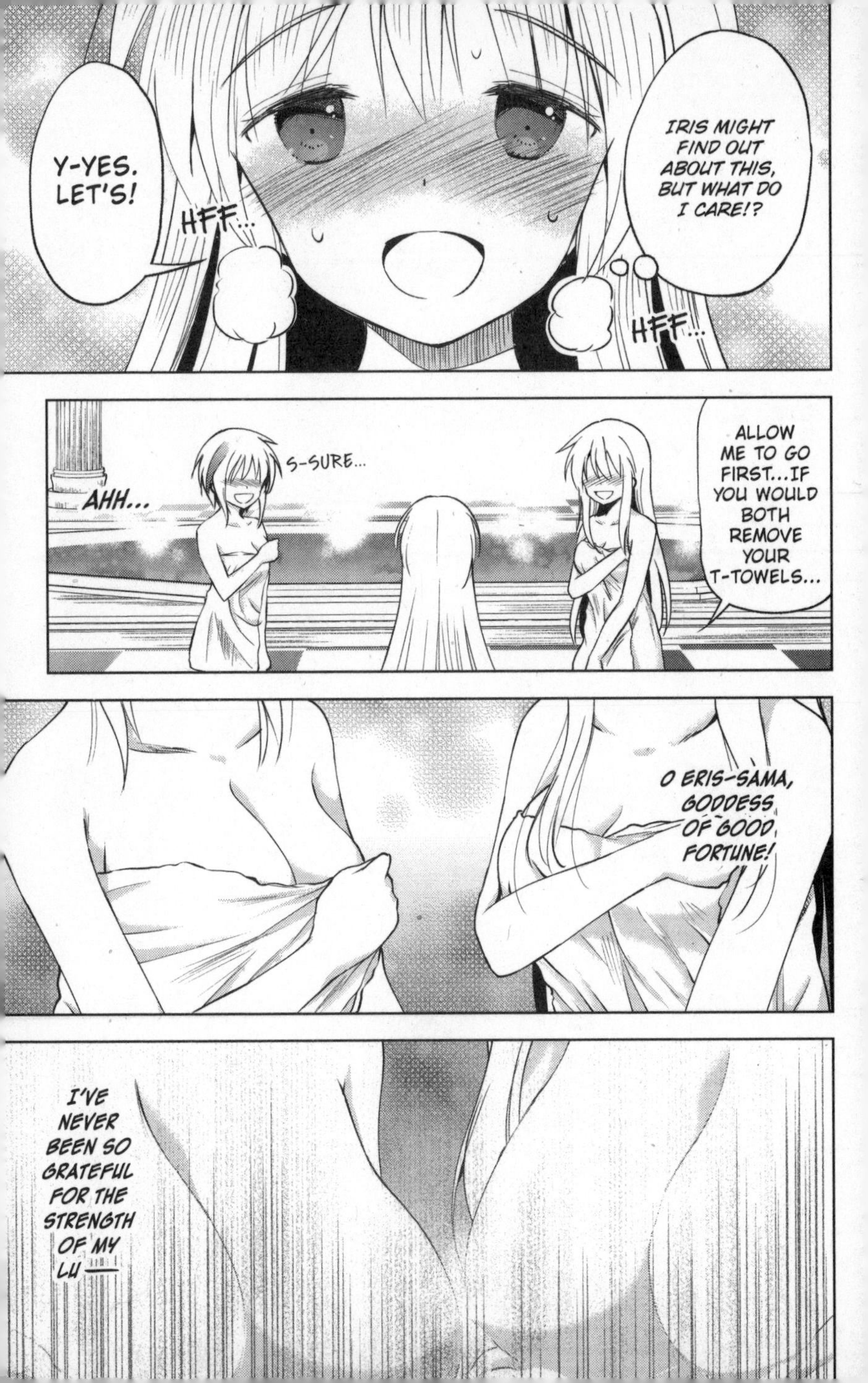
IRIS MIGHT FIND OUT ABOUT THIS, BUT WHAT DO I CARE!?
HFF...
Y-YES. LET'S!
HFF...
ALLOW ME TO GO FIRST...IF YOU WOULD BOTH REMOVE YOUR T-TOWELS...
S-SURE...
AHH...
O ERIS-SAMA, GODDESS OF GOOD FORTUNE!
I'VE NEVER BEEN SO GRATEFUL FOR THE STRENGTH OF MY LU—

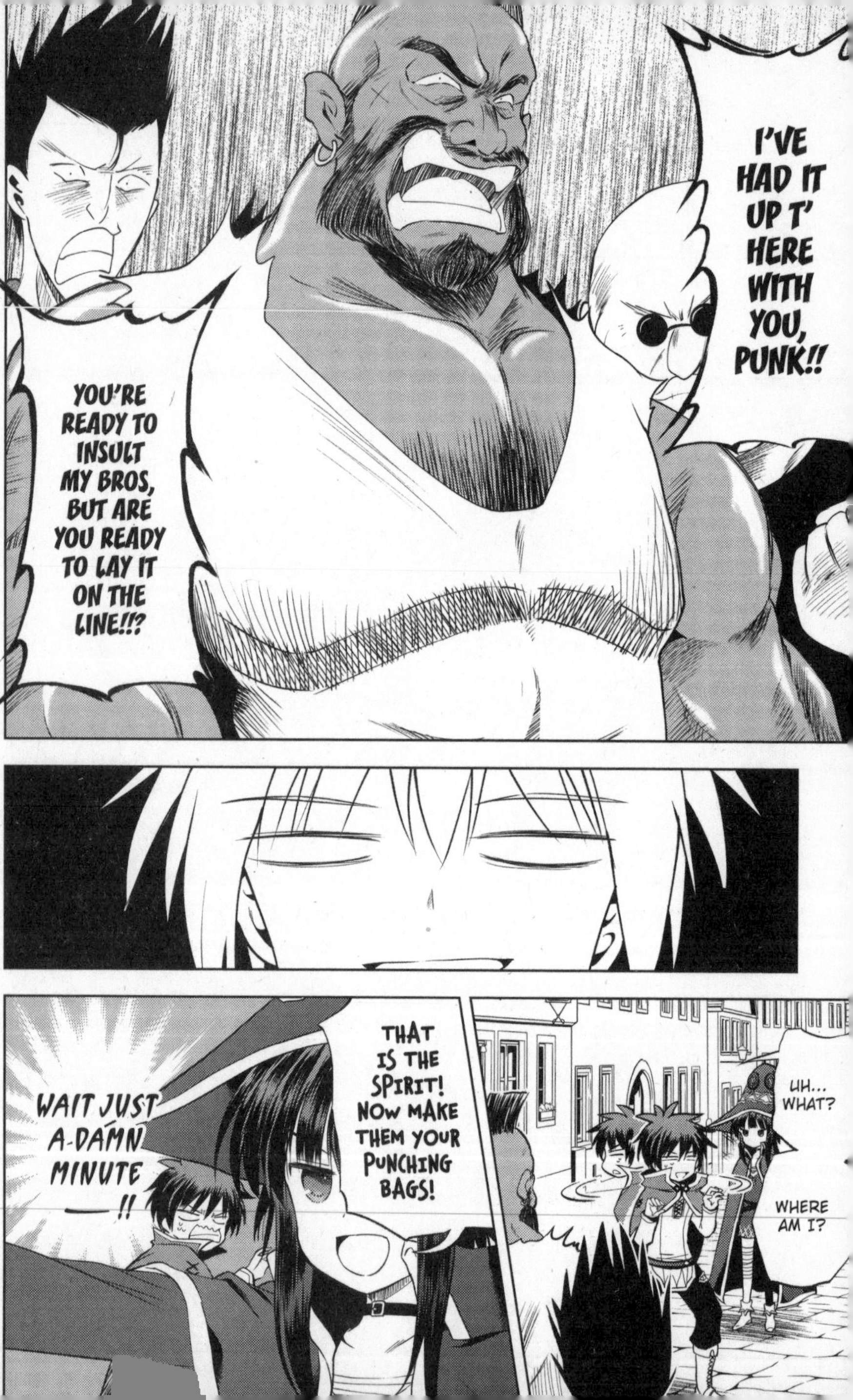
I'VE HAD IT UP T' HERE WITH YOU, PUNK!!
YOU'RE READY TO INSULT MY BROS, BUT ARE YOU READY TO LAY IT ON THE LINE!!?
UH... WHAT?
WHERE AM I?
THAT IS THE SPIRIT! NOW MAKE THEM YOUR PUNCHING BAGS!
WAIT JUST A-DAMN MINUTE —!!

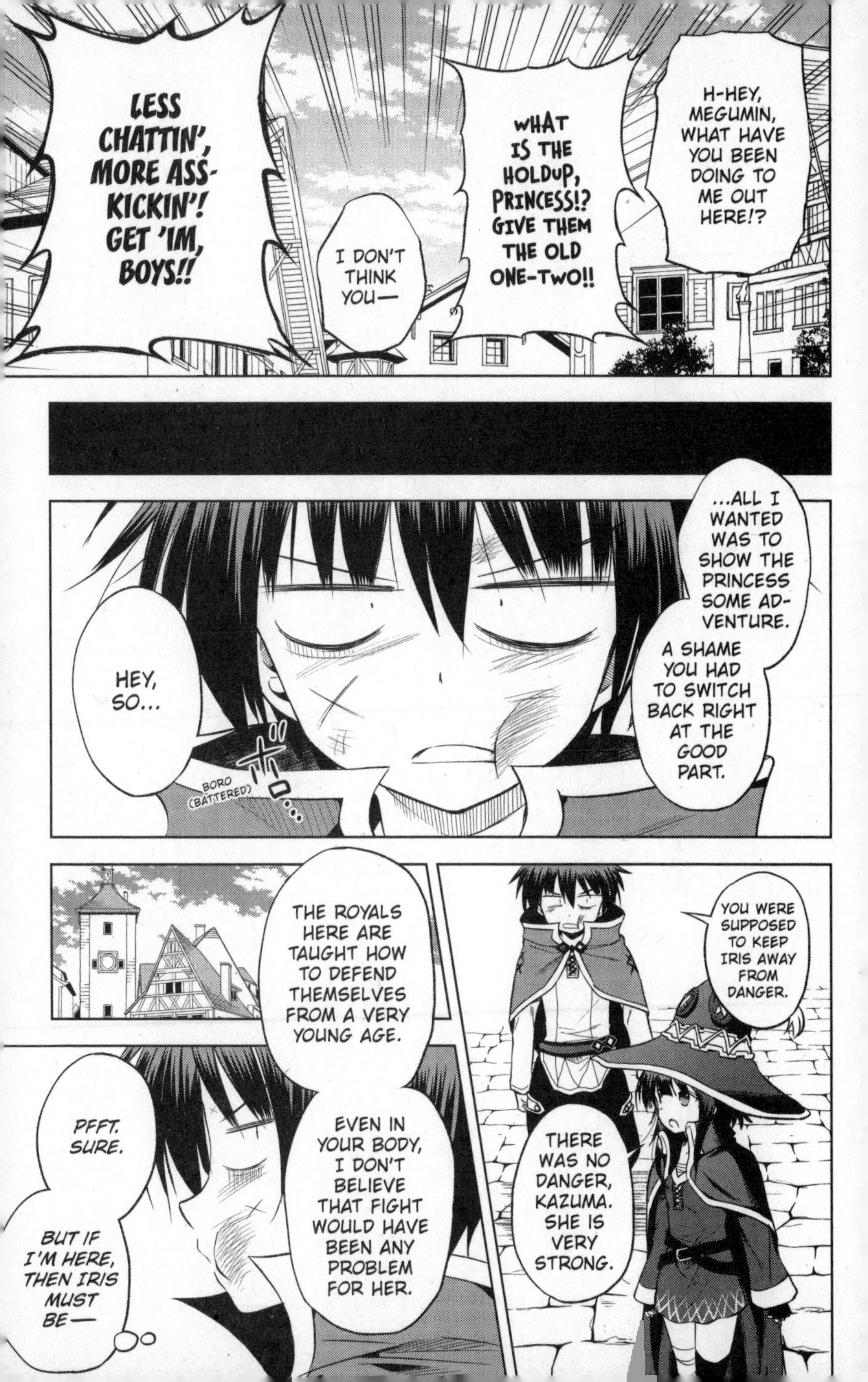
H-HEY, MEGUMIN, WHAT HAVE YOU BEEN DOING TO ME OUT HERE!?
WHAT IS THE HOLDUP, PRINCESS!? GIVE THEM THE OLD ONE-TWO!!
I DON'T THINK YOU—
LESS CHATTIN', MORE ASS-KICKIN'! GET 'IM, BOYS!!
...ALL I WANTED WAS TO SHOW THE PRINCESS SOME AD-VENTURE.
A SHAME YOU HAD TO SWITCH BACK RIGHT AT THE GOOD PART.
HEY, SO...
BORO (BATTERED)
YOU WERE SUPPOSED TO KEEP IRIS AWAY FROM DANGER.
THERE WAS NO DANGER, KAZUMA. SHE IS VERY STRONG.
THE ROYALS HERE ARE TAUGHT HOW TO DEFEND THEMSELVES FROM A VERY YOUNG AGE.
EVEN IN YOUR BODY, I DON'T BELIEVE THAT FIGHT WOULD HAVE BEEN ANY PROBLEM FOR HER.
PFFT. SURE.
BUT IF I'M HERE, THEN IRIS MUST BE—

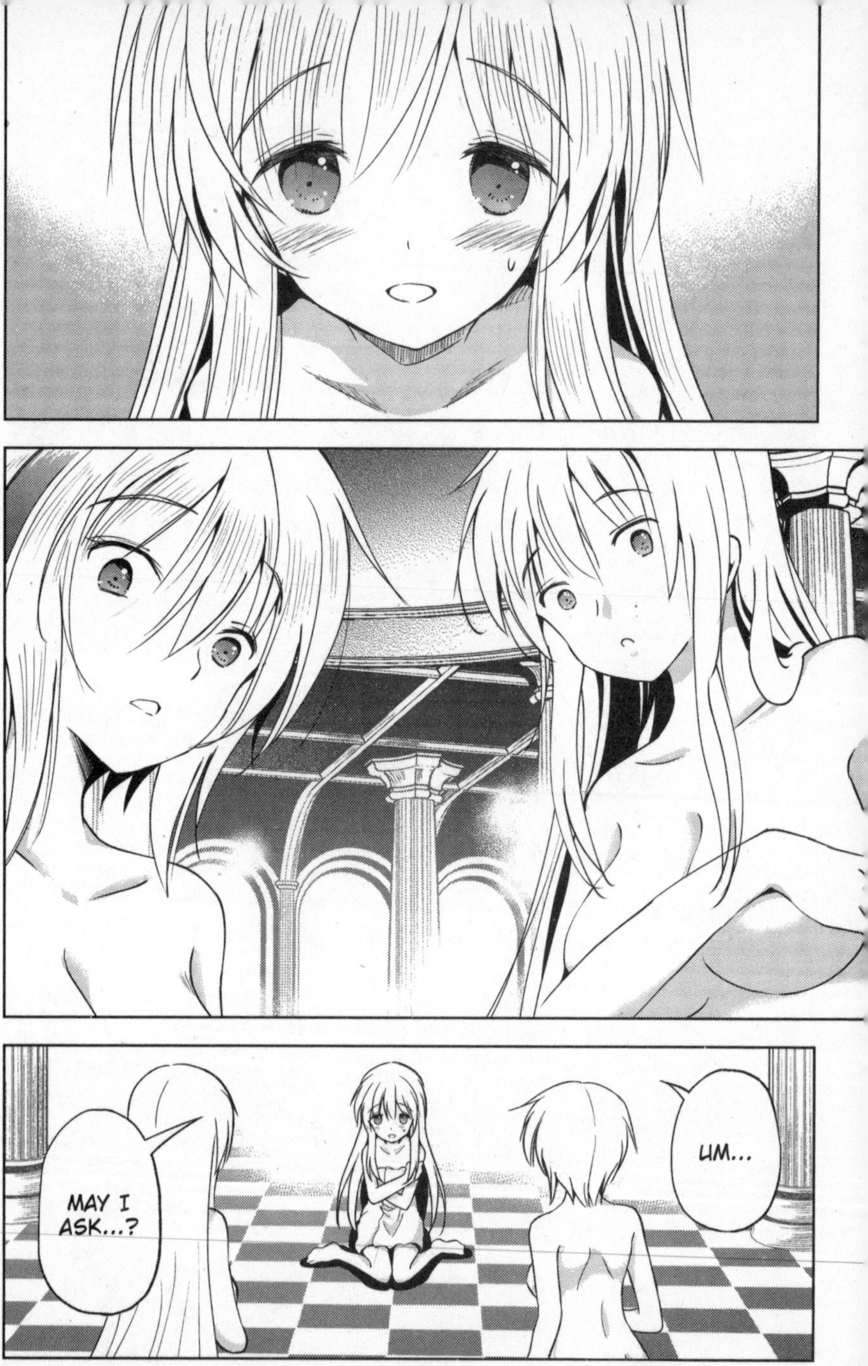
UM...
MAY I ASK...?

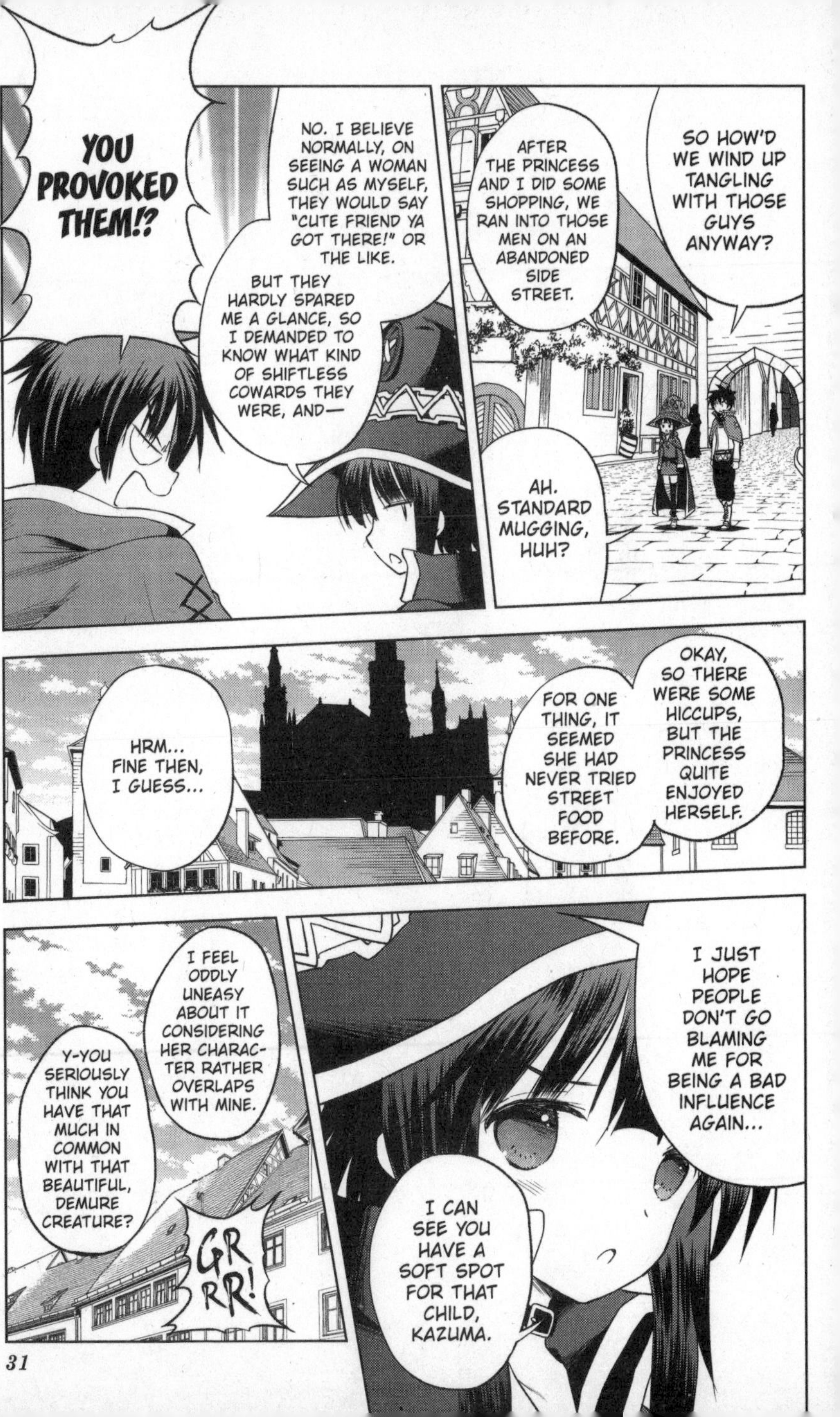
SO HOW'D WE WIND UP TANGLING WITH THOSE GUYS ANYWAY?
AFTER THE PRINCESS AND I DID SOME SHOPPING, WE RAN INTO THOSE MEN ON AN ABANDONED SIDE STREET.
AH. STANDARD MUGGING, HUH?
NO. I BELIEVE NORMALLY, ON SEEING A WOMAN SUCH AS MYSELF, THEY WOULD SAY "CUTE FRIEND YA GOT THERE!" OR THE LIKE.
BUT THEY HARDLY SPARED ME A GLANCE, SO I DEMANDED TO KNOW WHAT KIND OF SHIFTLESS COWARDS THEY WERE, AND—
YOU PROVOKED THEM!?
OKAY, SO THERE WERE SOME HICCUPS, BUT THE PRINCESS QUITE ENJOYED HERSELF.
FOR ONE THING, IT SEEMED SHE HAD NEVER TRIED STREET FOOD BEFORE.
HRM... FINE THEN, I GUESS...
I JUST HOPE PEOPLE DON'T GO BLAMING ME FOR BEING A BAD INFLUENCE AGAIN...
I CAN SEE YOU HAVE A SOFT SPOT FOR THAT CHILD, KAZUMA.
I FEEL ODDLY UNEASY ABOUT IT CONSIDERING HER CHARACTER RATHER OVERLAPS WITH MINE.
Y-YOU SERIOUSLY THINK YOU HAVE THAT MUCH IN COMMON WITH THAT BEAUTIFUL, DEMURE CREATURE?
GRRR!

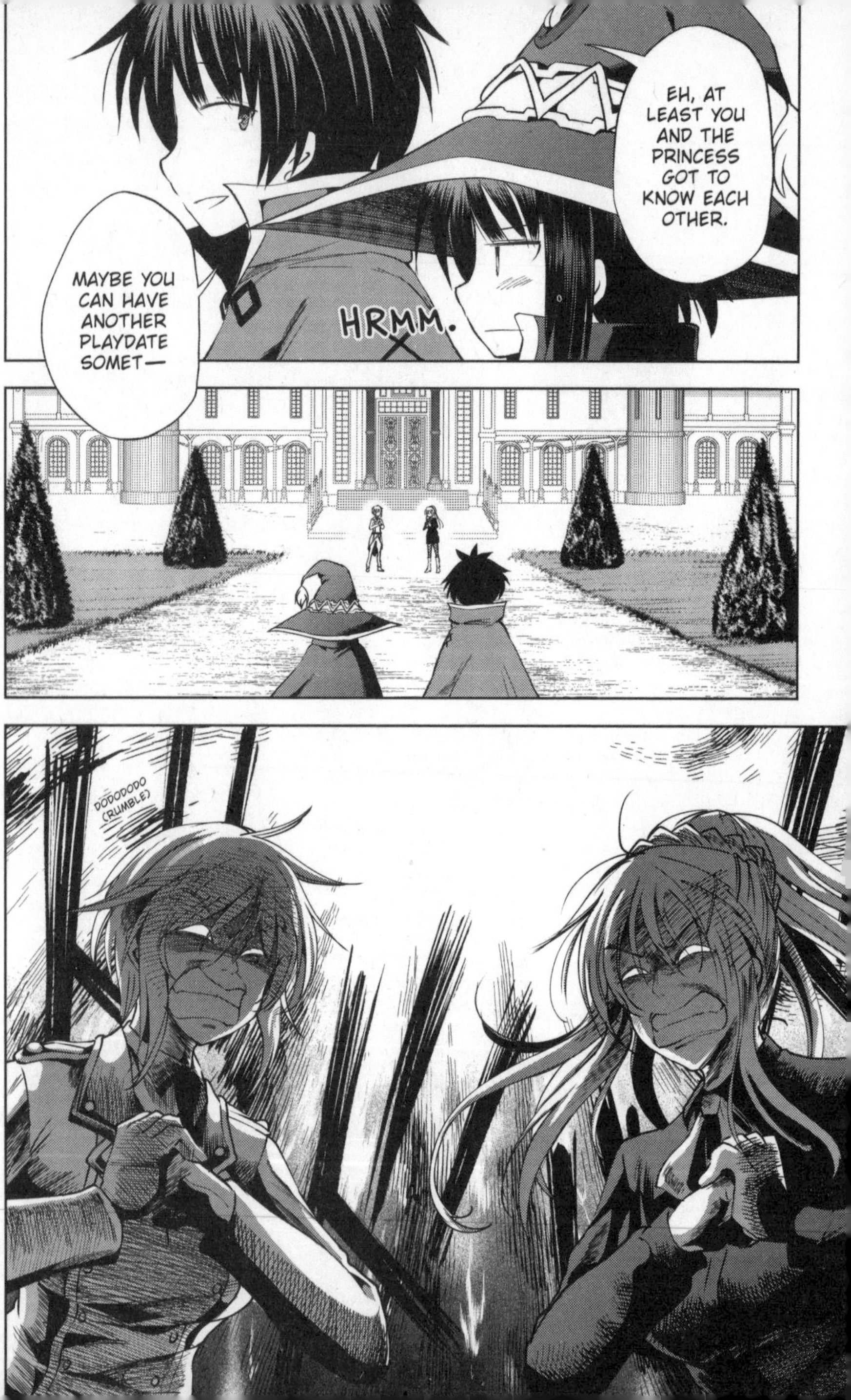
EH, AT LEAST YOU AND THE PRINCESS GOT TO KNOW EACH OTHER.
HRMM.
MAYBE YOU CAN HAVE ANOTHER PLAYDATE SOMET—
DODODODO (RUMBLE)

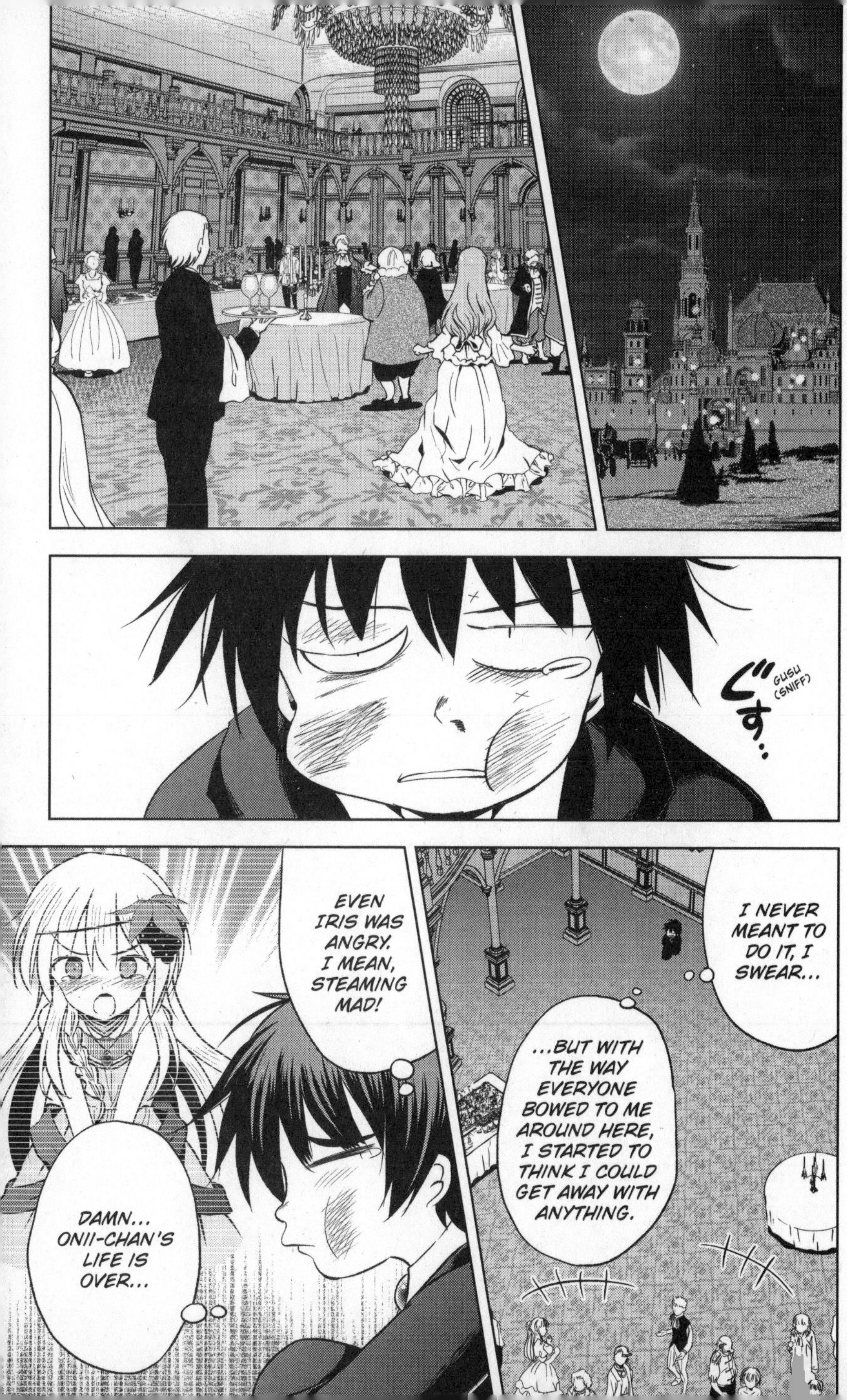
ぐす..
GUSU (SNIFF)
I NEVER MEANT TO DO IT, I SWEAR...
...BUT WITH THE WAY EVERYONE BOWED TO ME AROUND HERE, I STARTED TO THINK I COULD GET AWAY WITH ANYTHING.
EVEN IRIS WAS ANGRY. I MEAN, STEAMING MAD!
DAMN... ONII-CHAN'S LIFE IS OVER...

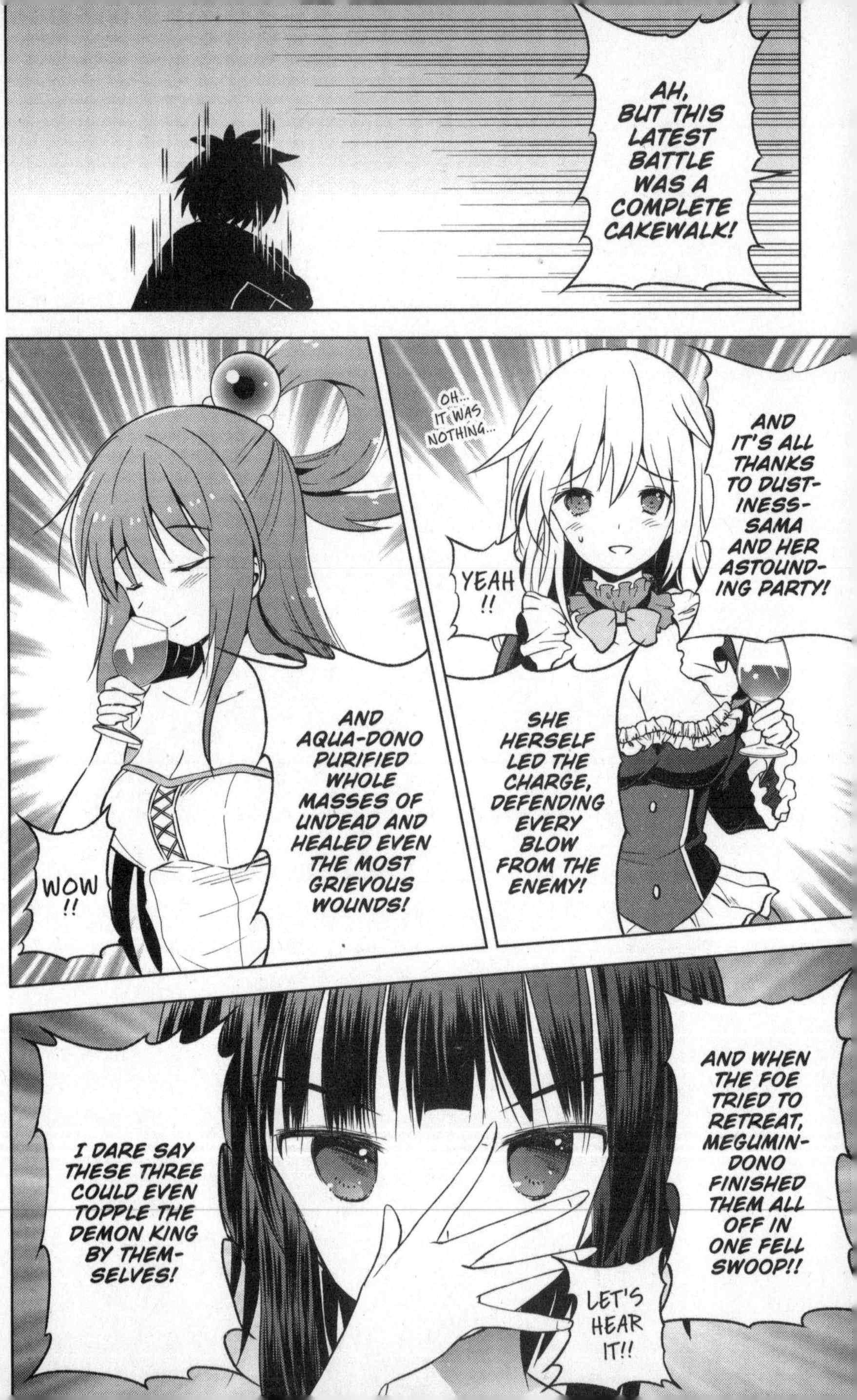
AH, BUT THIS LATEST BATTLE WAS A COMPLETE CAKEWALK!
AND IT'S ALL THANKS TO DUSTINESS-SAMA AND HER ASTOUNDING PARTY!
OH... IT WAS NOTHING...
YEAH!!
SHE HERSELF LED THE CHARGE, DEFENDING EVERY BLOW FROM THE ENEMY!
AND AQUA-DONO PURIFIED WHOLE MASSES OF UNDEAD AND HEALED EVEN THE MOST GRIEVOUS WOUNDS!
WOW!!
AND WHEN THE FOE TRIED TO RETREAT, MEGUMIN-DONO FINISHED THEM ALL OFF IN ONE FELL SWOOP!!
LET'S HEAR IT!!
I DARE SAY THESE THREE COULD EVEN TOPPLE THE DEMON KING BY THEM-SELVES!

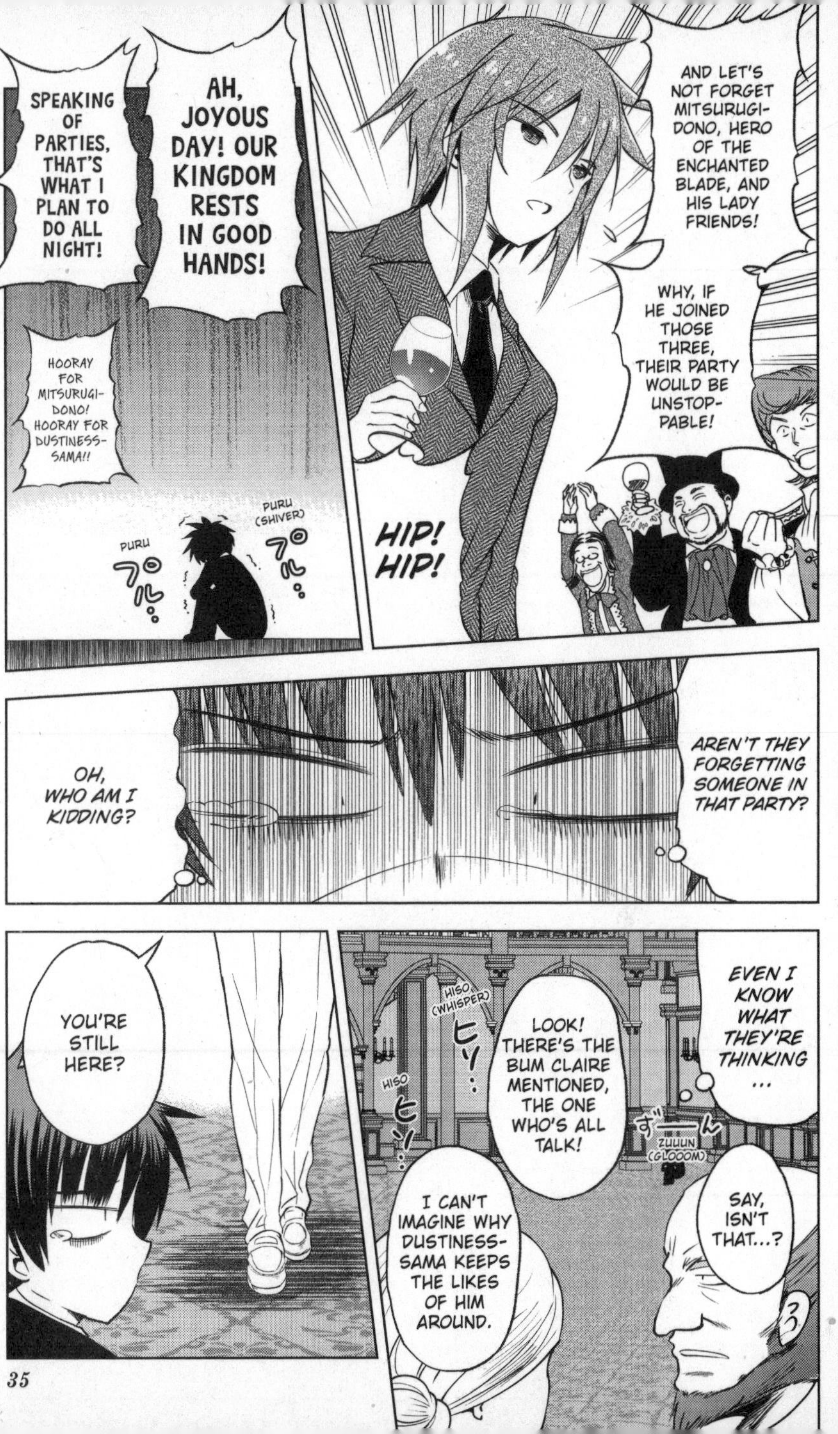
AND LET'S NOT FORGET MITSURUGI-DONO, HERO OF THE ENCHANTED BLADE, AND HIS LADY FRIENDS!
WHY, IF HE JOINED THOSE THREE, THEIR PARTY WOULD BE UNSTOP-PABLE!
HIP! HIP!
AH, JOYOUS DAY! OUR KINGDOM RESTS IN GOOD HANDS!
SPEAKING OF PARTIES, THAT'S WHAT I PLAN TO DO ALL NIGHT!
HOORAY FOR MITSURUGI-DONO! HOORAY FOR DUSTINESS-SAMA!!
PURU (SHIVER)
プル。
PURU
プル。
AREN'T THEY FORGETTING SOMEONE IN THAT PARTY?
OH, WHO AM I KIDDING?
EVEN I KNOW WHAT THEY'RE THINKING...
HISO (WHISPER)
ヒソ‥
LOOK! THERE'S THE BUM CLAIRE MENTIONED, THE ONE WHO'S ALL TALK!
HISO
ヒソ‥
ずーん
ZUUUN (GLOOOM)
SAY, ISN'T THAT...?
I CAN'T IMAGINE WHY DUSTINESS-SAMA KEEPS THE LIKES OF HIM AROUND.
YOU'RE STILL HERE?

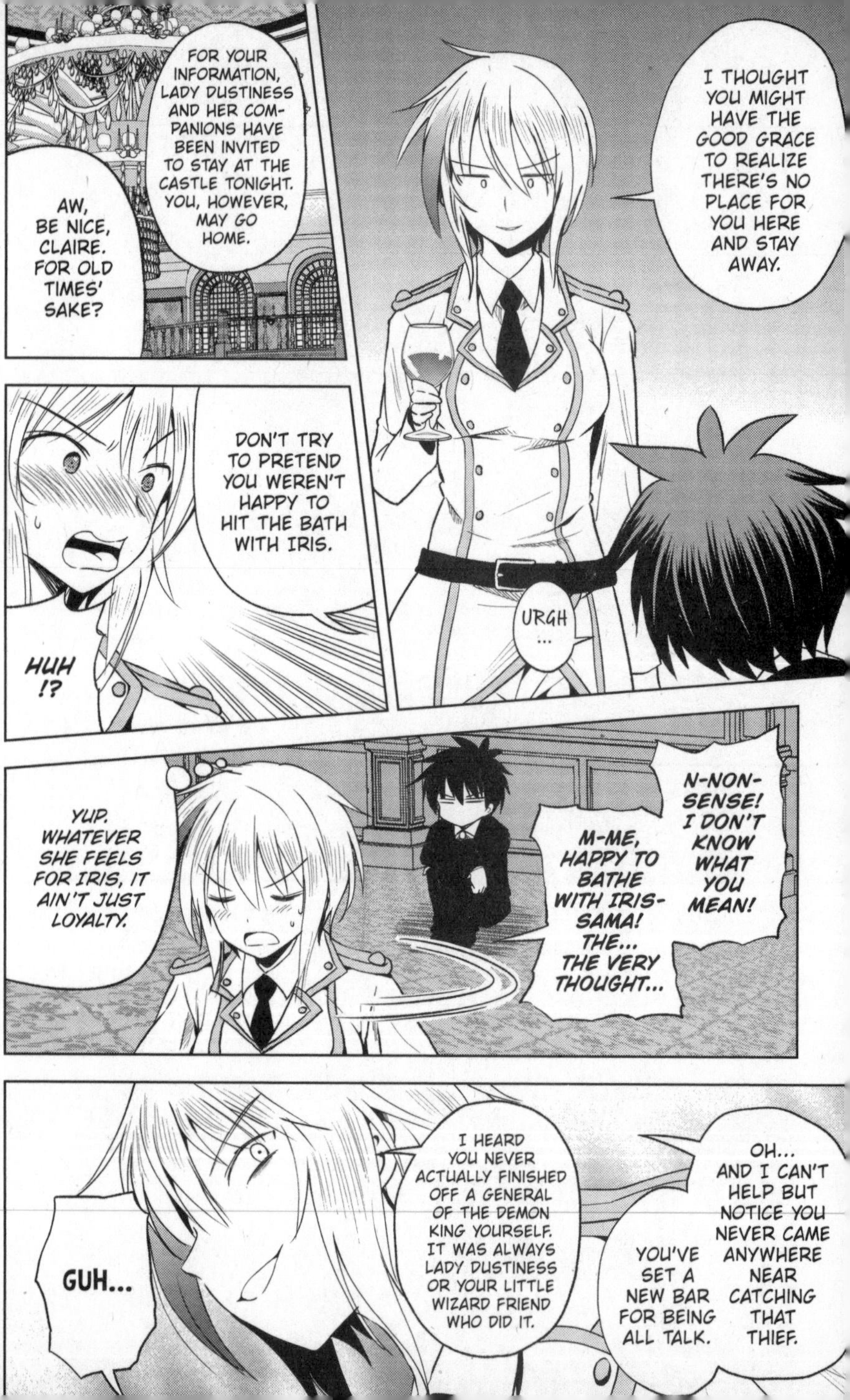

FOR YOUR INFORMATION, LADY DUSTINESS AND HER COMPANIONS HAVE BEEN INVITED TO STAY AT THE CASTLE TONIGHT. YOU, HOWEVER, MAY GO HOME.
AW, BE NICE, CLAIRE. FOR OLD TIMES' SAKE?
I THOUGHT YOU MIGHT HAVE THE GOOD GRACE TO REALIZE THERE'S NO PLACE FOR YOU HERE AND STAY AWAY.
DON'T TRY TO PRETEND YOU WEREN'T HAPPY TO HIT THE BATH WITH IRIS.
URGH...
HUH!?
N-NONSENSE! I DON'T KNOW WHAT YOU MEAN!
M-ME, HAPPY TO BATHE WITH IRIS-SAMA! THE... THE VERY THOUGHT...
YUP. WHATEVER SHE FEELS FOR IRIS, IT AIN'T JUST LOYALTY.
OH... AND I CAN'T HELP BUT NOTICE YOU NEVER CAME ANYWHERE NEAR CATCHING THAT THIEF.
YOU'VE SET A NEW BAR FOR BEING ALL TALK.
I HEARD YOU NEVER ACTUALLY FINISHED OFF A GENERAL OF THE DEMON KING YOURSELF. IT WAS ALWAYS LADY DUSTINESS OR YOUR LITTLE WIZARD FRIEND WHO DID IT.
GUH...

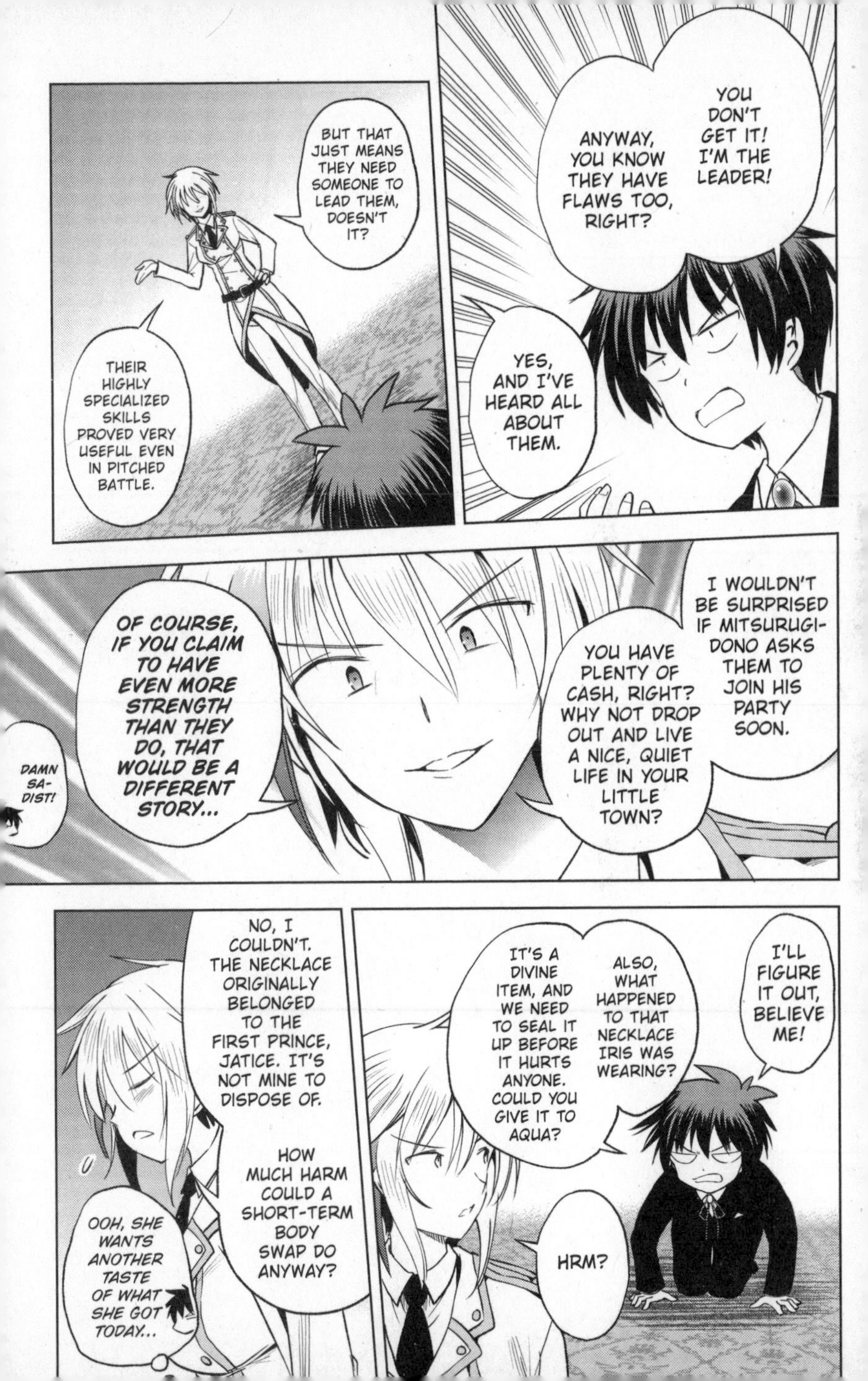

YOU DON'T GET IT! I'M THE LEADER!
ANYWAY, YOU KNOW THEY HAVE FLAWS TOO, RIGHT?
YES, AND I'VE HEARD ALL ABOUT THEM.
BUT THAT JUST MEANS THEY NEED SOMEONE TO LEAD THEM, DOESN'T IT?
THEIR HIGHLY SPECIALIZED SKILLS PROVED VERY USEFUL EVEN IN PITCHED BATTLE.
I WOULDN'T BE SURPRISED IF MITSURUGI-DONO ASKS THEM TO JOIN HIS PARTY SOON.
YOU HAVE PLENTY OF CASH, RIGHT? WHY NOT DROP OUT AND LIVE A NICE, QUIET LIFE IN YOUR LITTLE TOWN?
OF COURSE, IF YOU CLAIM TO HAVE EVEN MORE STRENGTH THAN THEY DO, THAT WOULD BE A DIFFERENT STORY...
DAMN SA-DIST!
I'LL FIGURE IT OUT, BELIEVE ME!
ALSO, WHAT HAPPENED TO THAT NECKLACE IRIS WAS WEARING?
IT'S A DIVINE ITEM, AND WE NEED TO SEAL IT UP BEFORE IT HURTS ANYONE. COULD YOU GIVE IT TO AQUA?
HRM?
NO, I COULDN'T. THE NECKLACE ORIGINALLY BELONGED TO THE FIRST PRINCE, JATICE. IT'S NOT MINE TO DISPOSE OF.
HOW MUCH HARM COULD A SHORT-TERM BODY SWAP DO ANYWAY?
OOH, SHE WANTS ANOTHER TASTE OF WHAT SHE GOT TODAY...

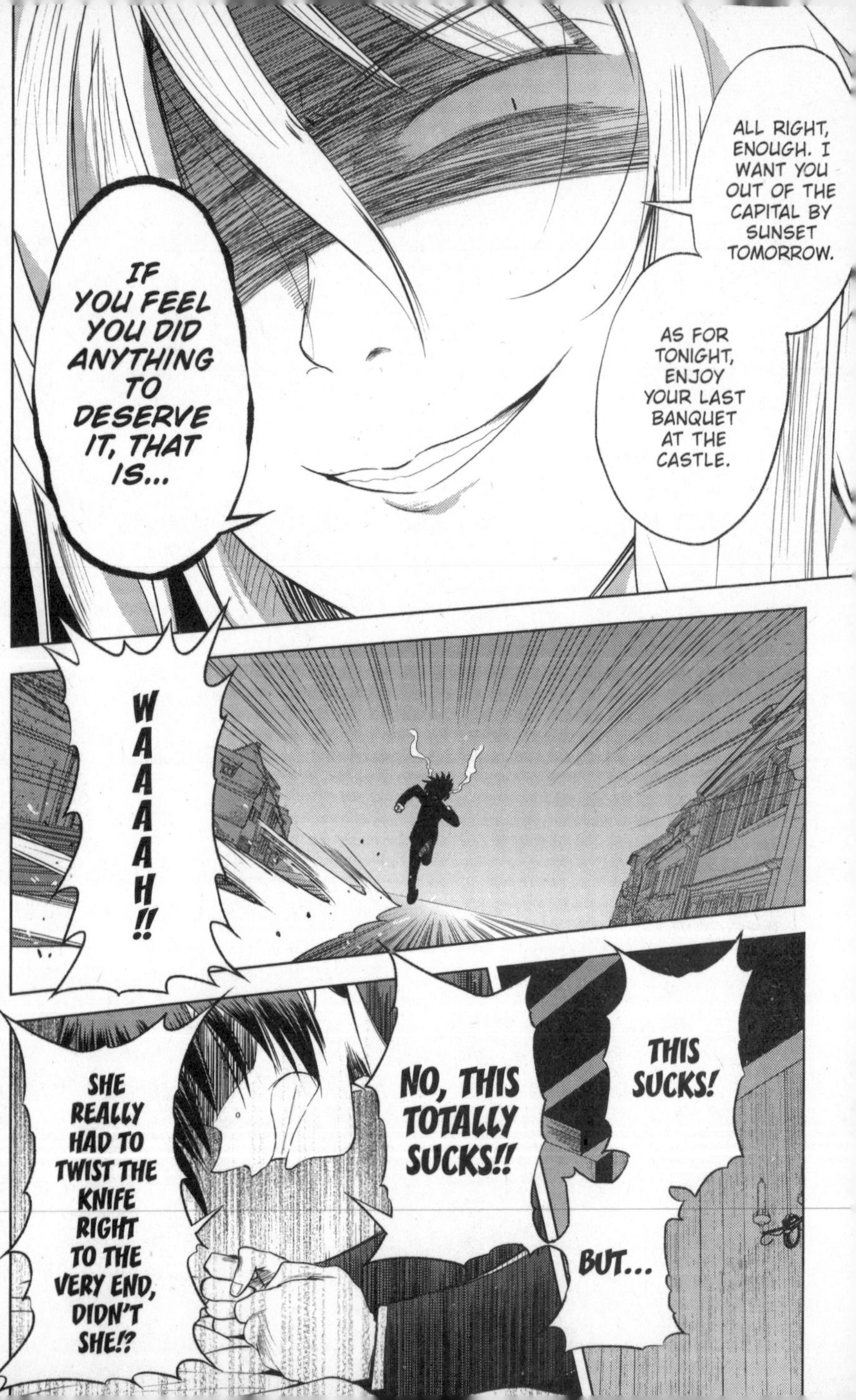
ALL RIGHT, ENOUGH. I WANT YOU OUT OF THE CAPITAL BY SUNSET TOMORROW.
AS FOR TONIGHT, ENJOY YOUR LAST BANQUET AT THE CASTLE.
IF YOU FEEL YOU DID ANYTHING TO DESERVE IT, THAT IS...
WAAAAAH!!
THIS SUCKS!
NO, THIS TOTALLY SUCKS!!
BUT...
SHE REALLY HAD TO TWIST THE KNIFE RIGHT TO THE VERY END, DIDN'T SHE!?

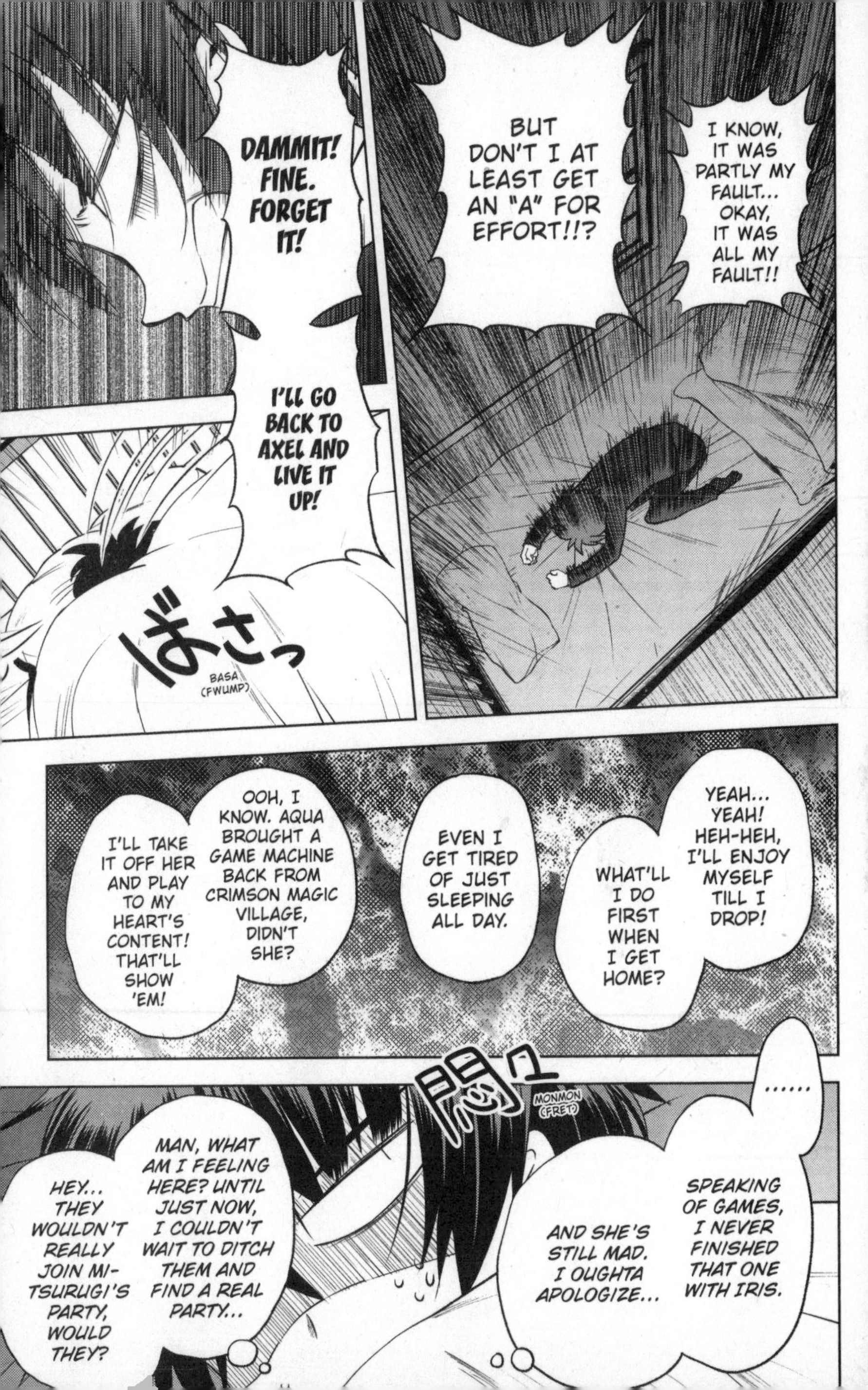
I KNOW, IT WAS PARTLY MY FAULT... OKAY, IT WAS ALL MY FAULT!!
BUT DON'T I AT LEAST GET AN "A" FOR EFFORT!!?
DAMMIT! FINE. FORGET IT!
I'LL GO BACK TO AXEL AND LIVE IT UP!
ばさっ
BASA (FWUMP)
YEAH... YEAH! HEH-HEH, I'LL ENJOY MYSELF TILL I DROP!
WHAT'LL I DO FIRST WHEN I GET HOME?
EVEN I GET TIRED OF JUST SLEEPING ALL DAY.
OOH, I KNOW. AQUA BROUGHT A GAME MACHINE BACK FROM CRIMSON MAGIC VILLAGE, DIDN'T SHE?
I'LL TAKE IT OFF HER AND PLAY TO MY HEART'S CONTENT! THAT'LL SHOW 'EM!
......
MONMON (FRET)
SPEAKING OF GAMES, I NEVER FINISHED THAT ONE WITH IRIS.
AND SHE'S STILL MAD. I OUGHTA APOLOGIZE...
MAN, WHAT AM I FEELING HERE? UNTIL JUST NOW, I COULDN'T WAIT TO DITCH THEM AND FIND A REAL PARTY...
HEY... THEY WOULDN'T REALLY JOIN MITSURUGI'S PARTY, WOULD THEY?

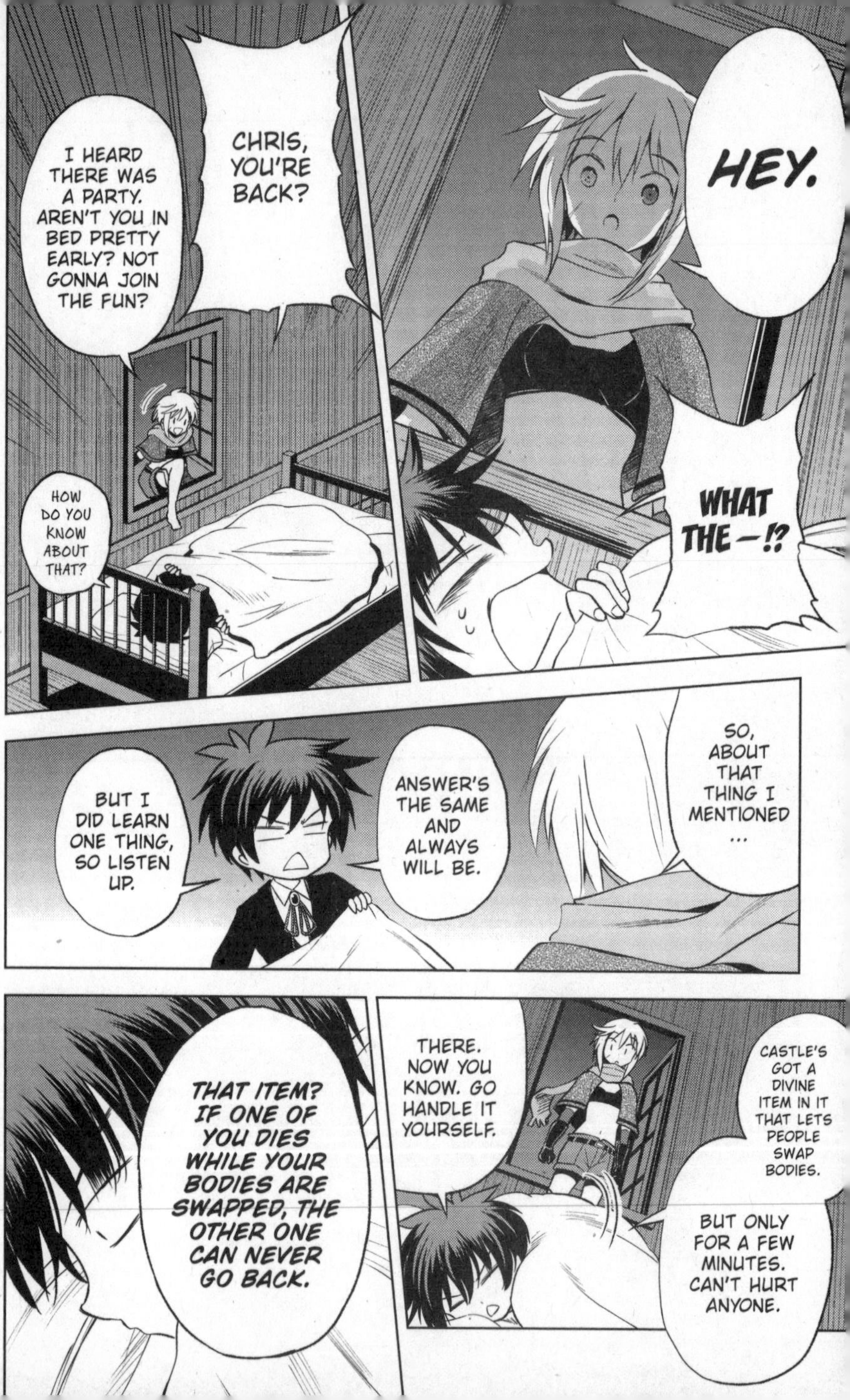
HEY.
WHAT THE—!?
CHRIS, YOU'RE BACK?
I HEARD THERE WAS A PARTY. AREN'T YOU IN BED PRETTY EARLY? NOT GONNA JOIN THE FUN?
HOW DO YOU KNOW ABOUT THAT?
SO, ABOUT THAT THING I MENTIONED...
ANSWER'S THE SAME AND ALWAYS WILL BE.
BUT I DID LEARN ONE THING, SO LISTEN UP.
CASTLE'S GOT A DIVINE ITEM IN IT THAT LETS PEOPLE SWAP BODIES.
THERE. NOW YOU KNOW. GO HANDLE IT YOURSELF.
BUT ONLY FOR A FEW MINUTES. CAN'T HURT ANYONE.
THAT ITEM? IF ONE OF YOU DIES WHILE YOUR BODIES ARE SWAPPED, THE OTHER ONE CAN NEVER GO BACK.

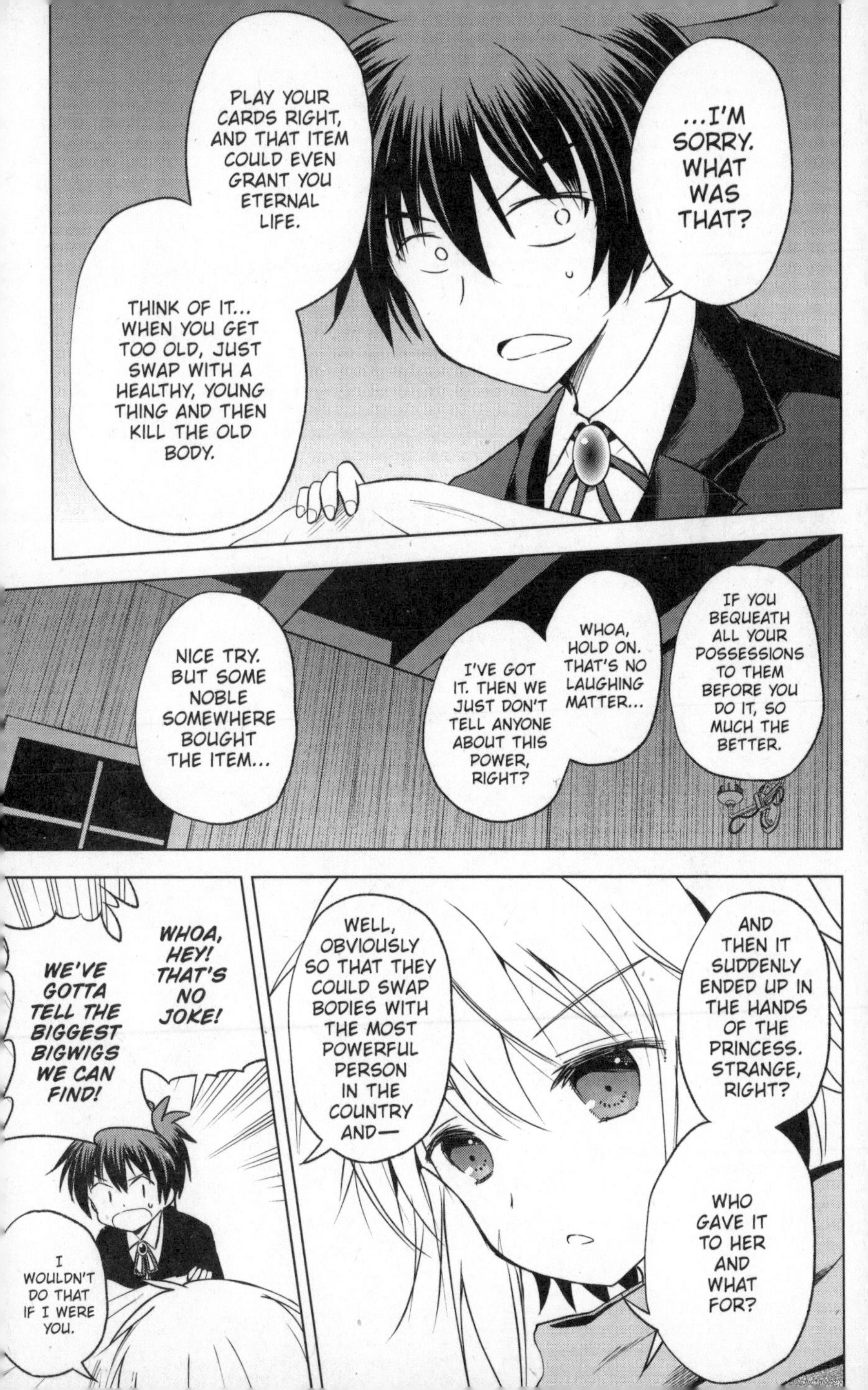
...I'M SORRY. WHAT WAS THAT?
PLAY YOUR CARDS RIGHT, AND THAT ITEM COULD EVEN GRANT YOU ETERNAL LIFE.
THINK OF IT... WHEN YOU GET TOO OLD, JUST SWAP WITH A HEALTHY, YOUNG THING AND THEN KILL THE OLD BODY.
IF YOU BEQUEATH ALL YOUR POSSESSIONS TO THEM BEFORE YOU DO IT, SO MUCH THE BETTER.
WHOA, HOLD ON. THAT'S NO LAUGHING MATTER...
I'VE GOT IT. THEN WE JUST DON'T TELL ANYONE ABOUT THIS POWER, RIGHT?
NICE TRY. BUT SOME NOBLE SOMEWHERE BOUGHT THE ITEM...
AND THEN IT SUDDENLY ENDED UP IN THE HANDS OF THE PRINCESS. STRANGE, RIGHT?
WHO GAVE IT TO HER AND WHAT FOR?
WELL, OBVIOUSLY SO THAT THEY COULD SWAP BODIES WITH THE MOST POWERFUL PERSON IN THE COUNTRY AND—
WHOA, HEY! THAT'S NO JOKE!
WE'VE GOTTA TELL THE BIGGEST BIGWIGS WE CAN FIND!
I WOULDN'T DO THAT IF I WERE YOU.

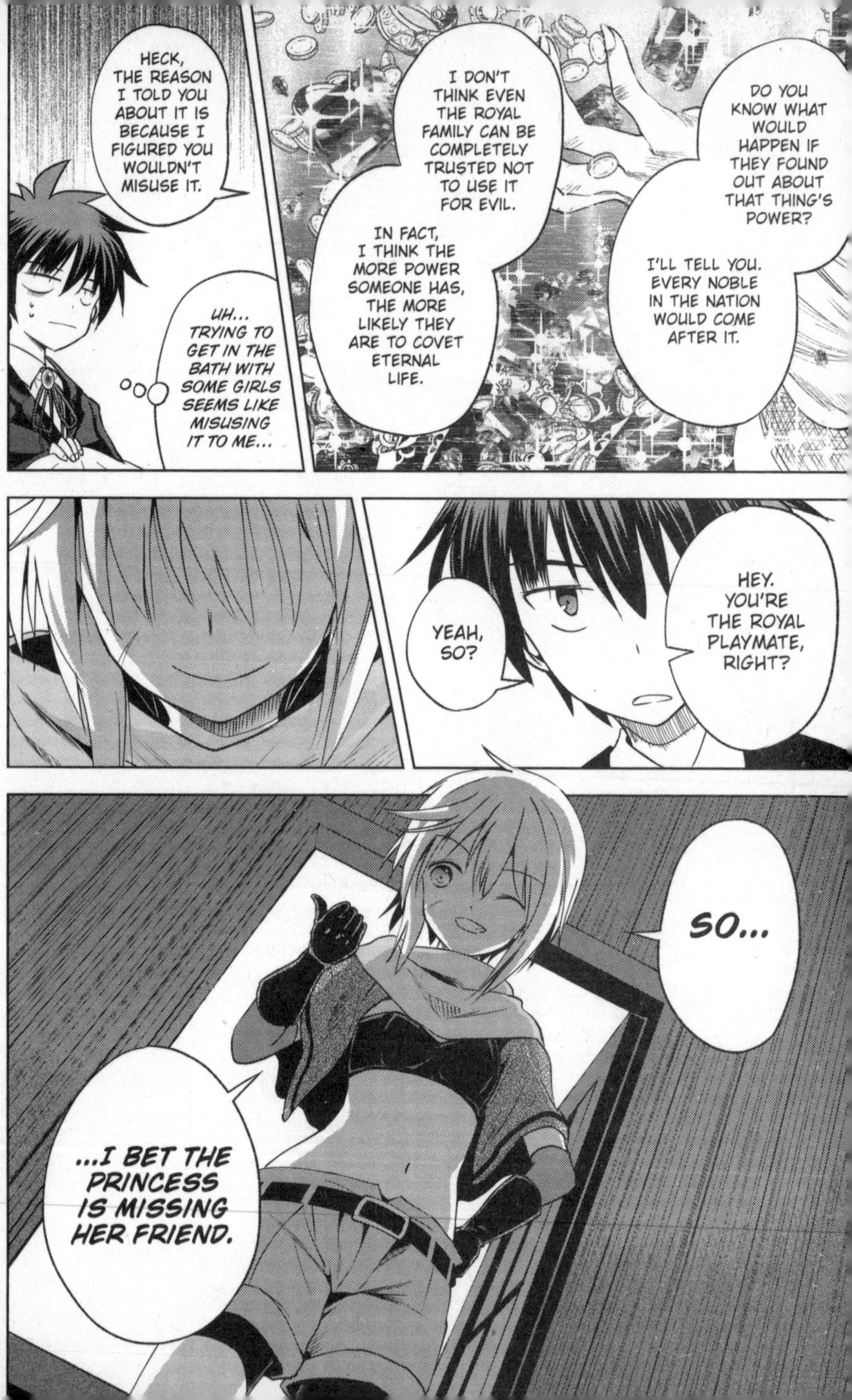
DO YOU KNOW WHAT WOULD HAPPEN IF THEY FOUND OUT ABOUT THAT THING'S POWER?
I'LL TELL YOU. EVERY NOBLE IN THE NATION WOULD COME AFTER IT.
I DON'T THINK EVEN THE ROYAL FAMILY CAN BE COMPLETELY TRUSTED NOT TO USE IT FOR EVIL.
IN FACT, I THINK THE MORE POWER SOMEONE HAS, THE MORE LIKELY THEY ARE TO COVET ETERNAL LIFE.
HECK, THE REASON I TOLD YOU ABOUT IT IS BECAUSE I FIGURED YOU WOULDN'T MISUSE IT.
UH... TRYING TO GET IN THE BATH WITH SOME GIRLS SEEMS LIKE MISUSING IT TO ME...
HEY. YOU'RE THE ROYAL PLAYMATE, RIGHT?
YEAH, SO?
SO...
...I BET THE PRINCESS IS MISSING HER FRIEND.

GOD'S
BLESSING
ON THIS
WONDERFUL
WORLD!

11

11

GOD'S
BLESSING
ON THIS
WONDERFUL
WORLD!

CHAPTER 62

MAY WE STOP THESE ACCURSED PLANS! ①

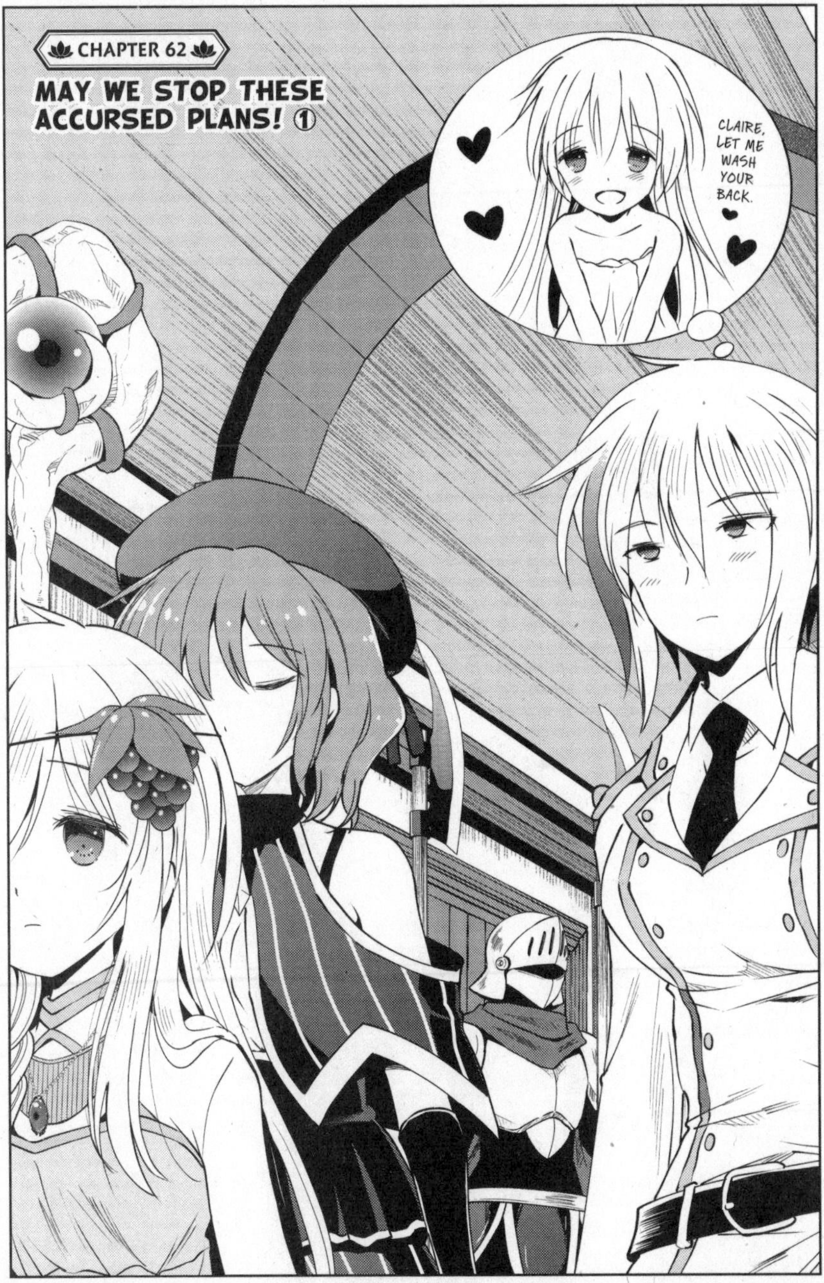
CLAIRE, LET ME WASH YOUR BACK.

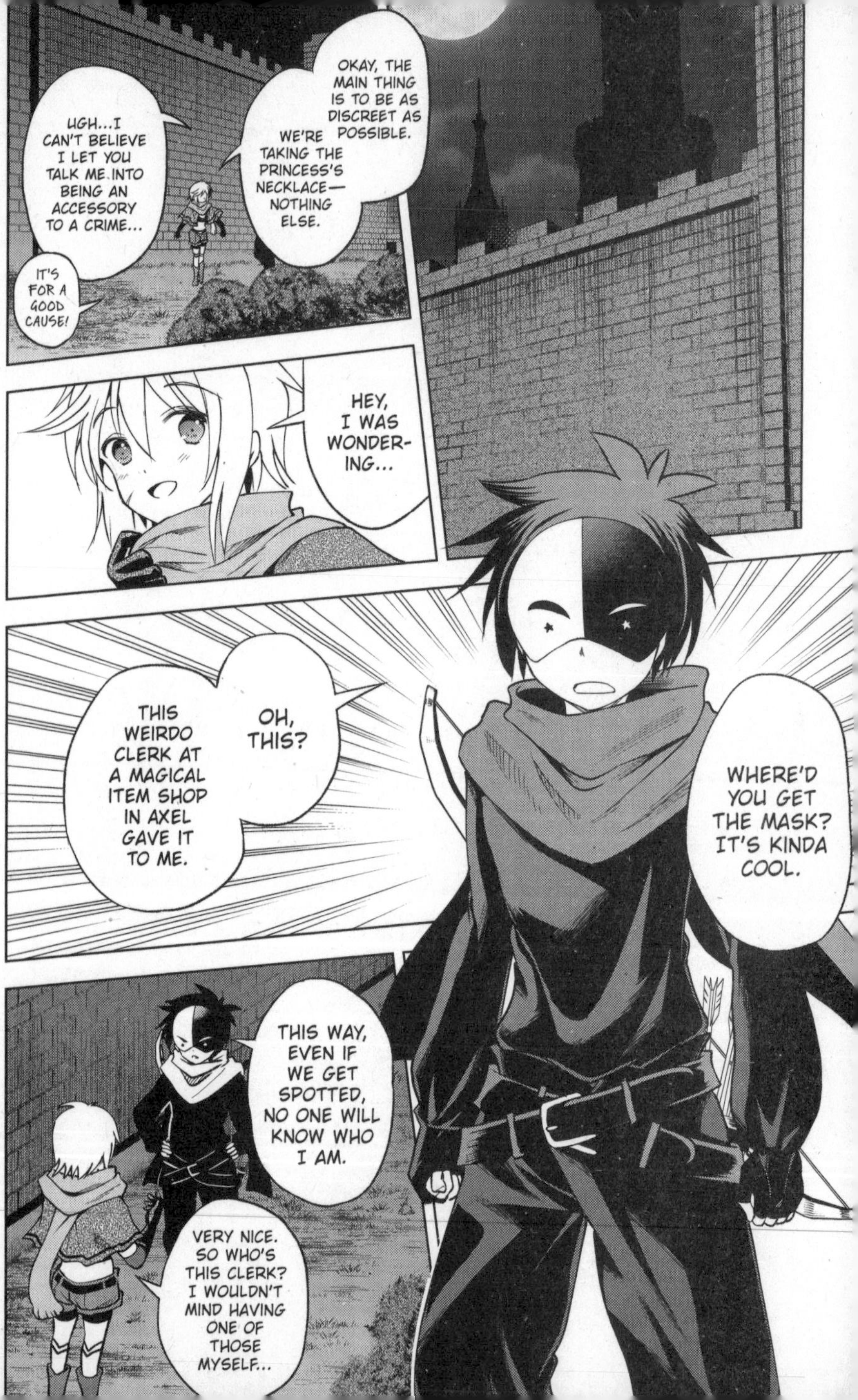
OKAY, THE MAIN THING IS TO BE AS DISCREET AS POSSIBLE.
WE'RE TAKING THE PRINCESS'S NECKLACE—NOTHING ELSE.
UGH...I CAN'T BELIEVE I LET YOU TALK ME INTO BEING AN ACCESSORY TO A CRIME...
IT'S FOR A GOOD CAUSE!
HEY, I WAS WONDER-ING...
WHERE'D YOU GET THE MASK? IT'S KINDA COOL.
OH, THIS?
THIS WEIRDO CLERK AT A MAGICAL ITEM SHOP IN AXEL GAVE IT TO ME.
THIS WAY, EVEN IF WE GET SPOTTED, NO ONE WILL KNOW WHO I AM.
VERY NICE. SO WHO'S THIS CLERK? I WOULDN'T MIND HAVING ONE OF THOSE MYSELF...

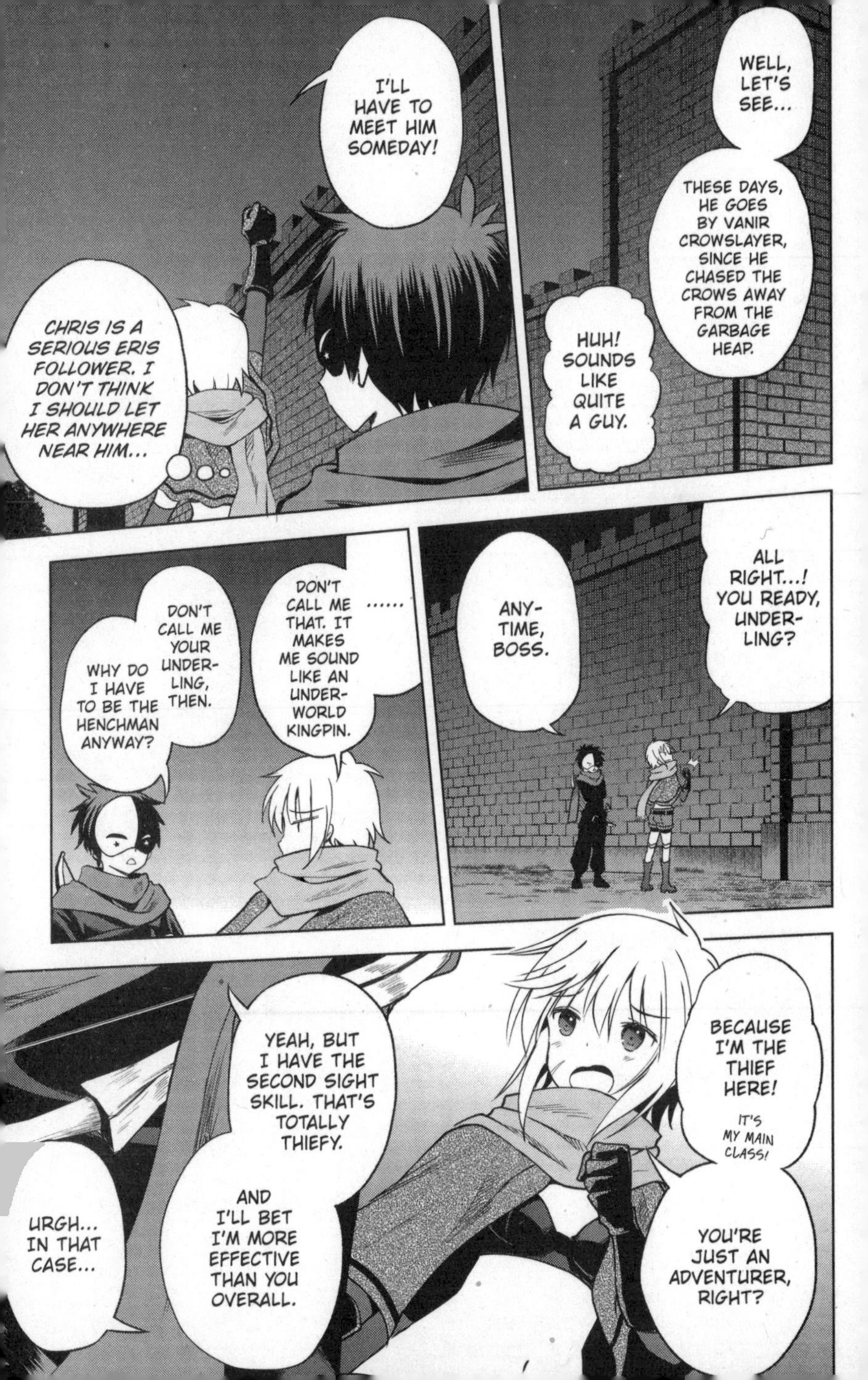
WELL, LET'S SEE...
THESE DAYS, HE GOES BY VANIR CROWSLAYER, SINCE HE CHASED THE CROWS AWAY FROM THE GARBAGE HEAP.
HUH! SOUNDS LIKE QUITE A GUY.
I'LL HAVE TO MEET HIM SOMEDAY!
CHRIS IS A SERIOUS ERIS FOLLOWER. I DON'T THINK I SHOULD LET HER ANYWHERE NEAR HIM...
ALL RIGHT...! YOU READY, UNDER-LING?
ANY-TIME, BOSS.
......
DON'T CALL ME THAT. IT MAKES ME SOUND LIKE AN UNDER-WORLD KINGPIN.
DON'T CALL ME YOUR UNDER-LING, THEN.
WHY DO I HAVE TO BE THE HENCHMAN ANYWAY?
BECAUSE I'M THE THIEF HERE!
IT'S MY MAIN CLASS!
YOU'RE JUST AN ADVENTURER, RIGHT?
YEAH, BUT I HAVE THE SECOND SIGHT SKILL. THAT'S TOTALLY THIEFY.
AND I'LL BET I'M MORE EFFECTIVE THAN YOU OVERALL.
URGH... IN THAT CASE...

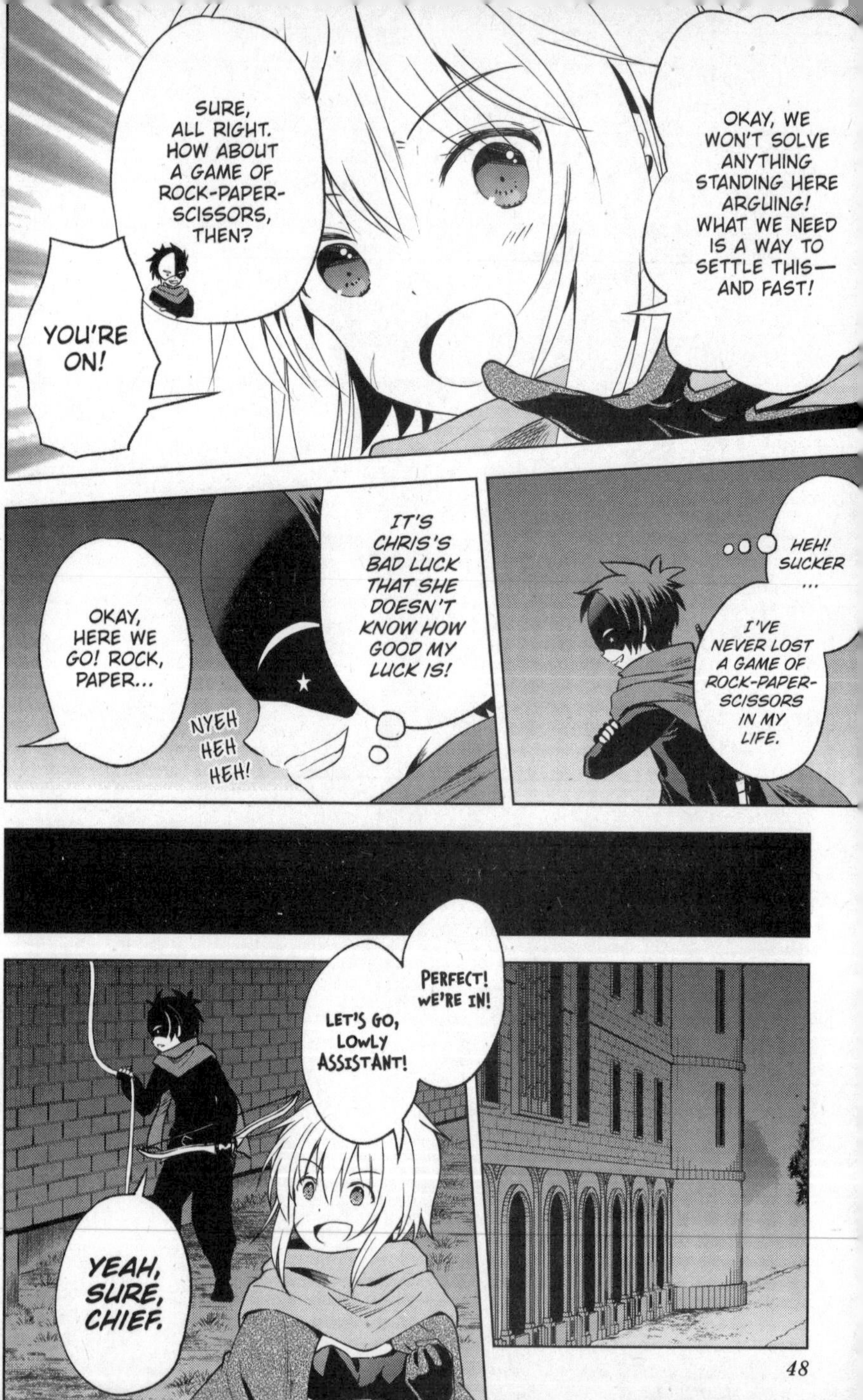
OKAY, WE WON'T SOLVE ANYTHING STANDING HERE ARGUING! WHAT WE NEED IS A WAY TO SETTLE THIS—AND FAST!
SURE, ALL RIGHT. HOW ABOUT A GAME OF ROCK-PAPER-SCISSORS, THEN?
YOU'RE ON!
HEH! SUCKER ...
I'VE NEVER LOST A GAME OF ROCK-PAPER-SCISSORS IN MY LIFE.
IT'S CHRIS'S BAD LUCK THAT SHE DOESN'T KNOW HOW GOOD MY LUCK IS!
OKAY, HERE WE GO! ROCK, PAPER...
NYEH HEH HEH!
PERFECT! WE'RE IN!
LET'S GO, LOWLY ASSISTANT!
YEAH, SURE, CHIEF.

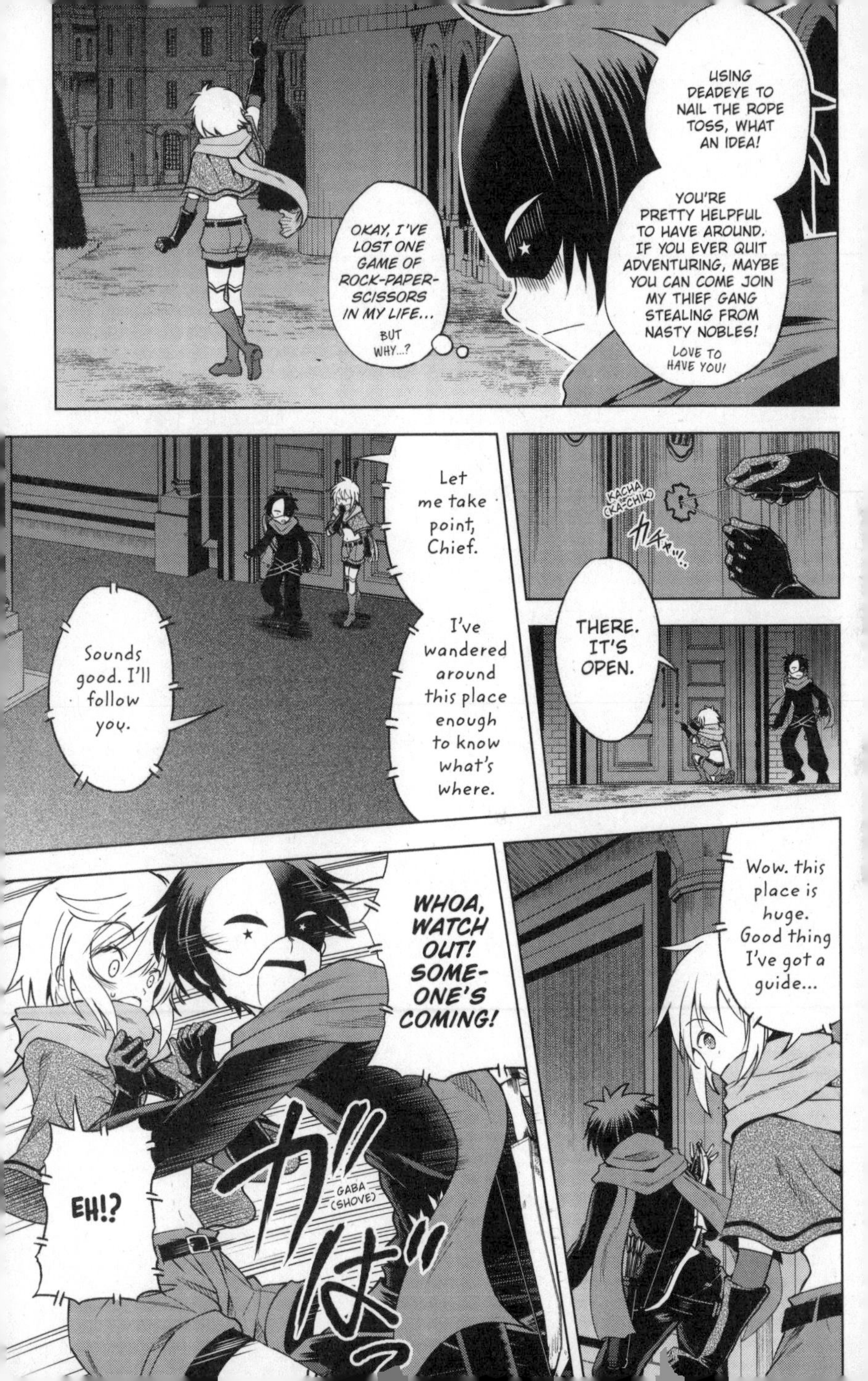
USING DEADEYE TO NAIL THE ROPE TOSS, WHAT AN IDEA!
YOU'RE PRETTY HELPFUL TO HAVE AROUND. IF YOU EVER QUIT ADVENTURING, MAYBE YOU CAN COME JOIN MY THIEF GANG STEALING FROM NASTY NOBLES!
LOVE TO HAVE YOU!
OKAY, I'VE LOST ONE GAME OF ROCK-PAPER-SCISSORS IN MY LIFE...
BUT WHY...?
KACHA (KA-CHIK)
THERE. IT'S OPEN.
Let me take point, Chief.
I've wandered around this place enough to know what's where.
Sounds good. I'll follow you.
Wow. this place is huge. Good thing I've got a guide...
WHOA, WATCH OUT! SOMEONE'S COMING!
GABA (SHOVE)
EH!?

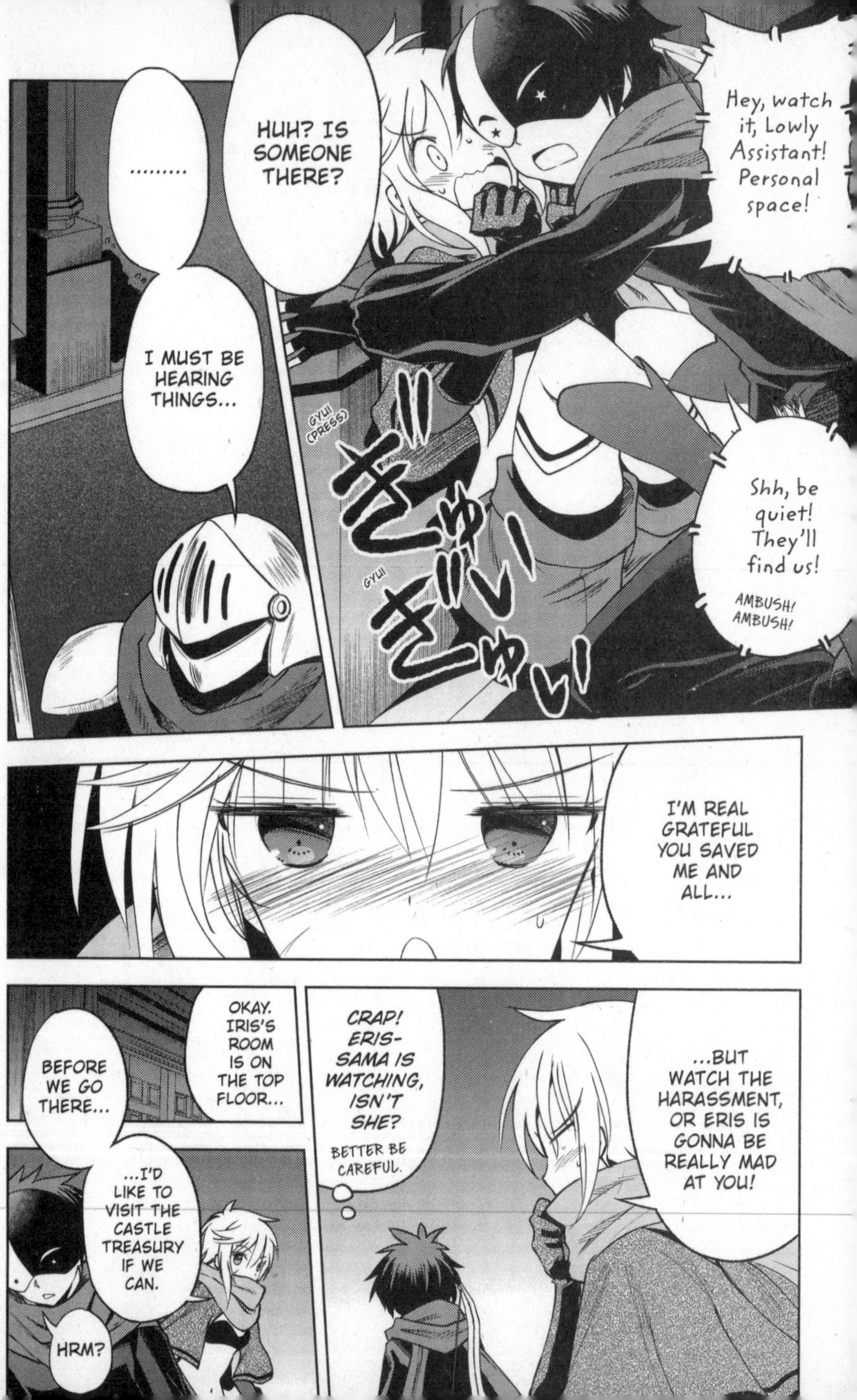
Hey, watch it, Lowly Assistant! Personal space!
HUH? IS SOMEONE THERE?
....
Shh, be quiet! They'll find us!
AMBUSH! AMBUSH!
I MUST BE HEARING THINGS...
GYUI (PRESS)
GYUI
I'M REAL GRATEFUL YOU SAVED ME AND ALL...
...BUT WATCH THE HARASSMENT, OR ERIS IS GONNA BE REALLY MAD AT YOU!
CRAP! ERIS-SAMA IS WATCHING, ISN'T SHE?
BETTER BE CAREFUL.
OKAY. IRIS'S ROOM IS ON THE TOP FLOOR...
BEFORE WE GO THERE...
...I'D LIKE TO VISIT THE CASTLE TREASURY IF WE CAN.
HRM?

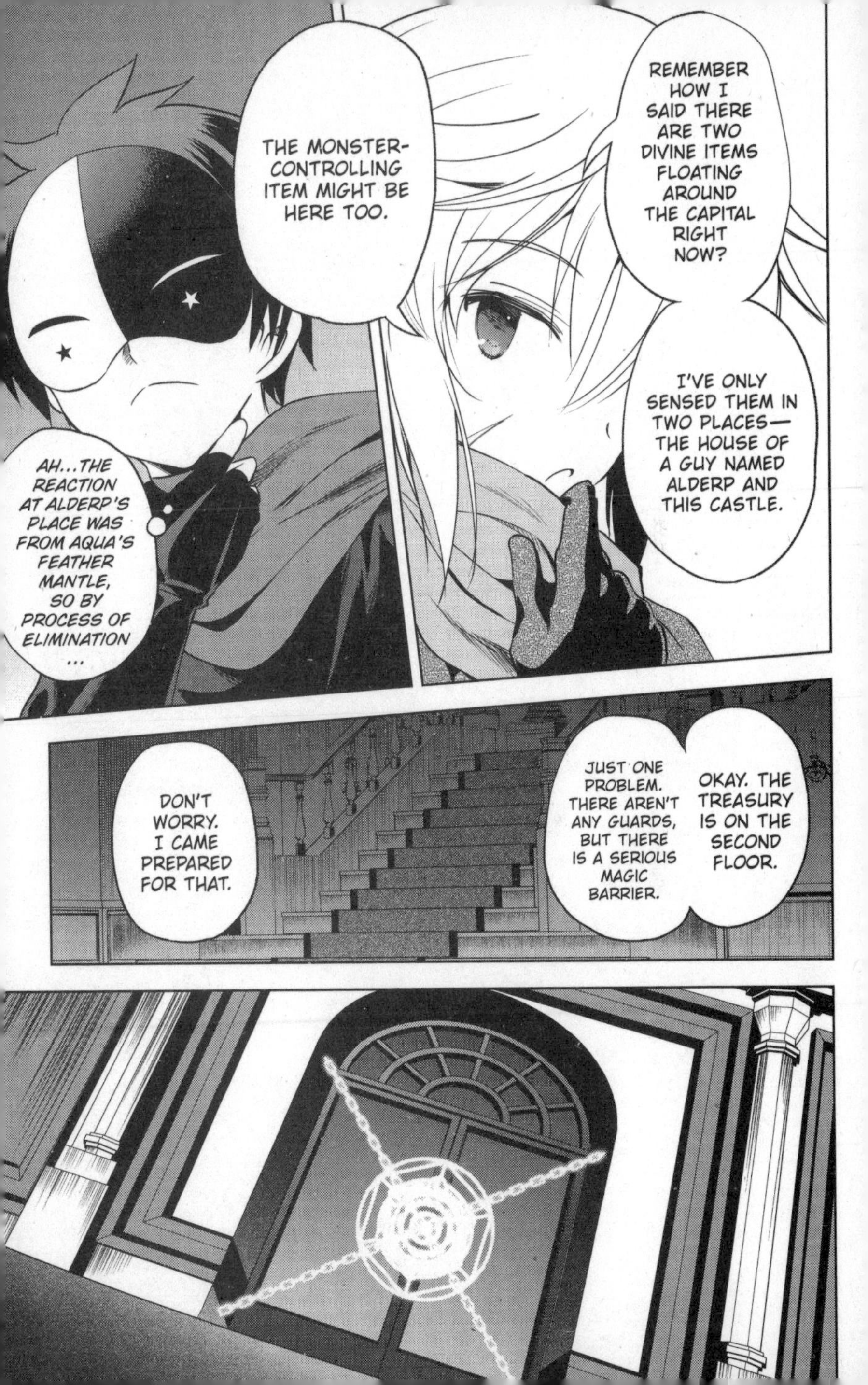
REMEMBER HOW I SAID THERE ARE TWO DIVINE ITEMS FLOATING AROUND THE CAPITAL RIGHT NOW?
I'VE ONLY SENSED THEM IN TWO PLACES— THE HOUSE OF A GUY NAMED ALDERP AND THIS CASTLE.
THE MONSTER-CONTROLLING ITEM MIGHT BE HERE TOO.
AH...THE REACTION AT ALDERP'S PLACE WAS FROM AQUA'S FEATHER MANTLE, SO BY PROCESS OF ELIMINATION ...
OKAY. THE TREASURY IS ON THE SECOND FLOOR.
JUST ONE PROBLEM. THERE AREN'T ANY GUARDS, BUT THERE IS A SERIOUS MAGIC BARRIER.
DON'T WORRY. I CAME PREPARED FOR THAT.

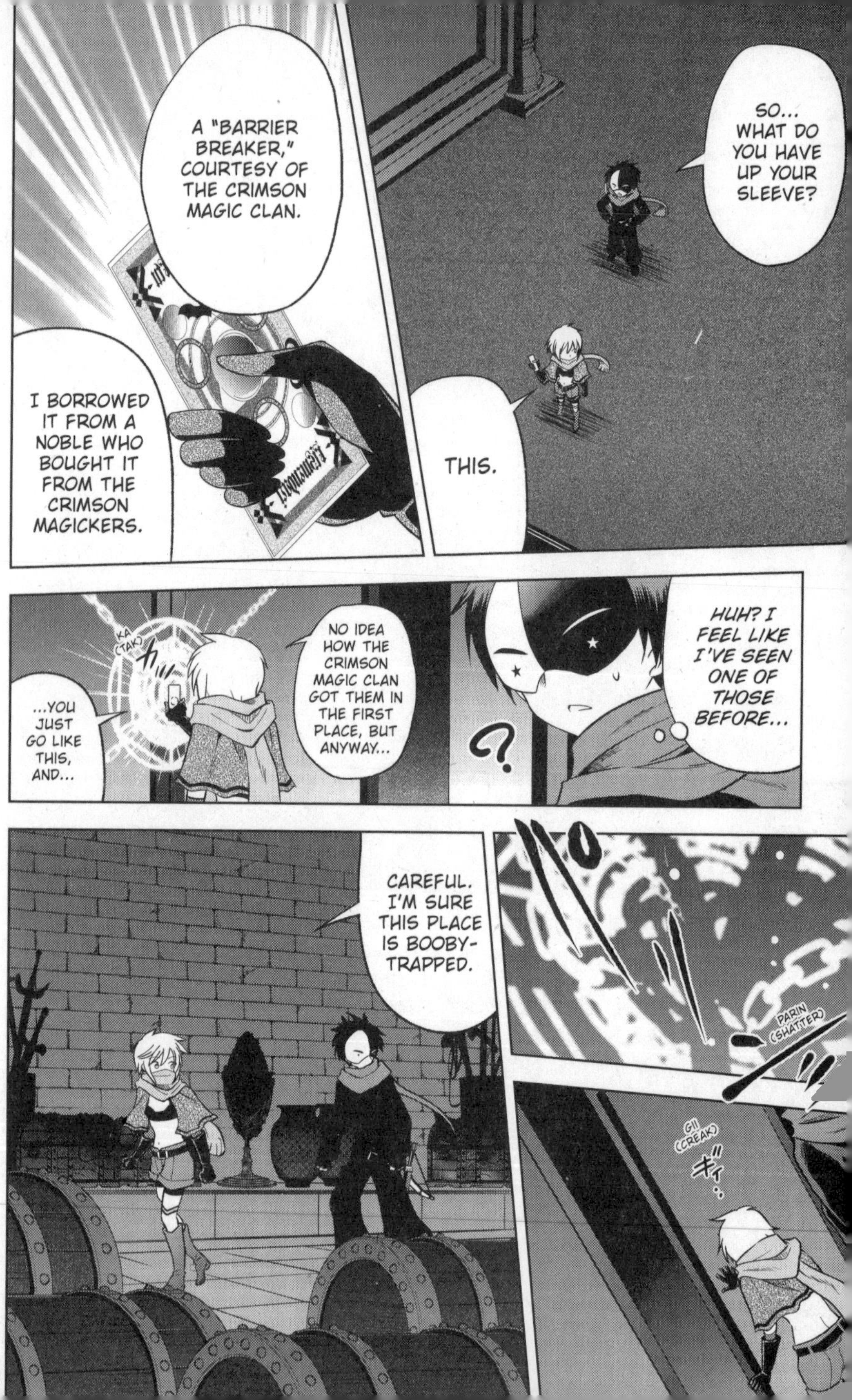
SO... WHAT DO YOU HAVE UP YOUR SLEEVE?
THIS.
A "BARRIER BREAKER," COURTESY OF THE CRIMSON MAGIC CLAN.
I BORROWED IT FROM A NOBLE WHO BOUGHT IT FROM THE CRIMSON MAGICKERS.
HUH? I FEEL LIKE I'VE SEEN ONE OF THOSE BEFORE...
NO IDEA HOW THE CRIMSON MAGIC CLAN GOT THEM IN THE FIRST PLACE, BUT ANYWAY...
KA (TAK)
...YOU JUST GO LIKE THIS, AND...
PARIN (SHATTER)
GII (CREAK)
CAREFUL. I'M SURE THIS PLACE IS BOOBY-TRAPPED.

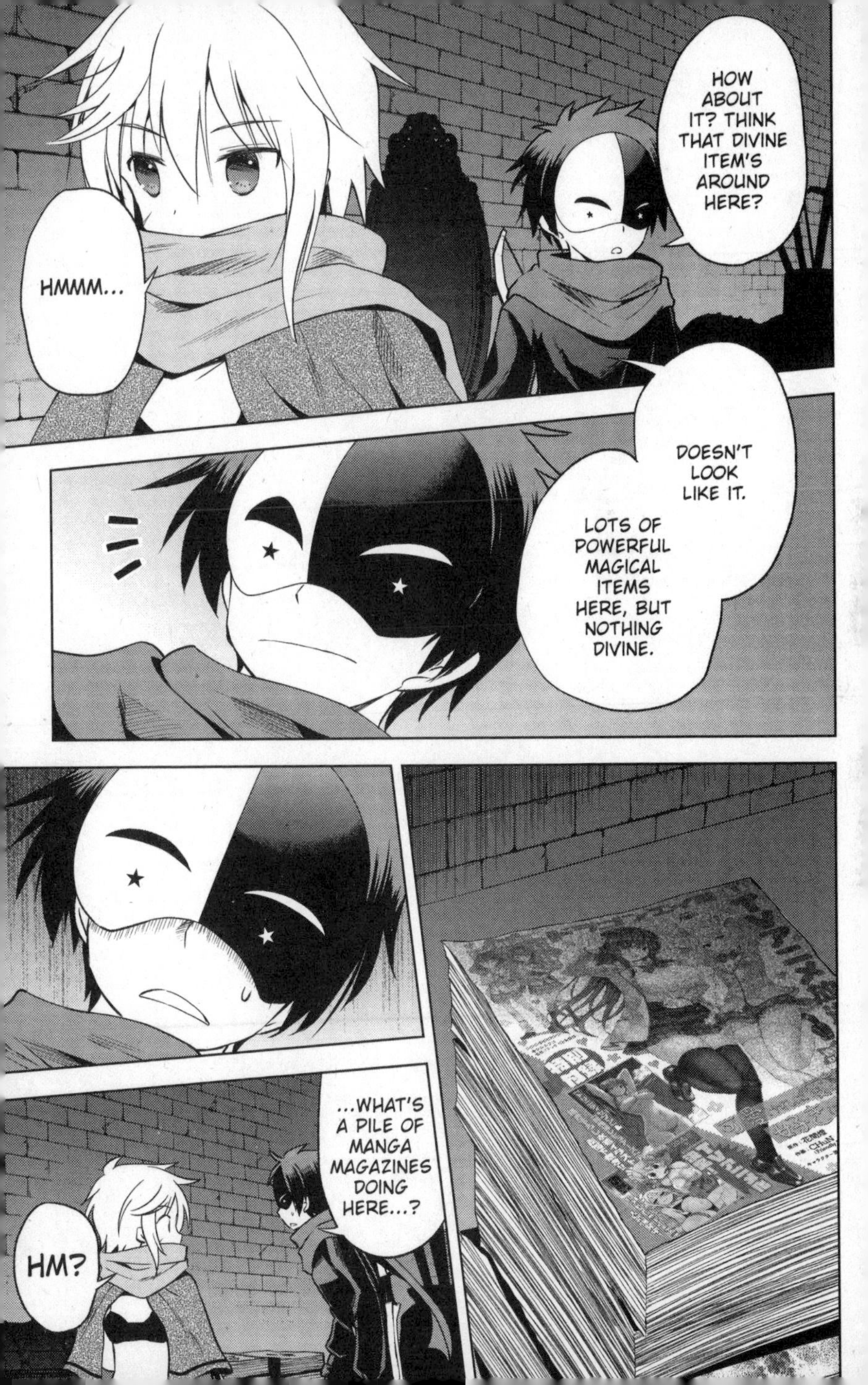
HOW ABOUT IT? THINK THAT DIVINE ITEM'S AROUND HERE?
HMMM...
DOESN'T LOOK LIKE IT.
LOTS OF POWERFUL MAGICAL ITEMS HERE, BUT NOTHING DIVINE.
...WHAT'S A PILE OF MANGA MAGAZINES DOING HERE...?
HM?

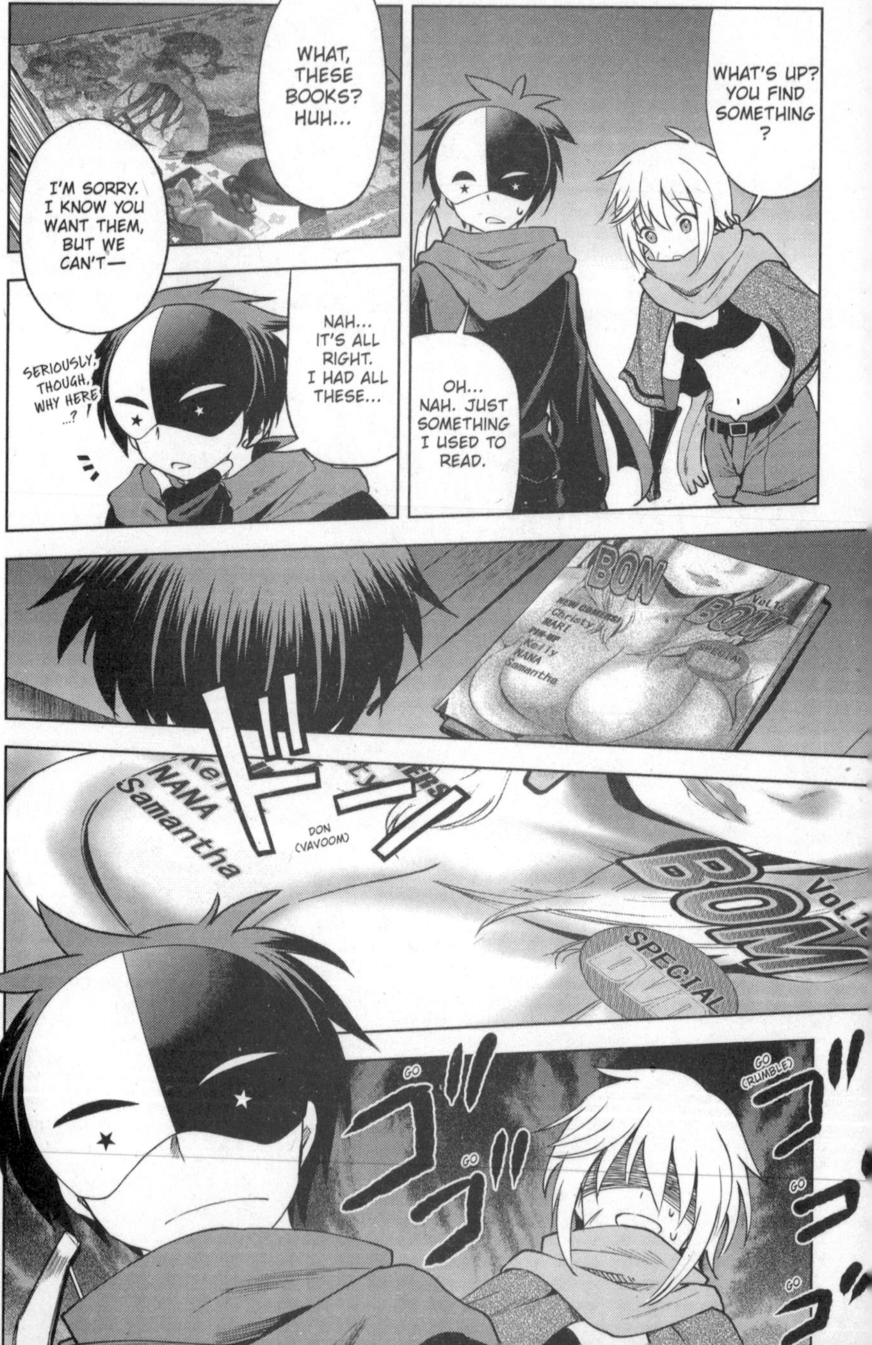
WHAT'S UP? YOU FIND SOMETHING?
OH... NAH. JUST SOMETHING I USED TO READ.
WHAT, THESE BOOKS? HUH...
I'M SORRY. I KNOW YOU WANT THEM, BUT WE CAN'T—
NAH... IT'S ALL RIGHT. I HAD ALL THESE...
SERIOUSLY, THOUGH, WHY HERE ...?!
BON BON
Christy
MARI
Kelly
NANA
Samantha
SPECIAL
DON (VAVOOM)
GO (RUMBLE)
GO
GO
GO
GO

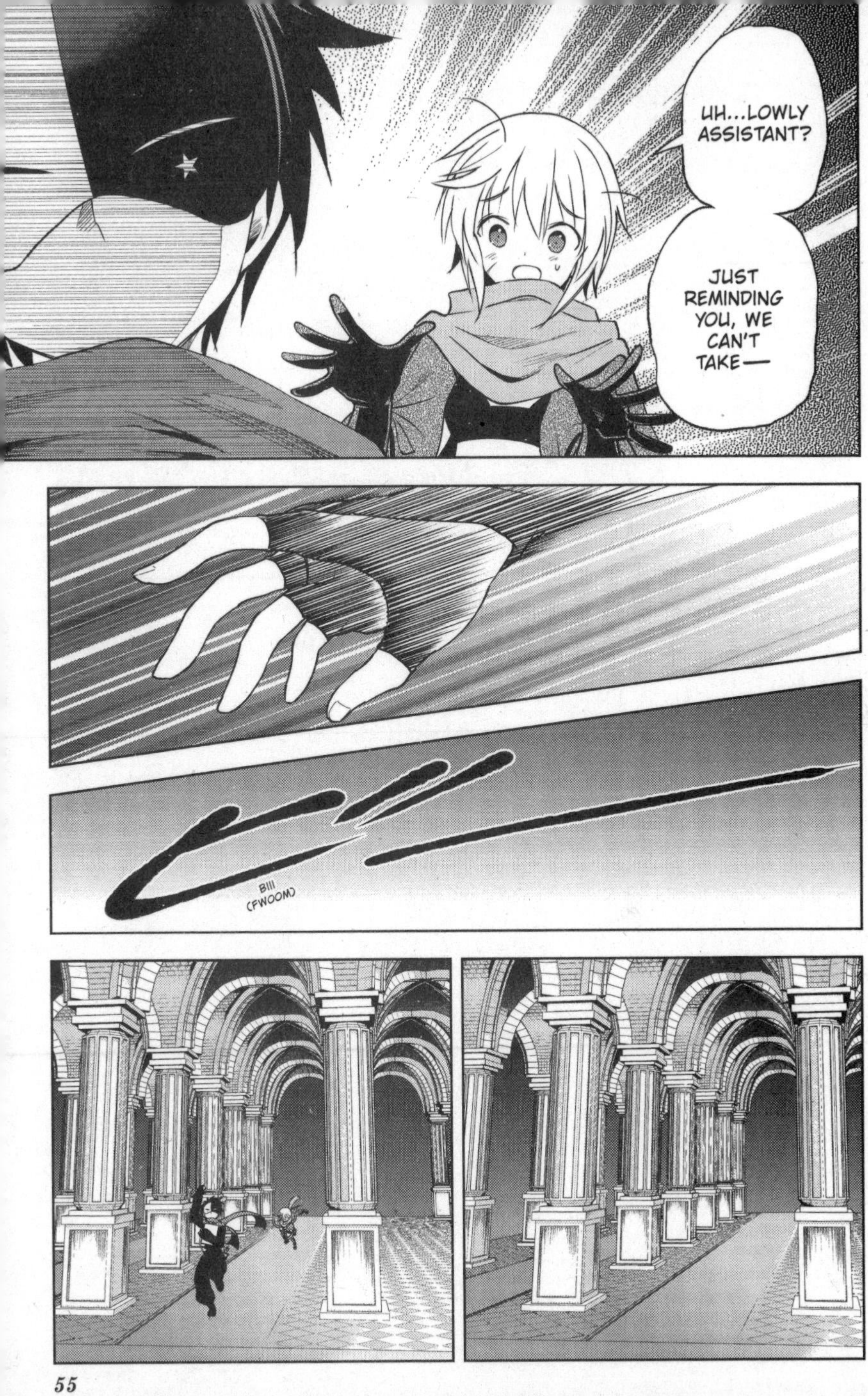
UH...LOWLY ASSISTANT?
JUST REMINDING YOU, WE CAN'T TAKE—
BIII (FWOOM)

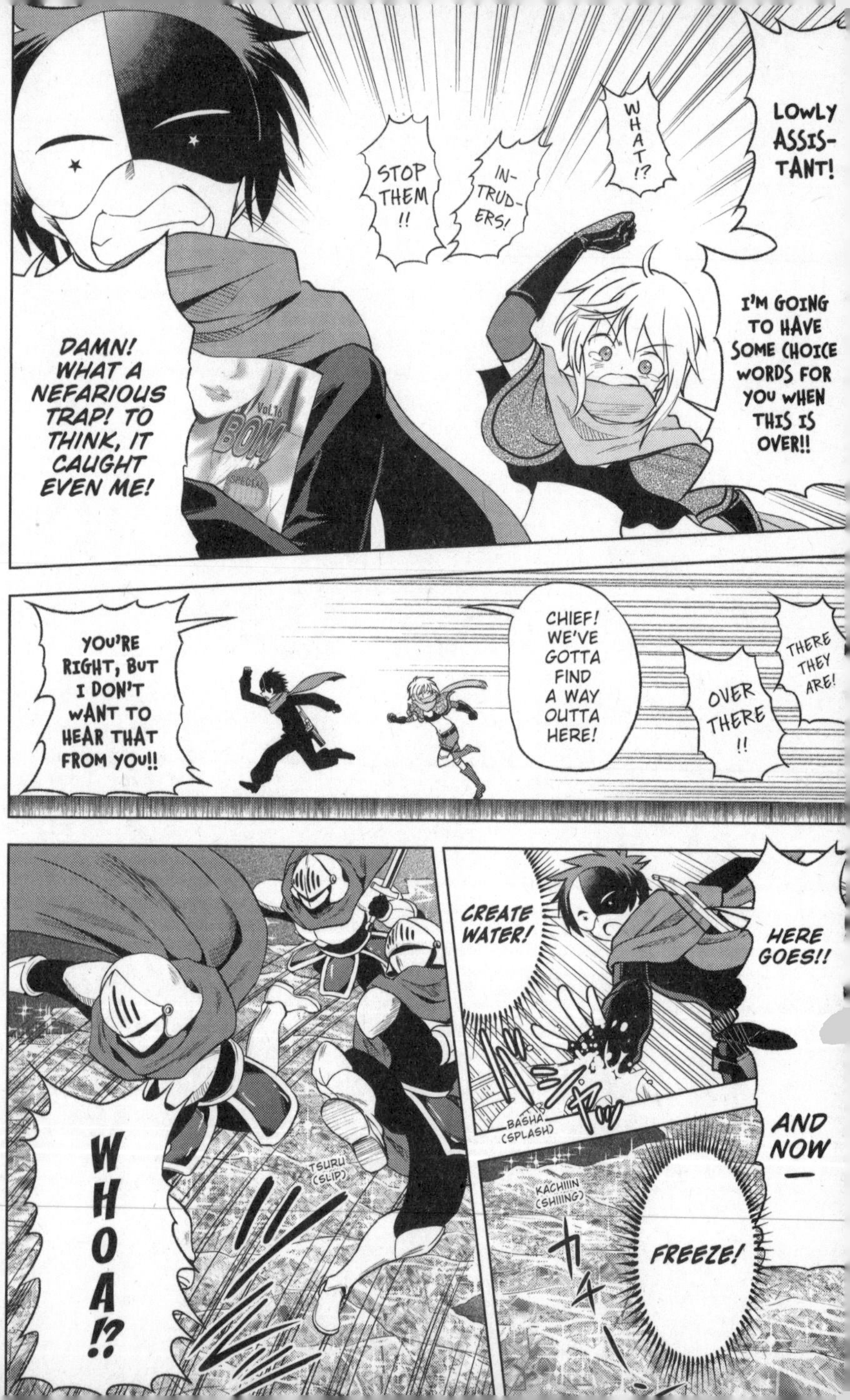
LOWLY ASSIS-TANT!
I'M GOING TO HAVE SOME CHOICE WORDS FOR YOU WHEN THIS IS OVER!!
WHAT!?
IN-TRUD-ERS!
STOP THEM!!
Vol.16
BOM
SPECIAL
DAMN! WHAT A NEFARIOUS TRAP! TO THINK, IT CAUGHT EVEN ME!
THERE THEY ARE!
OVER THERE!!
CHIEF! WE'VE GOTTA FIND A WAY OUTTA HERE!
YOU'RE RIGHT, BUT I DON'T WANT TO HEAR THAT FROM YOU!!
HERE GOES!!
CREATE WATER!
BASHA (SPLASH)
AND NOW—
KACHIIIN (SHIIING)
FREEZE!
TSURU (SLIP)
WHOA!?

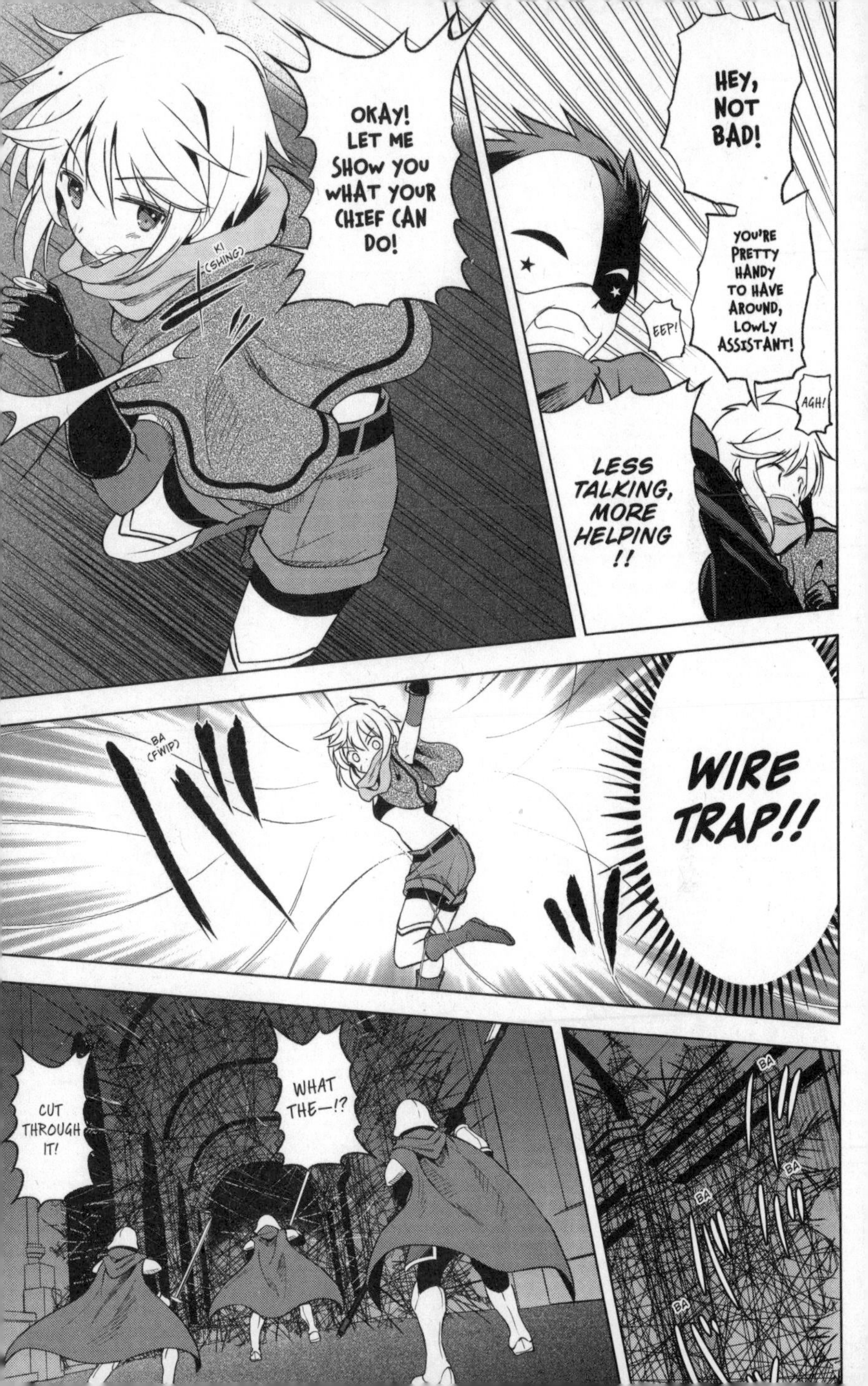
HEY, NOT BAD!
YOU'RE PRETTY HANDY TO HAVE AROUND, LOWLY ASSISTANT!
EEP!
AGH!
LESS TALKING, MORE HELPING !!
OKAY! LET ME SHOW YOU WHAT YOUR CHIEF CAN DO!
KI (SHING)
WIRE TRAP!!
BA (FWIP)
BA
BA
BA
BA
WHAT THE—!?
CUT THROUGH IT!

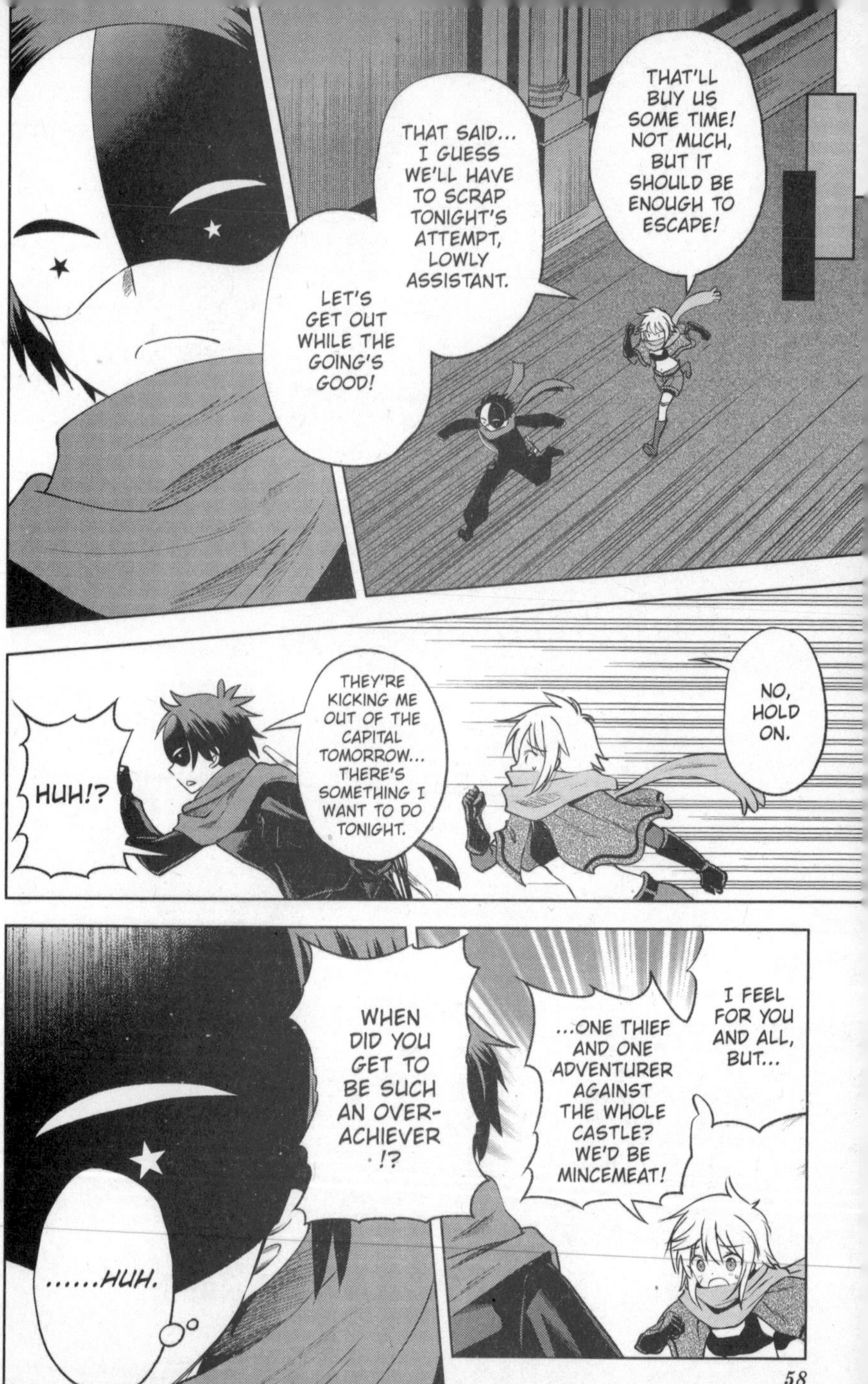
THAT'LL BUY US SOME TIME! NOT MUCH, BUT IT SHOULD BE ENOUGH TO ESCAPE!
THAT SAID... I GUESS WE'LL HAVE TO SCRAP TONIGHT'S ATTEMPT, LOWLY ASSISTANT.
LET'S GET OUT WHILE THE GOING'S GOOD!
NO, HOLD ON.
THEY'RE KICKING ME OUT OF THE CAPITAL TOMORROW... THERE'S SOMETHING I WANT TO DO TONIGHT.
HUH!?
I FEEL FOR YOU AND ALL, BUT...
...ONE THIEF AND ONE ADVENTURER AGAINST THE WHOLE CASTLE? WE'D BE MINCEMEAT!
WHEN DID YOU GET TO BE SUCH AN OVER-ACHIEVER!?
......HUH.

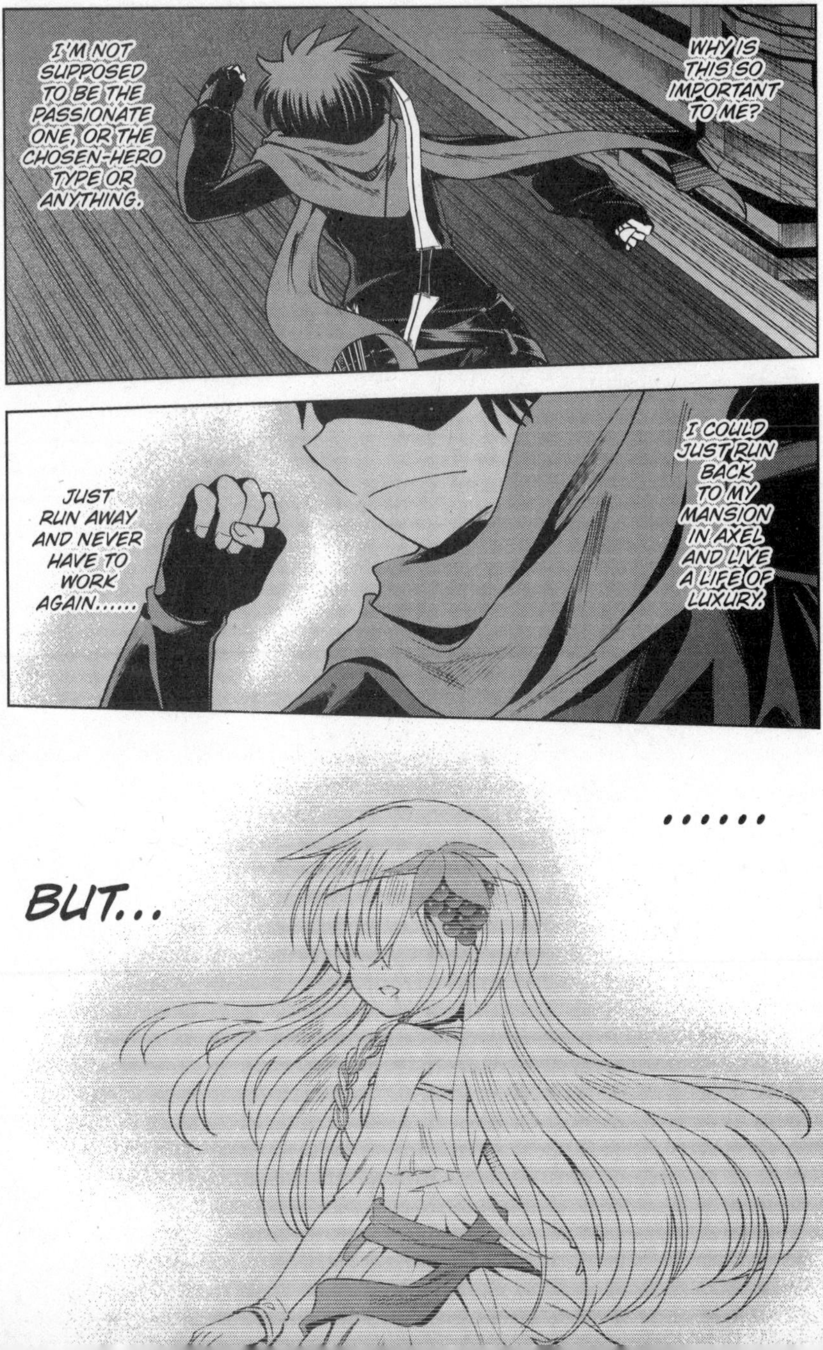
WHY IS THIS SO IMPORTANT TO ME?
I'M NOT SUPPOSED TO BE THE PASSIONATE ONE, OR THE CHOSEN-HERO TYPE OR ANYTHING.
I COULD JUST RUN BACK TO MY MANSION IN AXEL AND LIVE A LIFE OF LUXURY.
JUST RUN AWAY AND NEVER HAVE TO WORK AGAIN......
......
BUT...

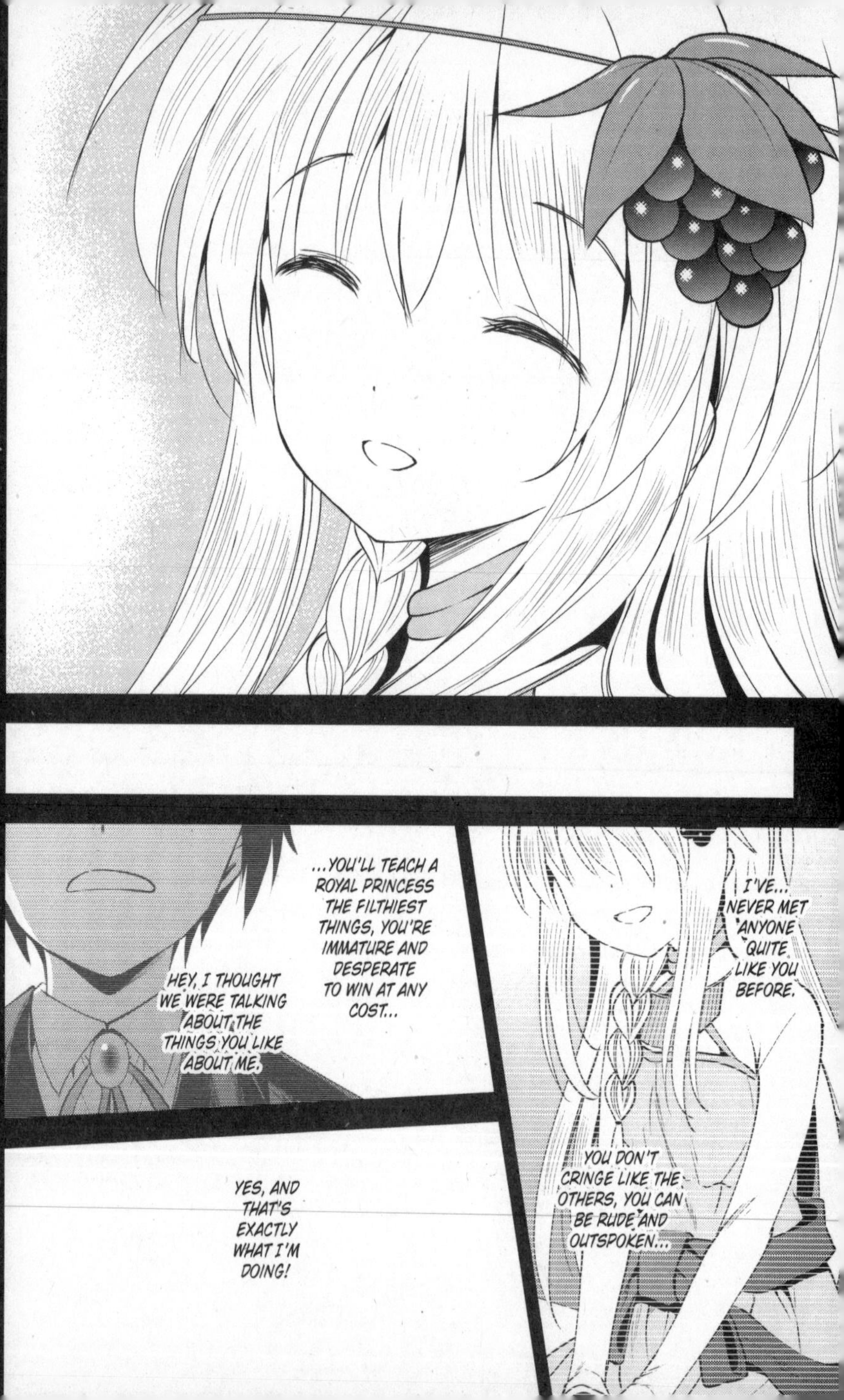
I'VE... NEVER MET ANYONE QUITE LIKE YOU BEFORE.
YOU DON'T CRINGE LIKE THE OTHERS, YOU CAN BE RUDE AND OUTSPOKEN...
...YOU'LL TEACH A ROYAL PRINCESS THE FILTHIEST THINGS, YOU'RE IMMATURE AND DESPERATE TO WIN AT ANY COST...
HEY, I THOUGHT WE WERE TALKING ABOUT THE THINGS YOU LIKE ABOUT ME.
YES, AND THAT'S EXACTLY WHAT I'M DOING!

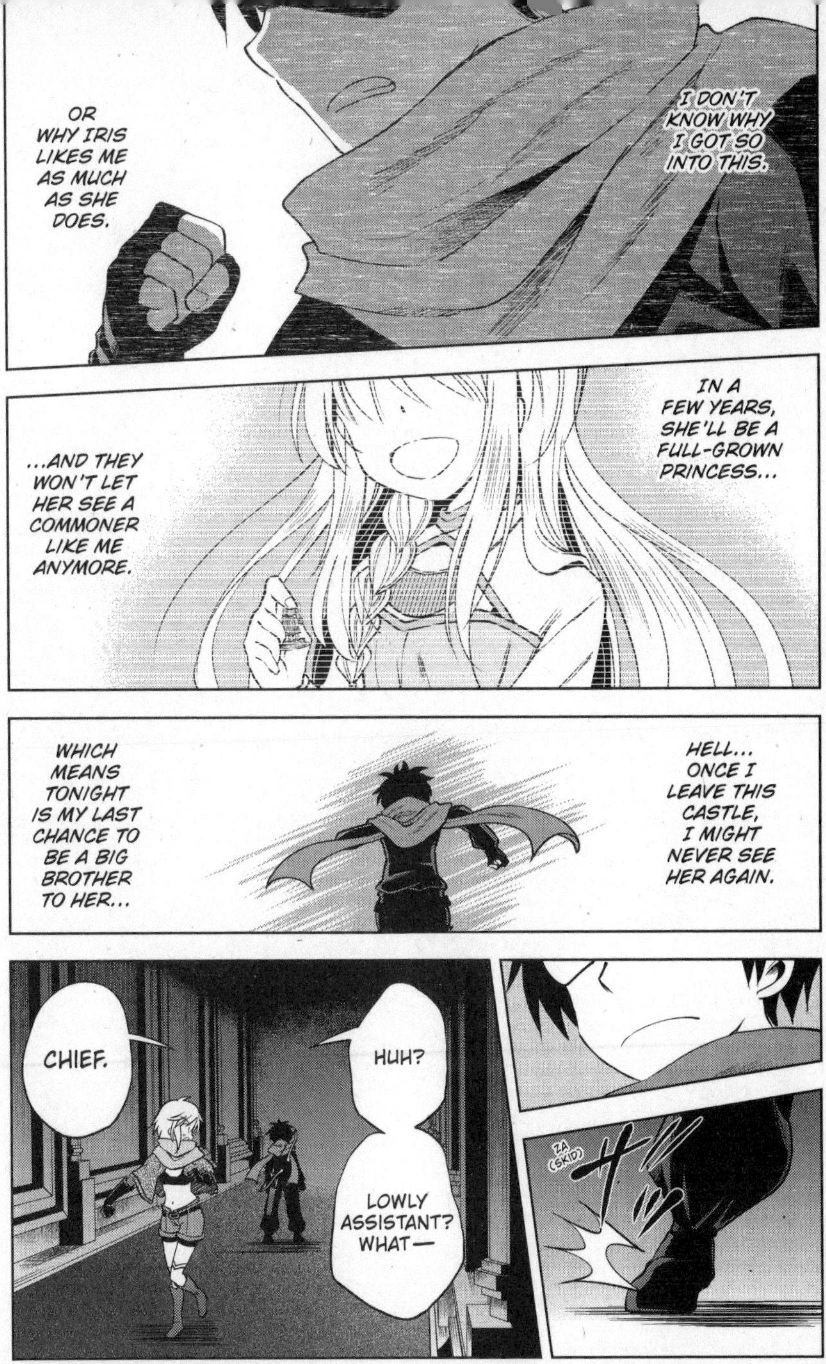
I DON'T KNOW WHY I GOT SO INTO THIS.
OR WHY IRIS LIKES ME AS MUCH AS SHE DOES.
IN A FEW YEARS, SHE'LL BE A FULL-GROWN PRINCESS...
...AND THEY WON'T LET HER SEE A COMMONER LIKE ME ANYMORE.
HELL... ONCE I LEAVE THIS CASTLE, I MIGHT NEVER SEE HER AGAIN.
WHICH MEANS TONIGHT IS MY LAST CHANCE TO BE A BIG BROTHER TO HER...
ZA (SKID)
HUH?
LOWLY ASSISTANT? WHAT—
CHIEF.

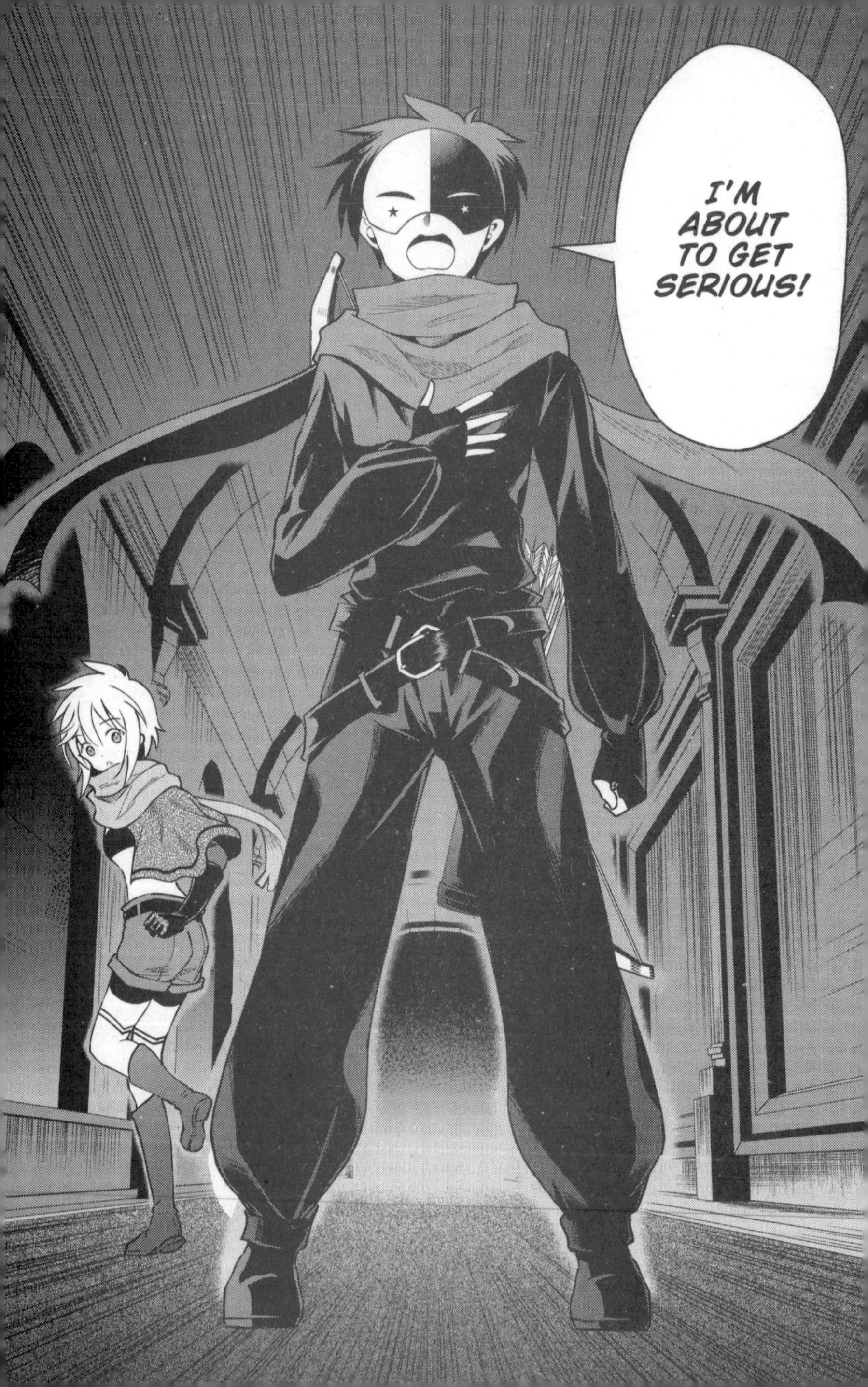
I'M ABOUT TO GET SERIOUS!

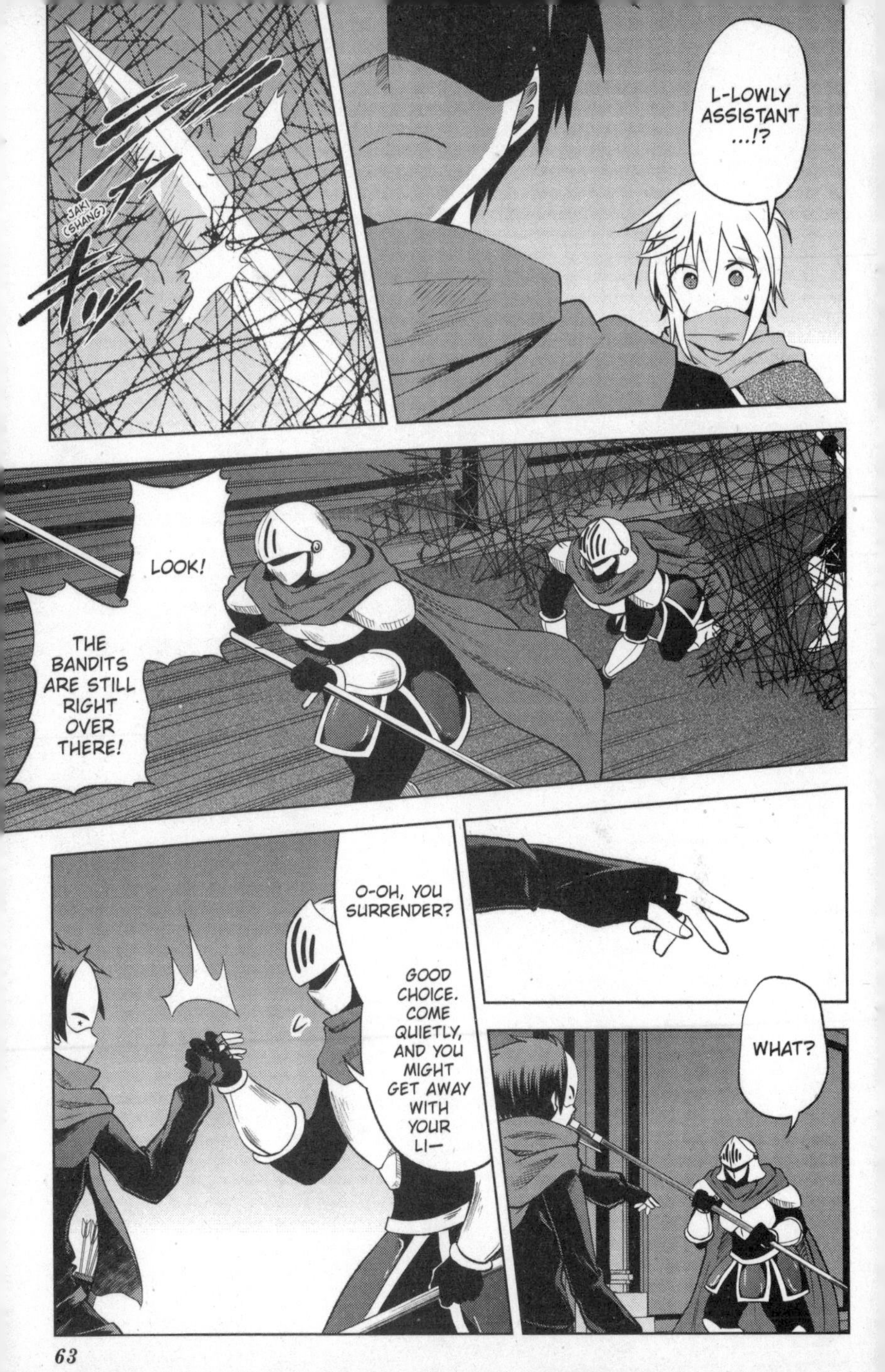
L-LOWLY ASSISTANT ...!?
JAKI (SHANG)
LOOK!
THE BANDITS ARE STILL RIGHT OVER THERE!
O-OH, YOU SURRENDER?
GOOD CHOICE. COME QUIETLY, AND YOU MIGHT GET AWAY WITH YOUR LI—
WHAT?

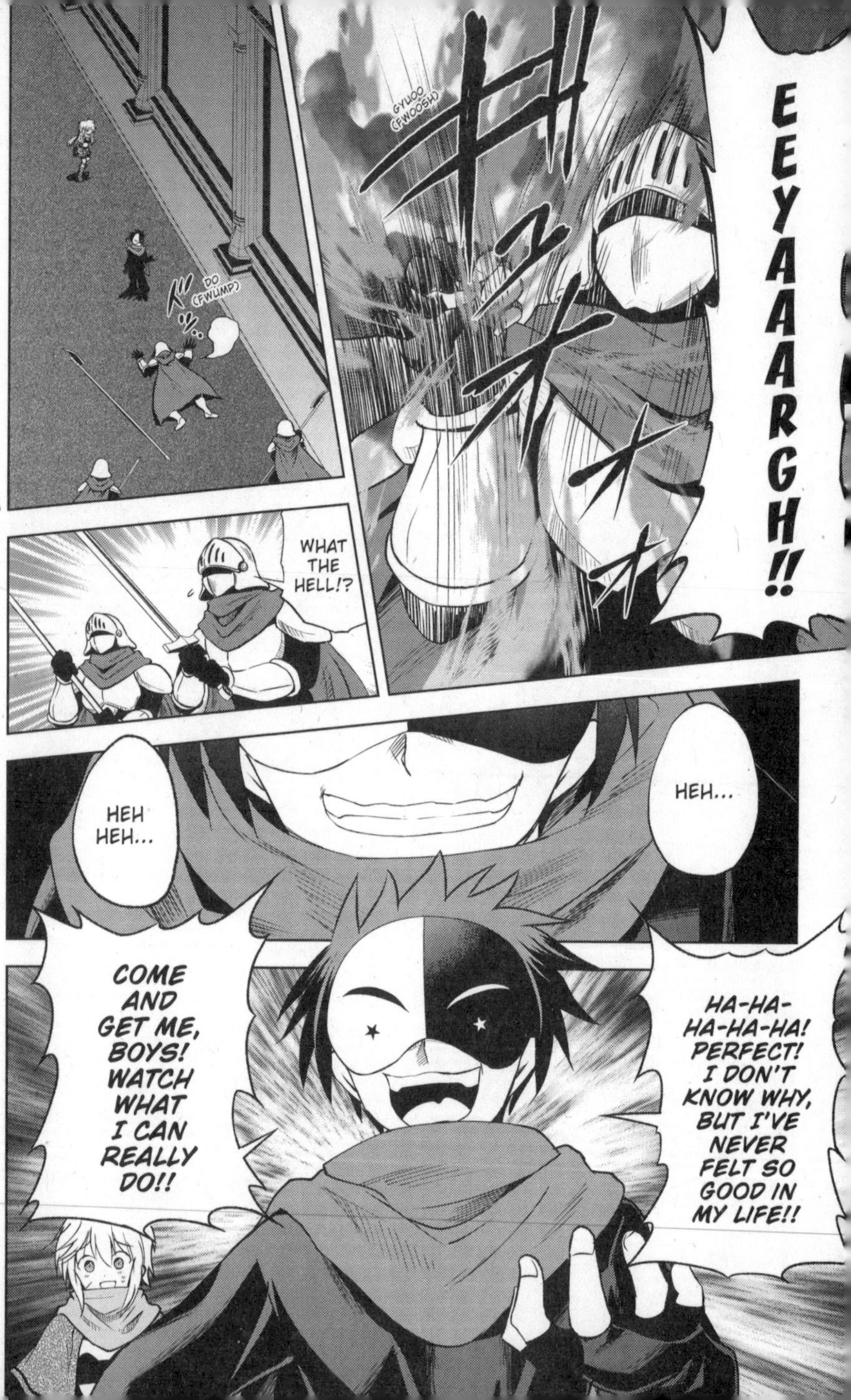
EEYAAARGH!!
GYUOO (FWOOSH)
DO (FWUMP)
WHAT THE HELL!?
HEH...
HEH HEH...
HA-HA-HA-HA-HA! PERFECT! I DON'T KNOW WHY, BUT I'VE NEVER FELT SO GOOD IN MY LIFE!!
COME AND GET ME, BOYS! WATCH WHAT I CAN REALLY DO!!

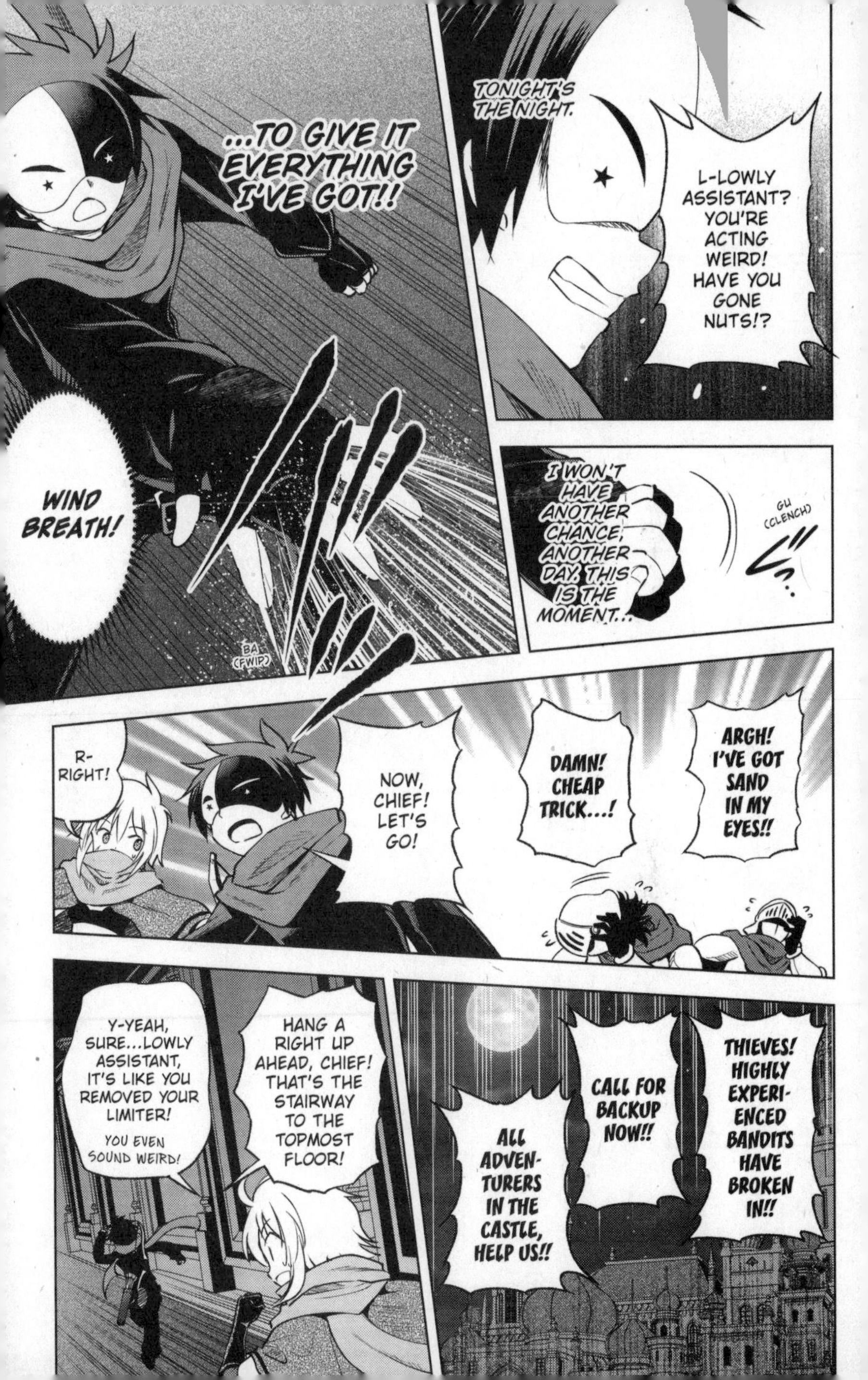
L-LOWLY ASSISTANT? YOU'RE ACTING WEIRD! HAVE YOU GONE NUTS!?
TONIGHT'S THE NIGHT.
GU (CLENCH)
I WON'T HAVE ANOTHER CHANCE, ANOTHER DAY. THIS IS THE MOMENT...
...TO GIVE IT EVERYTHING I'VE GOT!!
WIND BREATH!
BA (FWIP)
ARGH! I'VE GOT SAND IN MY EYES!!
DAMN! CHEAP TRICK...!
NOW, CHIEF! LET'S GO!
R- RIGHT!
THIEVES! HIGHLY EXPERI-ENCED BANDITS HAVE BROKEN IN!!
CALL FOR BACKUP NOW!!
ALL ADVEN-TURERS IN THE CASTLE, HELP US!!
HANG A RIGHT UP AHEAD, CHIEF! THAT'S THE STAIRWAY TO THE TOPMOST FLOOR!
Y-YEAH, SURE...LOWLY ASSISTANT, IT'S LIKE YOU REMOVED YOUR LIMITER!
YOU EVEN SOUND WEIRD!

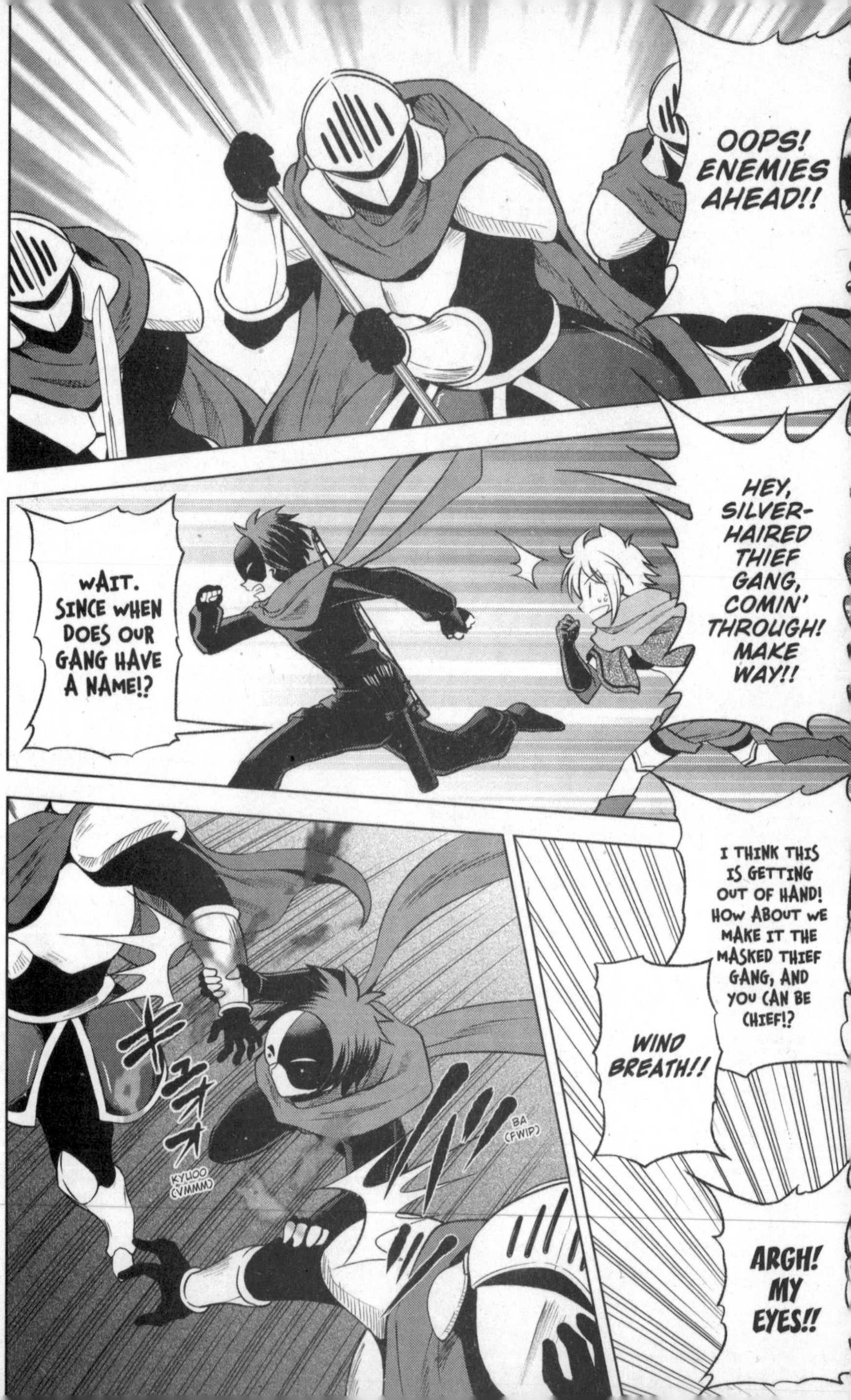
OOPS! ENEMIES AHEAD!!
HEY, SILVER-HAIRED THIEF GANG, COMIN' THROUGH! MAKE WAY!!
WAIT. SINCE WHEN DOES OUR GANG HAVE A NAME!?
I THINK THIS IS GETTING OUT OF HAND! HOW ABOUT WE MAKE IT THE MASKED THIEF GANG, AND YOU CAN BE CHIEF!?
WIND BREATH!!
BA (FWIP)
ARGH! MY EYES!!
KYUOO (VMMM)

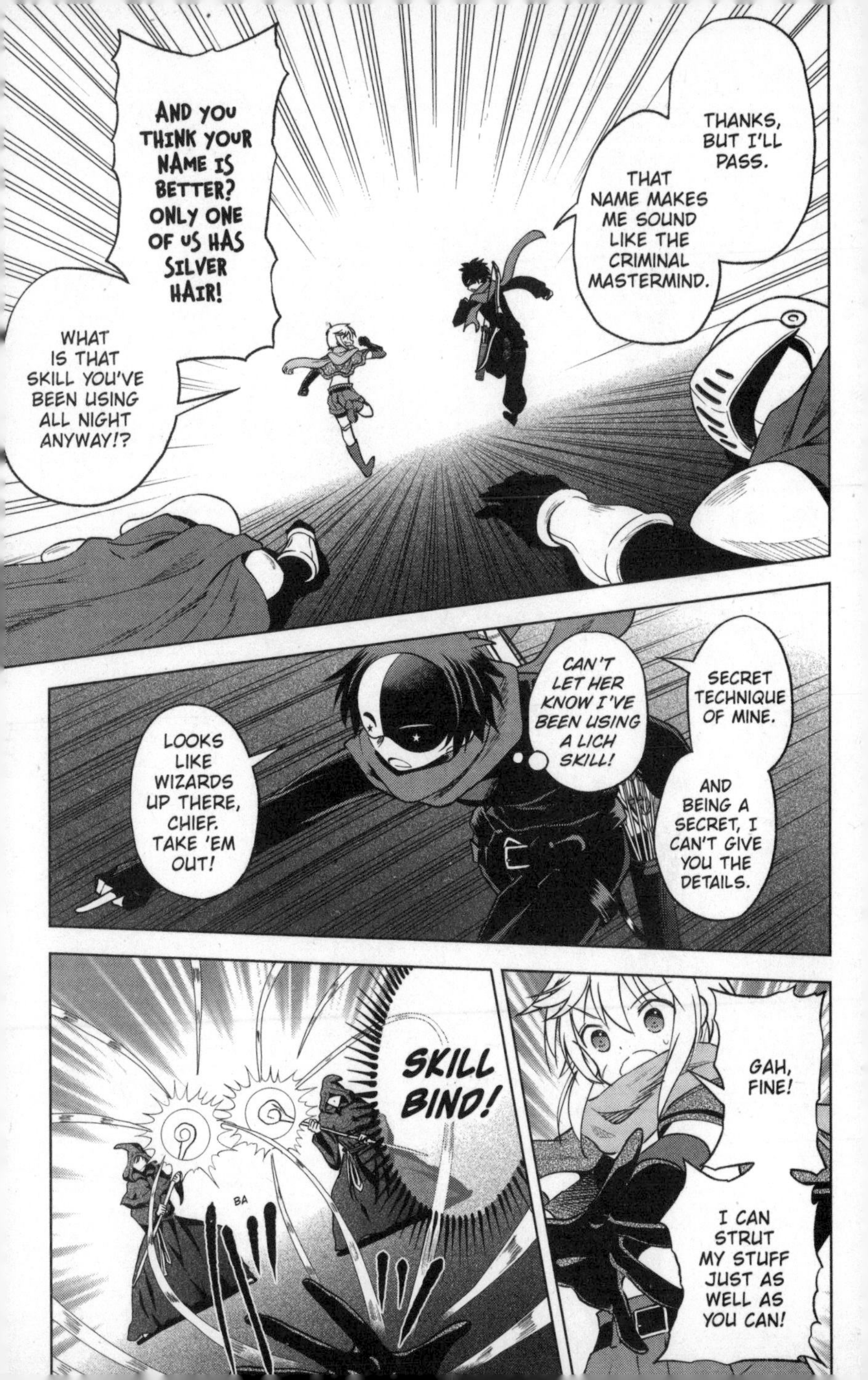
THANKS, BUT I'LL PASS.
THAT NAME MAKES ME SOUND LIKE THE CRIMINAL MASTERMIND.
AND YOU THINK YOUR NAME IS BETTER? ONLY ONE OF US HAS SILVER HAIR!
WHAT IS THAT SKILL YOU'VE BEEN USING ALL NIGHT ANYWAY!?
SECRET TECHNIQUE OF MINE.
AND BEING A SECRET, I CAN'T GIVE YOU THE DETAILS.
CAN'T LET HER KNOW I'VE BEEN USING A LICH SKILL!
LOOKS LIKE WIZARDS UP THERE, CHIEF. TAKE 'EM OUT!
GAH, FINE!
I CAN STRUT MY STUFF JUST AS WELL AS YOU CAN!
SKILL BIND!
BA

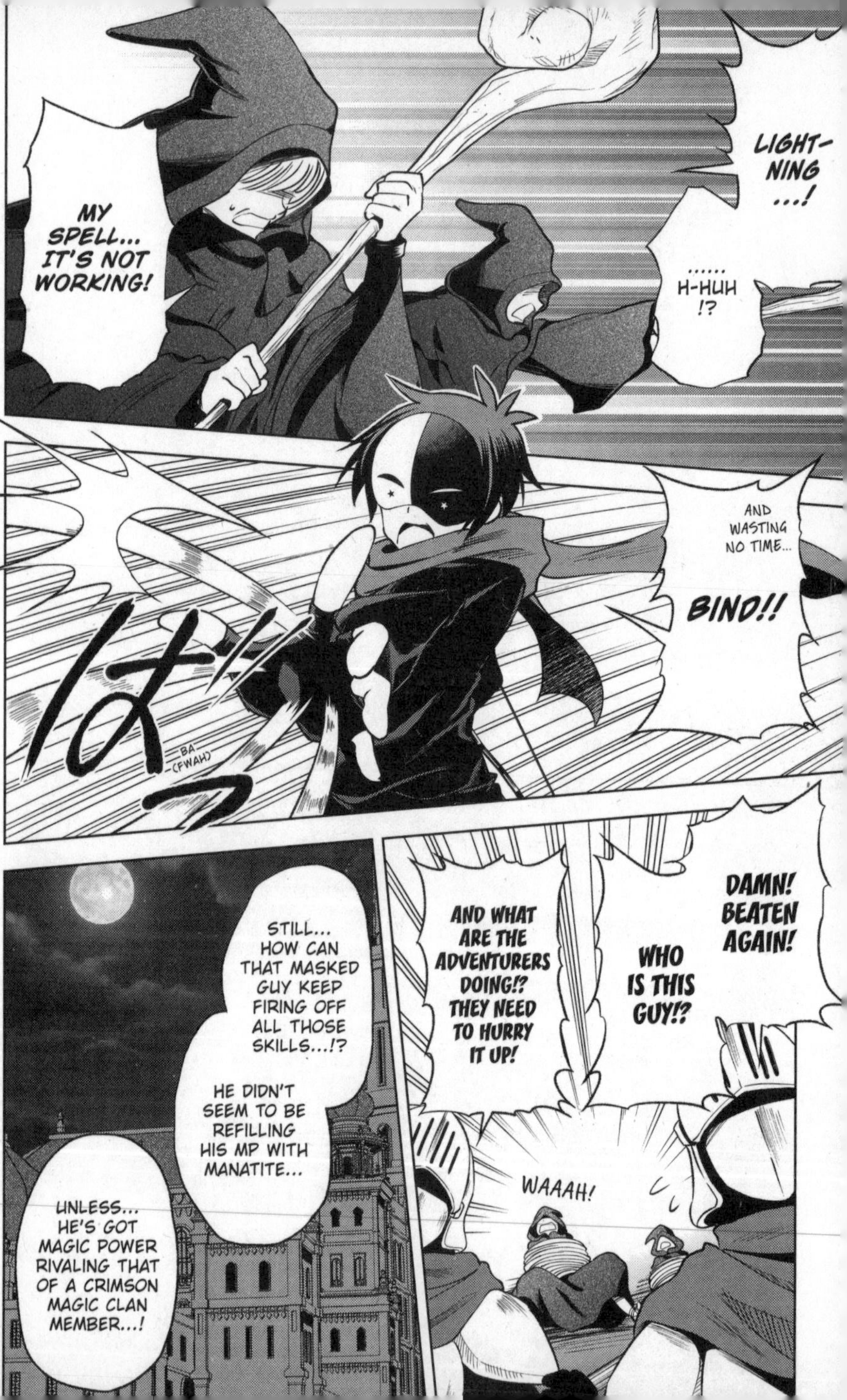
LIGHT-
NING
...!
......
H-HUH
!?
MY SPELL... IT'S NOT WORKING!
AND WASTING NO TIME...
BIND!!
BA (FWAH)
DAMN! BEATEN AGAIN!
WHO IS THIS GUY!?
AND WHAT ARE THE ADVENTURERS DOING!? THEY NEED TO HURRY IT UP!
WAAAH!
STILL... HOW CAN THAT MASKED GUY KEEP FIRING OFF ALL THOSE SKILLS...!?
HE DIDN'T SEEM TO BE REFILLING HIS MP WITH MANATITE...
UNLESS... HE'S GOT MAGIC POWER RIVALING THAT OF A CRIMSON MAGIC CLAN MEMBER...!

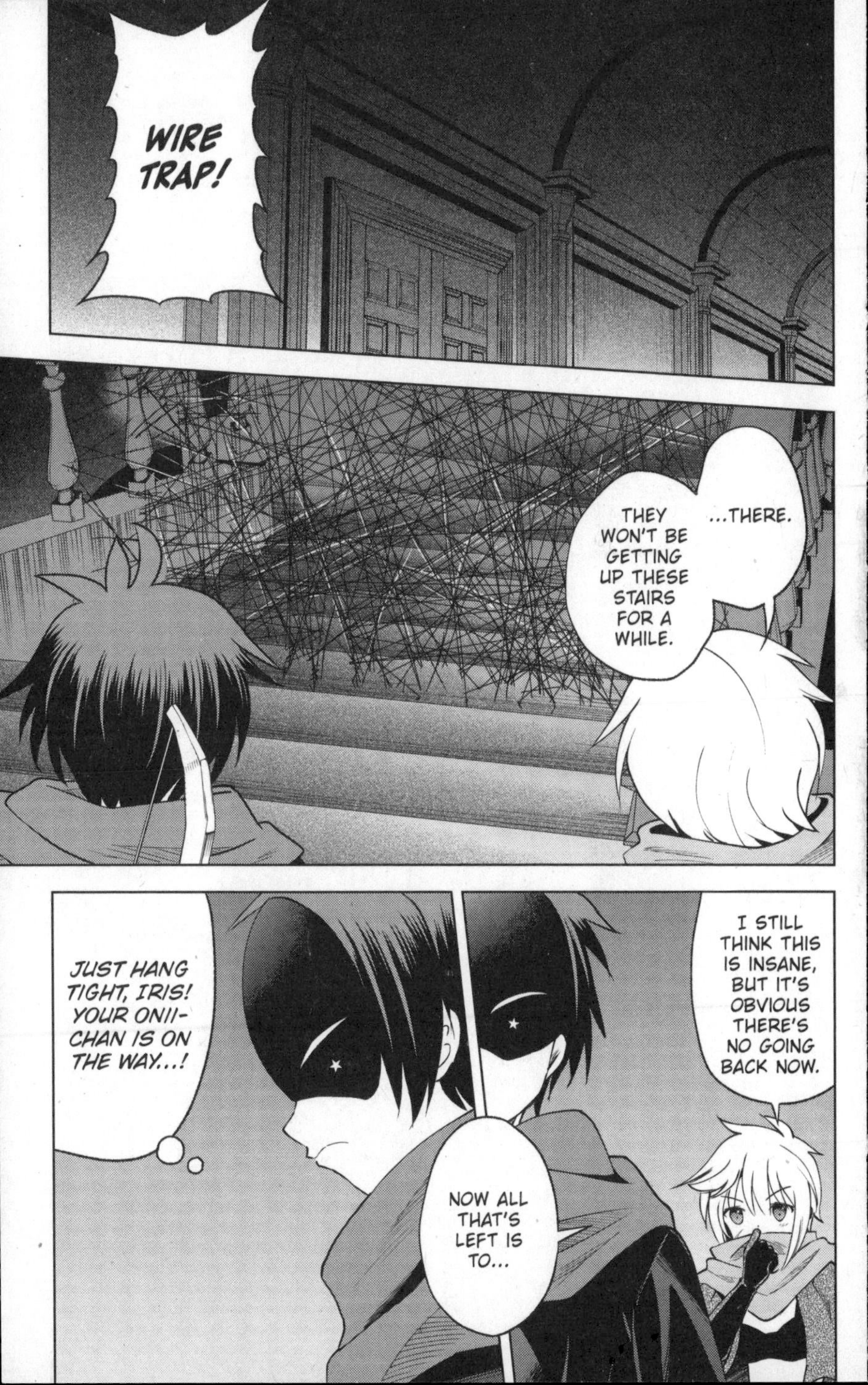
WIRE TRAP!
...THERE.
THEY WON'T BE GETTING UP THESE STAIRS FOR A WHILE.
I STILL THINK THIS IS INSANE, BUT IT'S OBVIOUS THERE'S NO GOING BACK NOW.
NOW ALL THAT'S LEFT IS TO...
JUST HANG TIGHT, IRIS! YOUR ONII-CHAN IS ON THE WAY...!

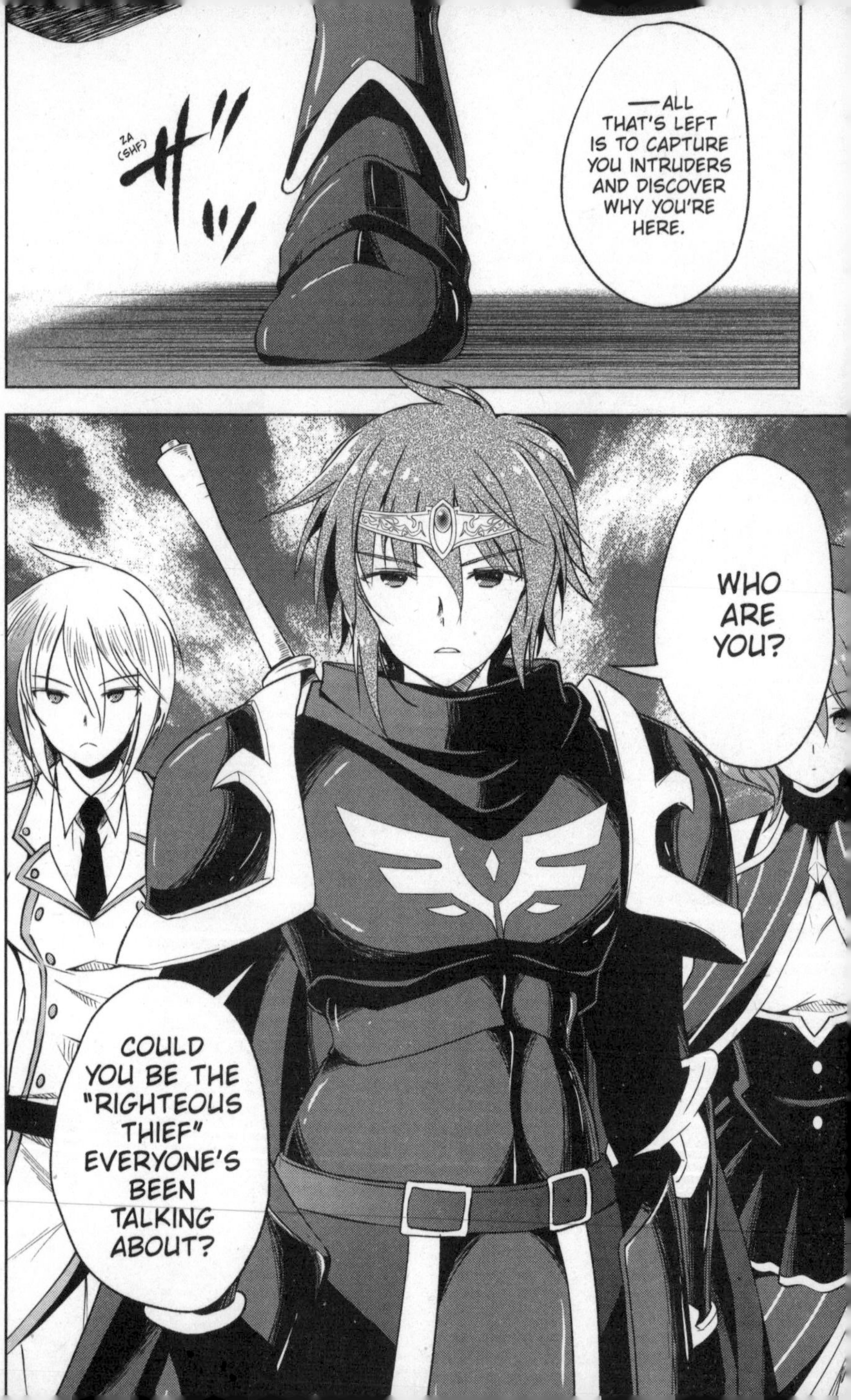
—ALL THAT'S LEFT IS TO CAPTURE YOU INTRUDERS AND DISCOVER WHY YOU'RE HERE.
ZA (SHF)
WHO ARE YOU?
COULD YOU BE THE "RIGHTEOUS THIEF" EVERYONE'S BEEN TALKING ABOUT?

GOD'S
BLESSING
ON THIS
WONDERFUL
WORLD!

11

11

GOD'S
BLESSING
ON THIS
WONDERFUL
WORLD!

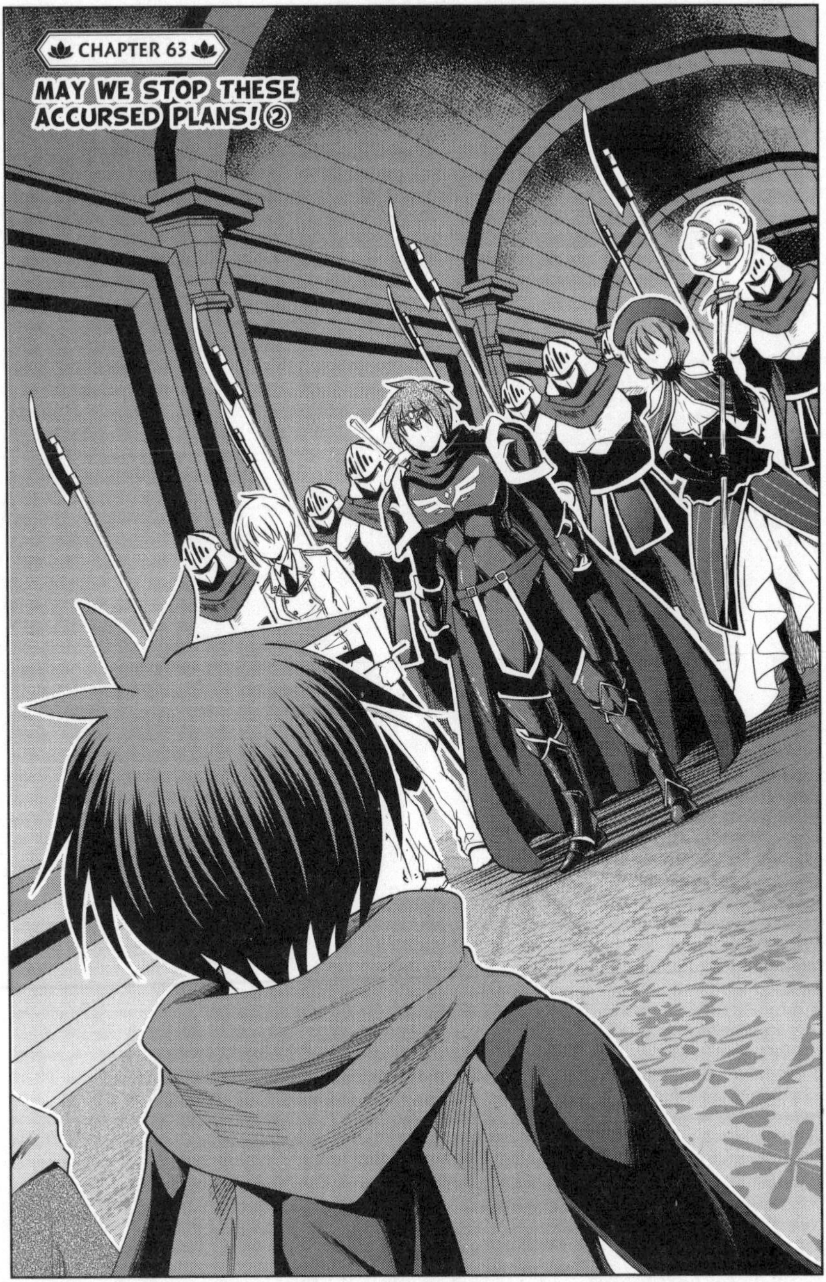
CHAPTER 63
MAY WE STOP THESE ACCURSED PLANS! ②

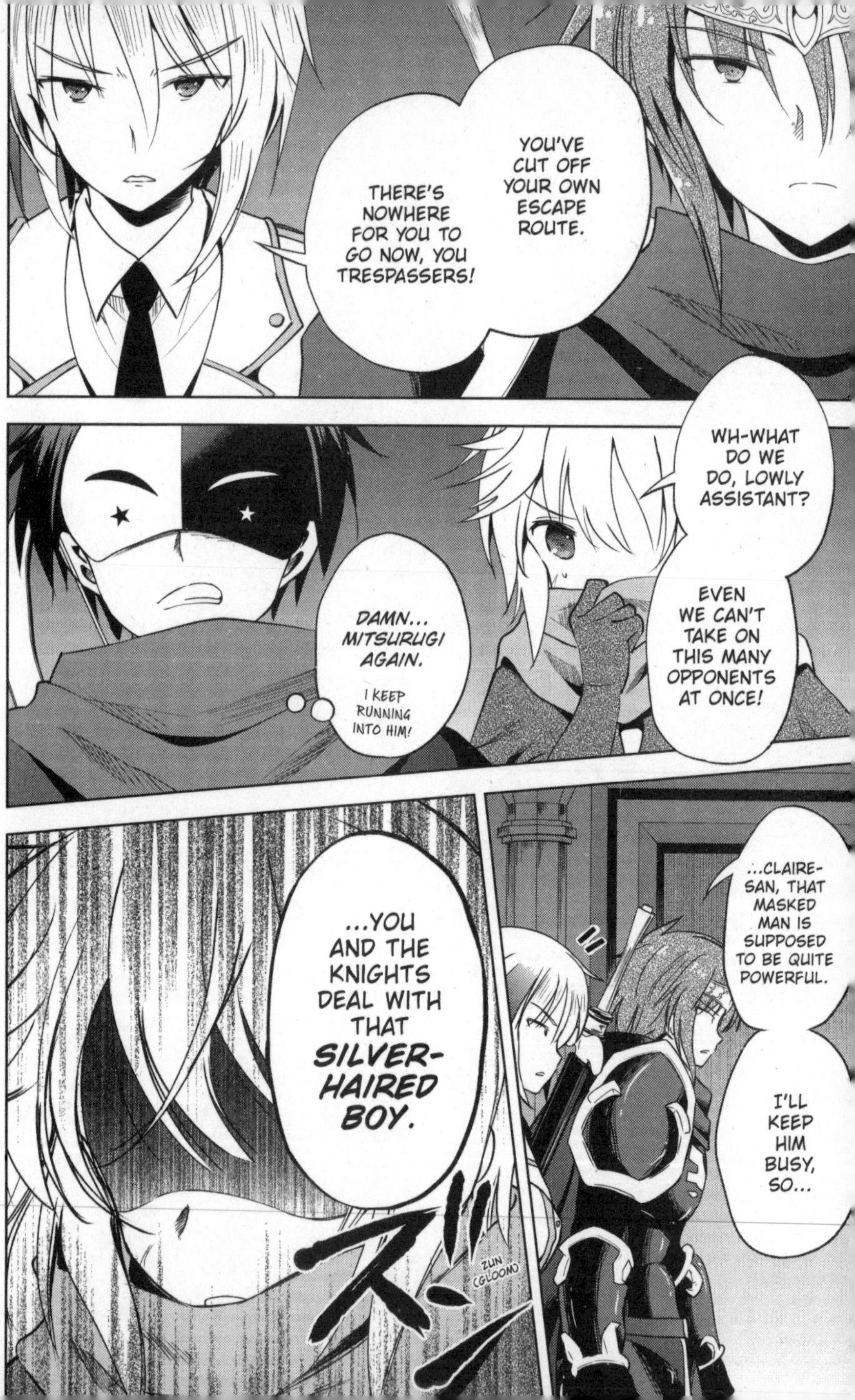
YOU'VE CUT OFF YOUR OWN ESCAPE ROUTE.
THERE'S NOWHERE FOR YOU TO GO NOW, YOU TRESPASSERS!
WH-WHAT DO WE DO, LOWLY ASSISTANT?
EVEN WE CAN'T TAKE ON THIS MANY OPPONENTS AT ONCE!
DAMN... MITSURUGI AGAIN.
I KEEP RUNNING INTO HIM!
...CLAIRE-SAN, THAT MASKED MAN IS SUPPOSED TO BE QUITE POWERFUL.
I'LL KEEP HIM BUSY, SO...
...YOU AND THE KNIGHTS DEAL WITH THAT ***SILVER-HAIRED BOY.***
ZUN (GLOOM)

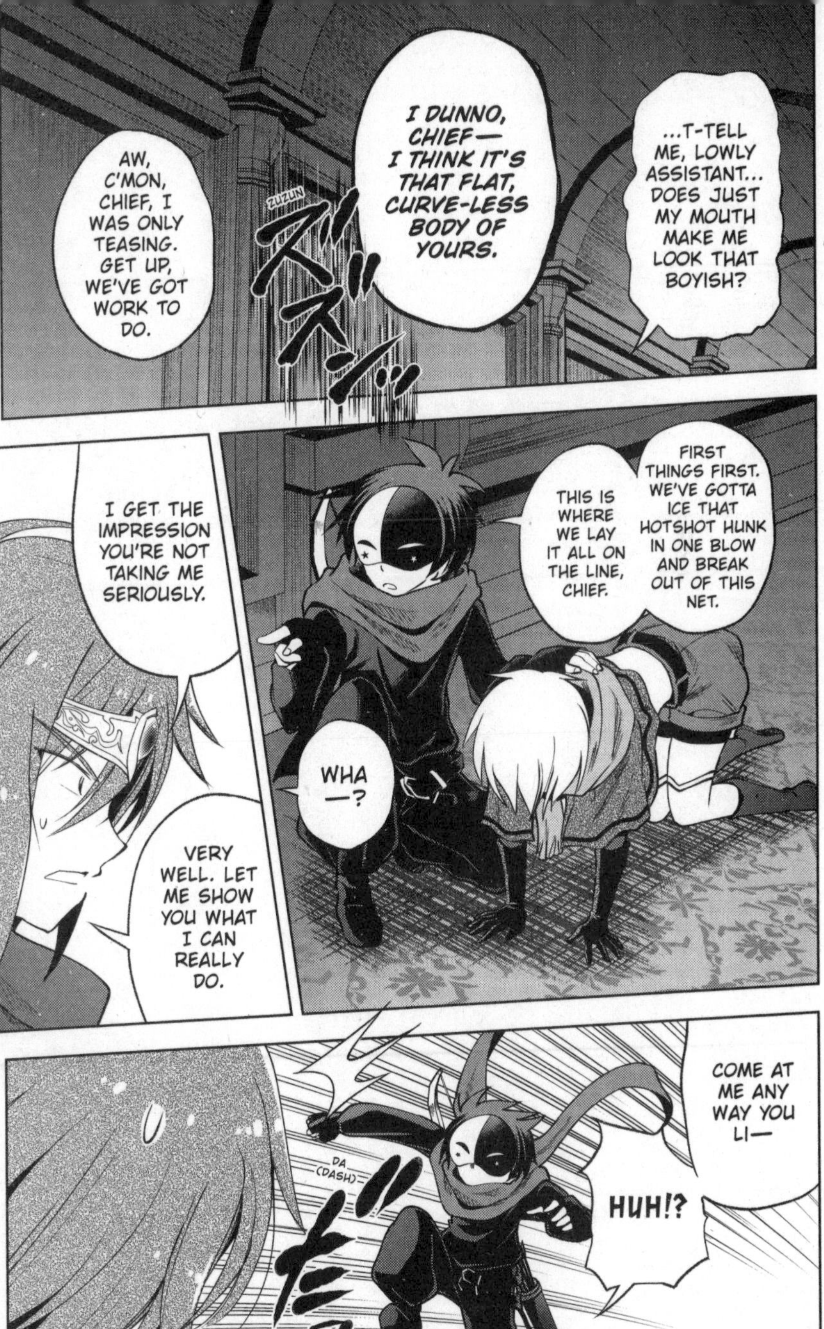
...T-TELL ME, LOWLY ASSISTANT... DOES JUST MY MOUTH MAKE ME LOOK THAT BOYISH?
I DUNNO, CHIEF— I THINK IT'S THAT FLAT, CURVE-LESS BODY OF YOURS.
ZUZUN
AW, C'MON, CHIEF, I WAS ONLY TEASING. GET UP, WE'VE GOT WORK TO DO.
FIRST THINGS FIRST. WE'VE GOTTA ICE THAT HOTSHOT HUNK IN ONE BLOW AND BREAK OUT OF THIS NET.
THIS IS WHERE WE LAY IT ALL ON THE LINE, CHIEF.
WHA —?
I GET THE IMPRESSION YOU'RE NOT TAKING ME SERIOUSLY.
VERY WELL. LET ME SHOW YOU WHAT I CAN REALLY DO.
COME AT ME ANY WAY YOU LI—
HUH!?
DA (DASH)

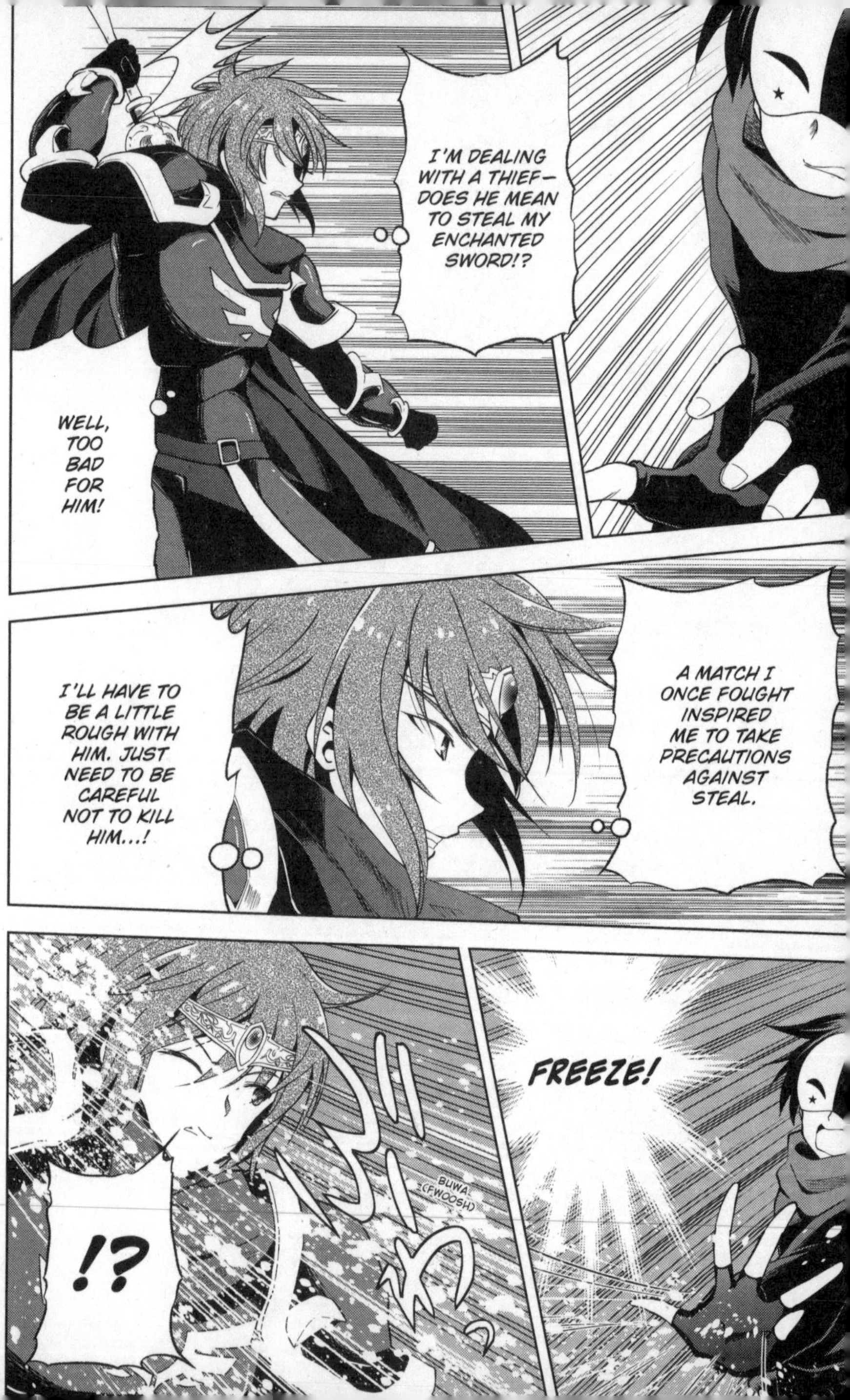
I'M DEALING WITH A THIEF—DOES HE MEAN TO STEAL MY ENCHANTED SWORD!?
WELL, TOO BAD FOR HIM!
A MATCH I ONCE FOUGHT INSPIRED ME TO TAKE PRECAUTIONS AGAINST STEAL.
I'LL HAVE TO BE A LITTLE ROUGH WITH HIM. JUST NEED TO BE CAREFUL NOT TO KILL HIM...!
FREEZE!
BUWA (FWOOSH)
!?

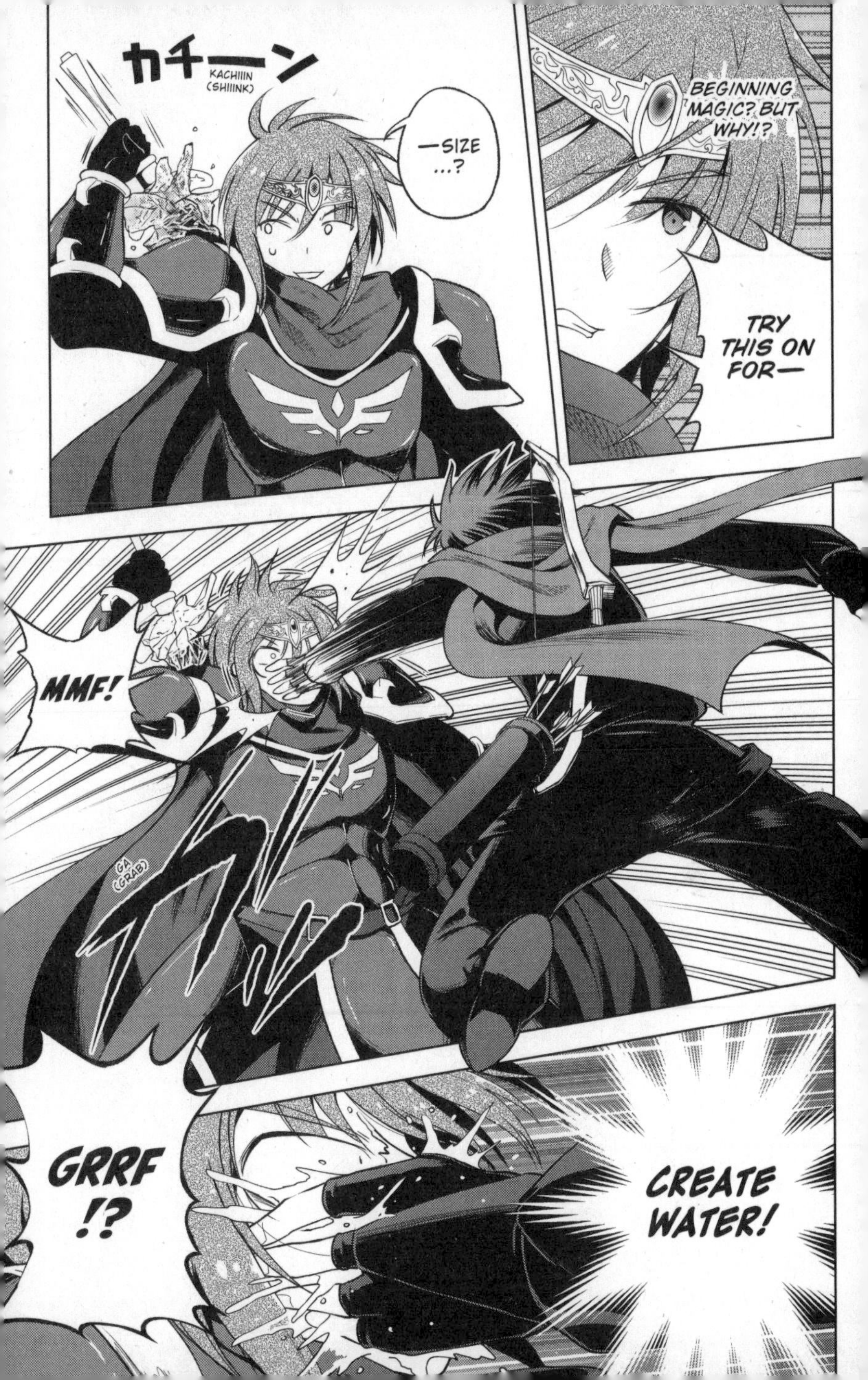
BEGINNING MAGIC? BUT WHY!?
TRY THIS ON FOR—
カチーン
KACHIIIN (SHIIINK)
—SIZE ...?
MMF!
GA (GRAB)
CREATE WATER!
GRRF !?

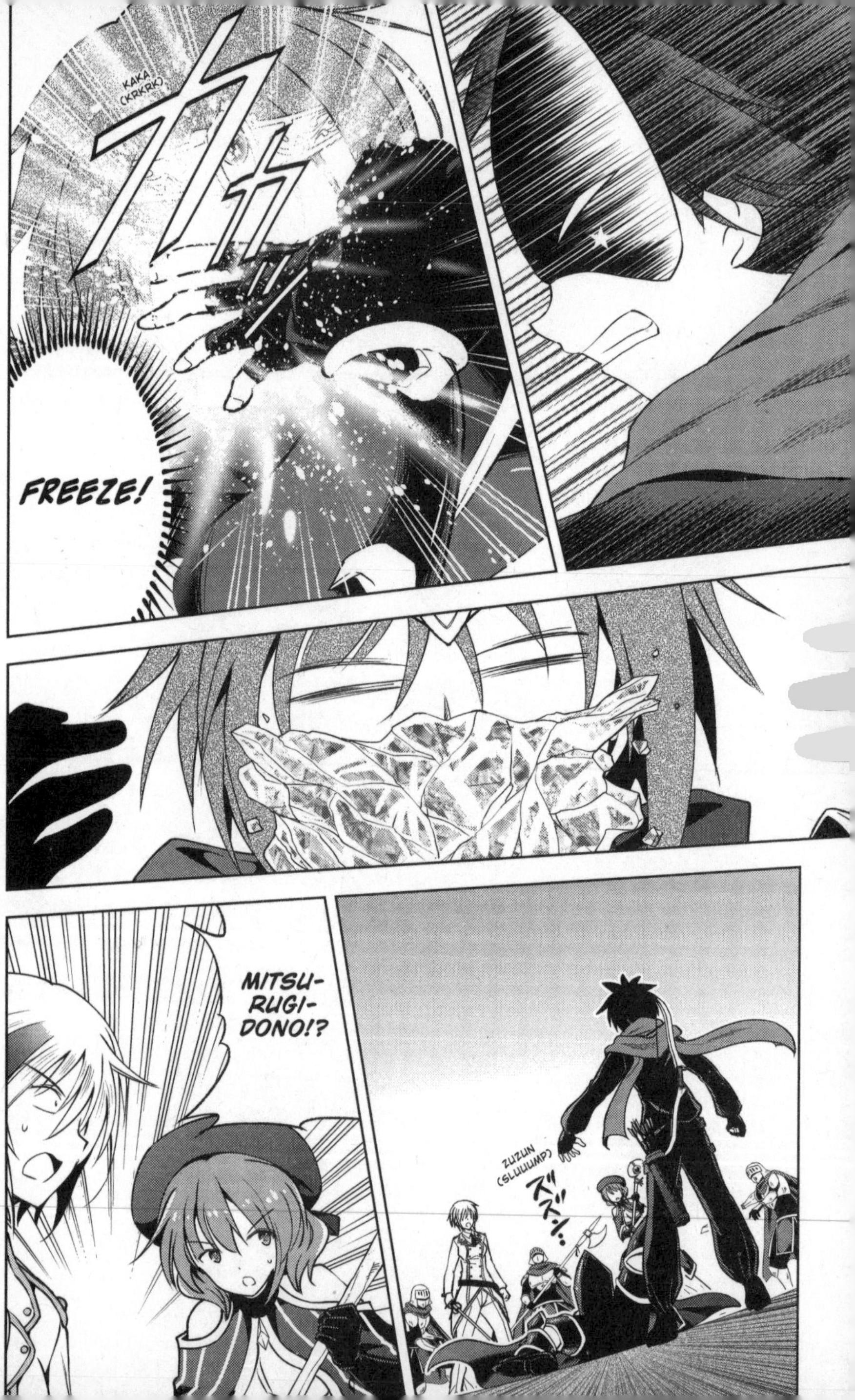
KAKA (KRKRK)
カカッ
FREEZE!
ZUZUN (SLUUUMP)
ズズン…
MITSU-RUGI-DONO!?

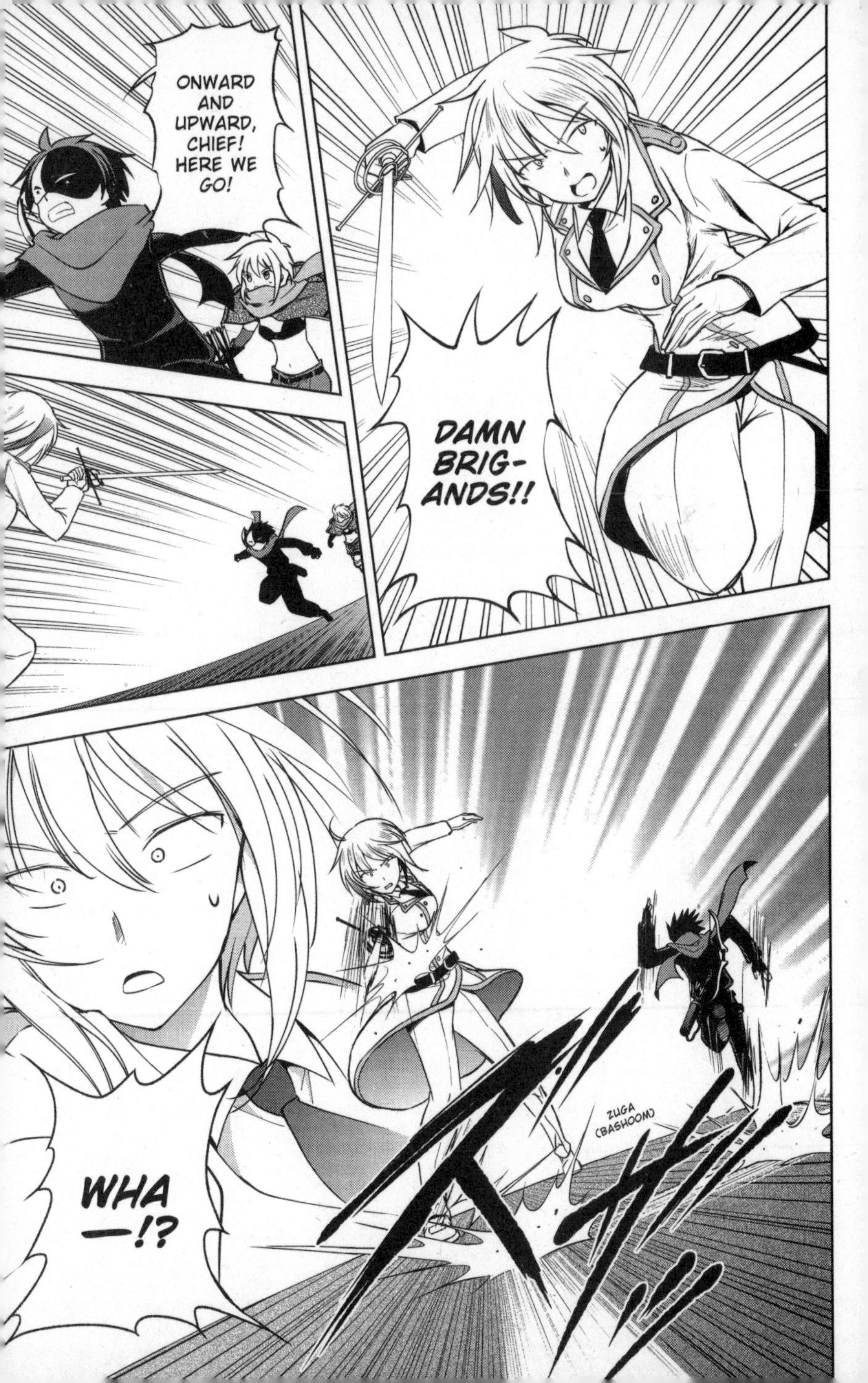
DAMN BRIG-ANDS!!
ONWARD AND UPWARD, CHIEF! HERE WE GO!
ZUGA (BASHOOM)
WHA—!?

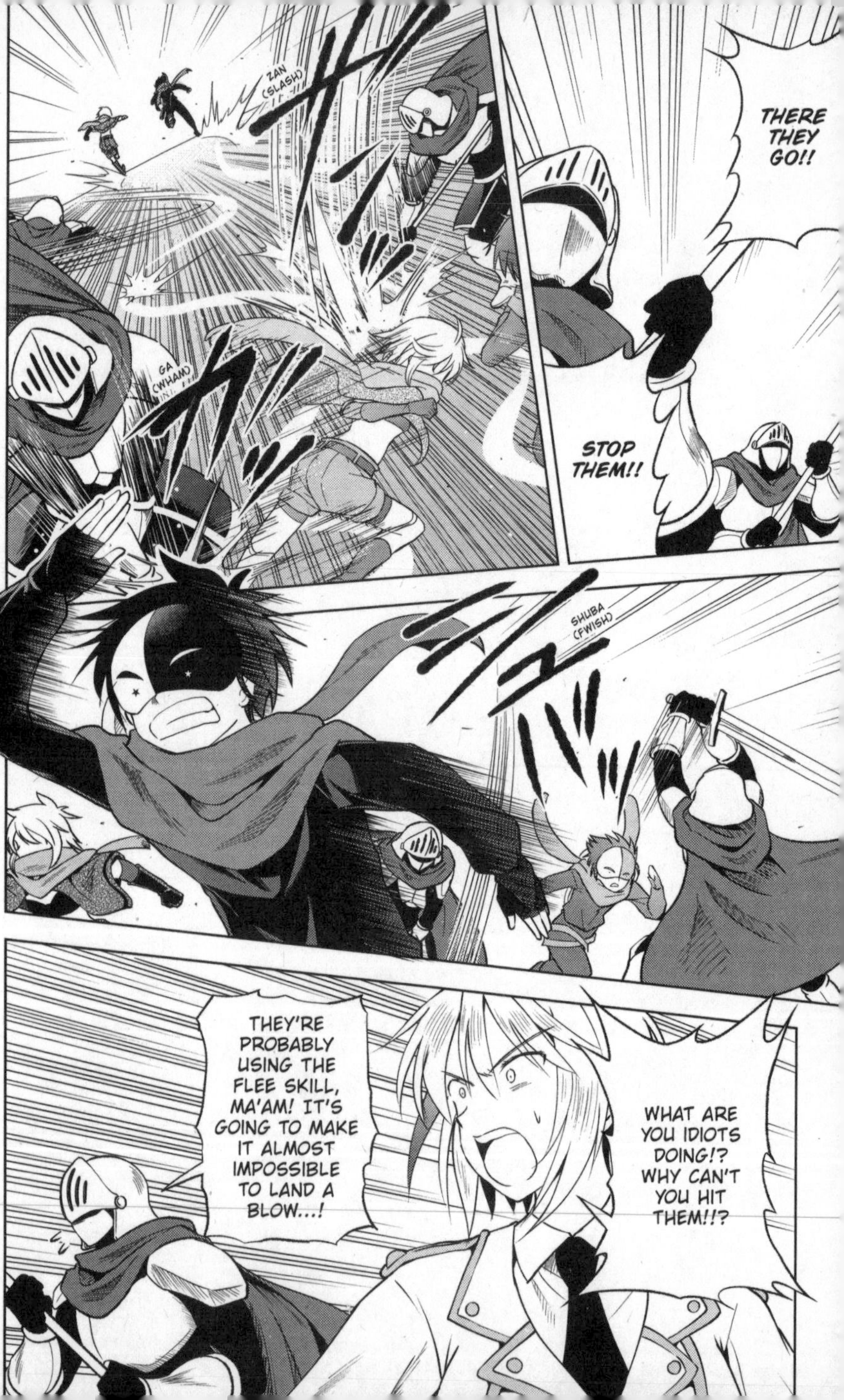
THERE THEY GO!!
STOP THEM!!
ZAN (SLASH)
GA (WHAM)
SHUBA (FWISH)
WHAT ARE YOU IDIOTS DOING!? WHY CAN'T YOU HIT THEM!!?
THEY'RE PROBABLY USING THE FLEE SKILL, MA'AM! IT'S GOING TO MAKE IT ALMOST IMPOSSIBLE TO LAND A BLOW...!

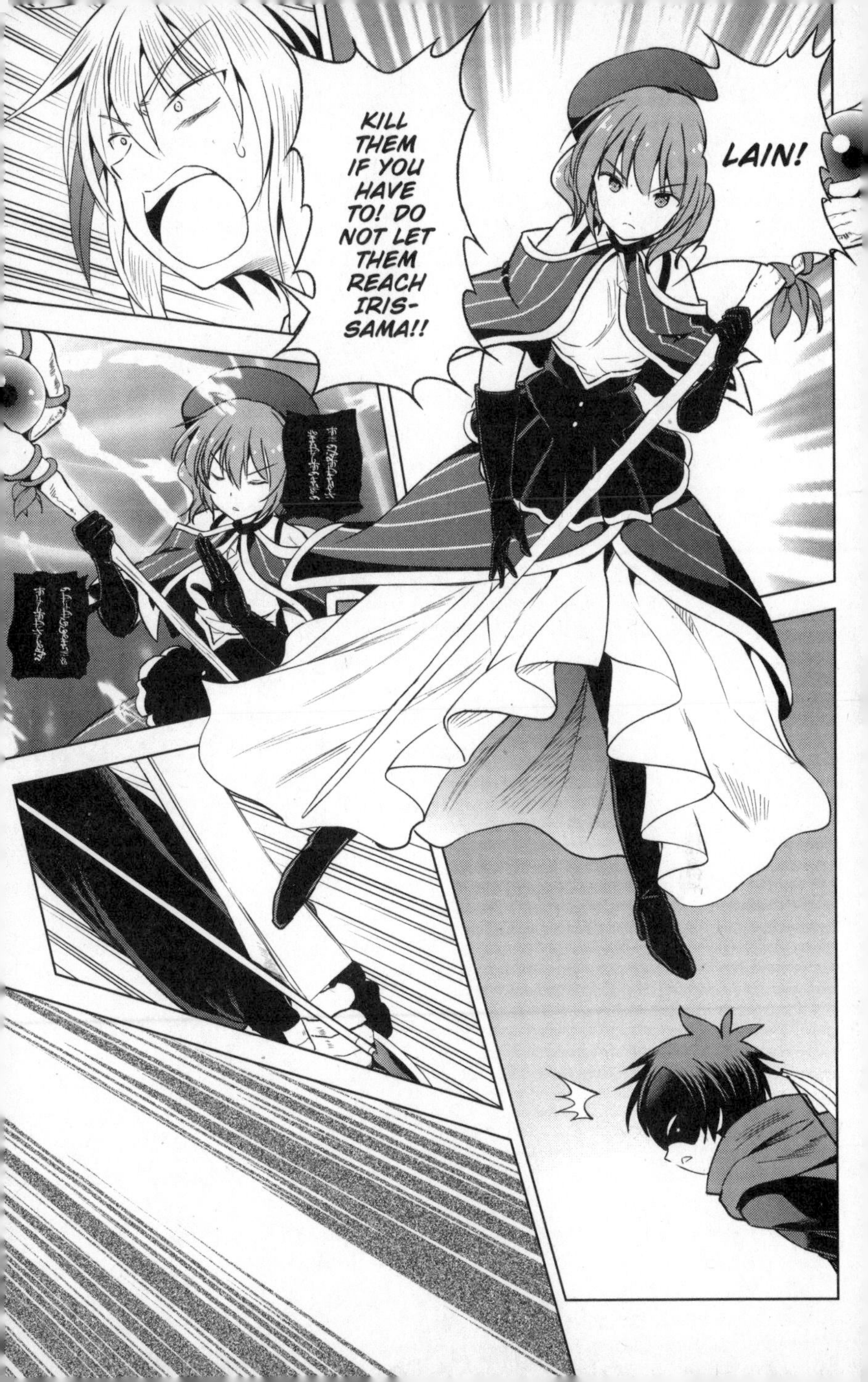
LAIN!
KILL THEM IF YOU HAVE TO! DO NOT LET THEM REACH IRIS-SAMA!!

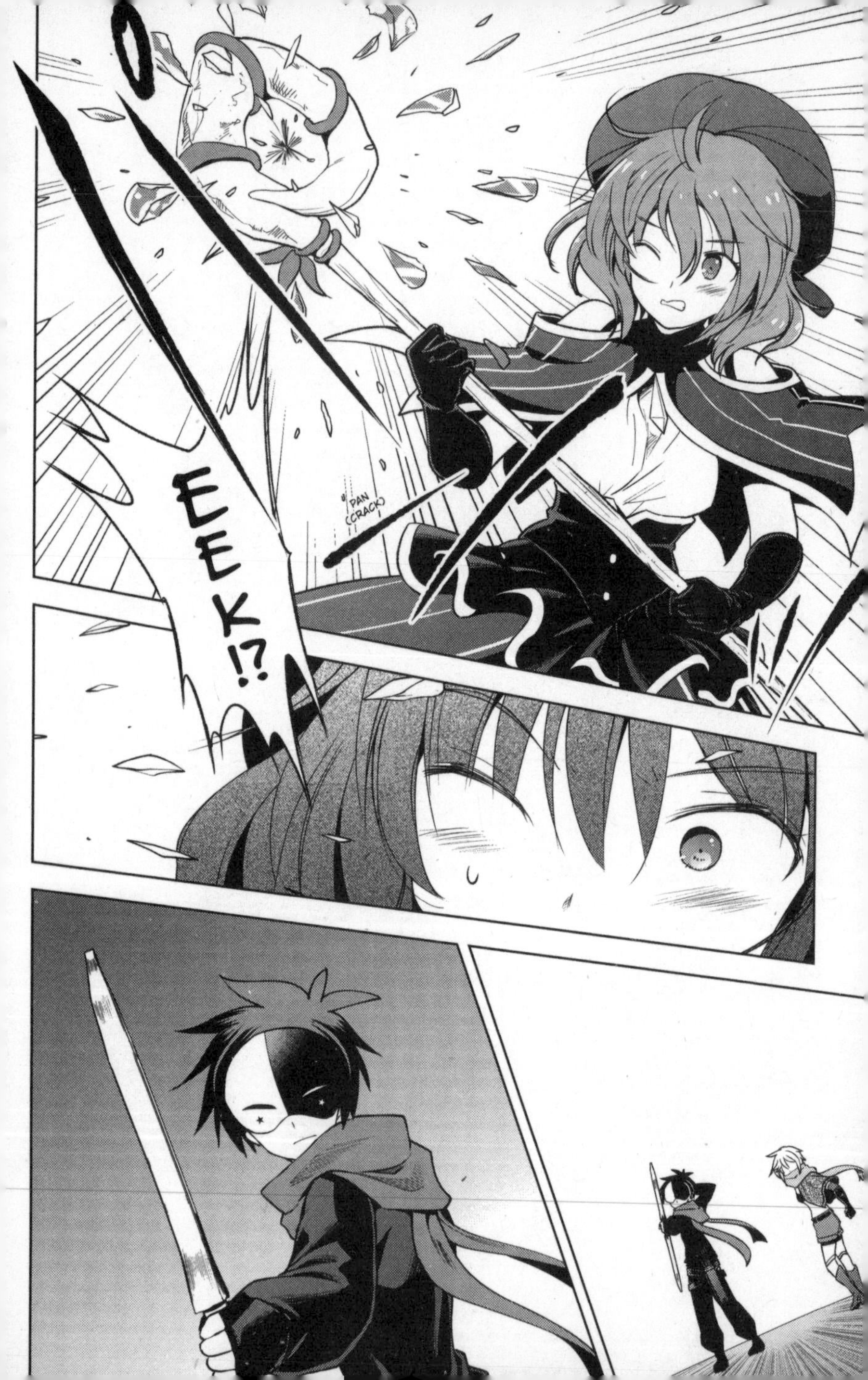
PAN (CRACK)
EEEK!?

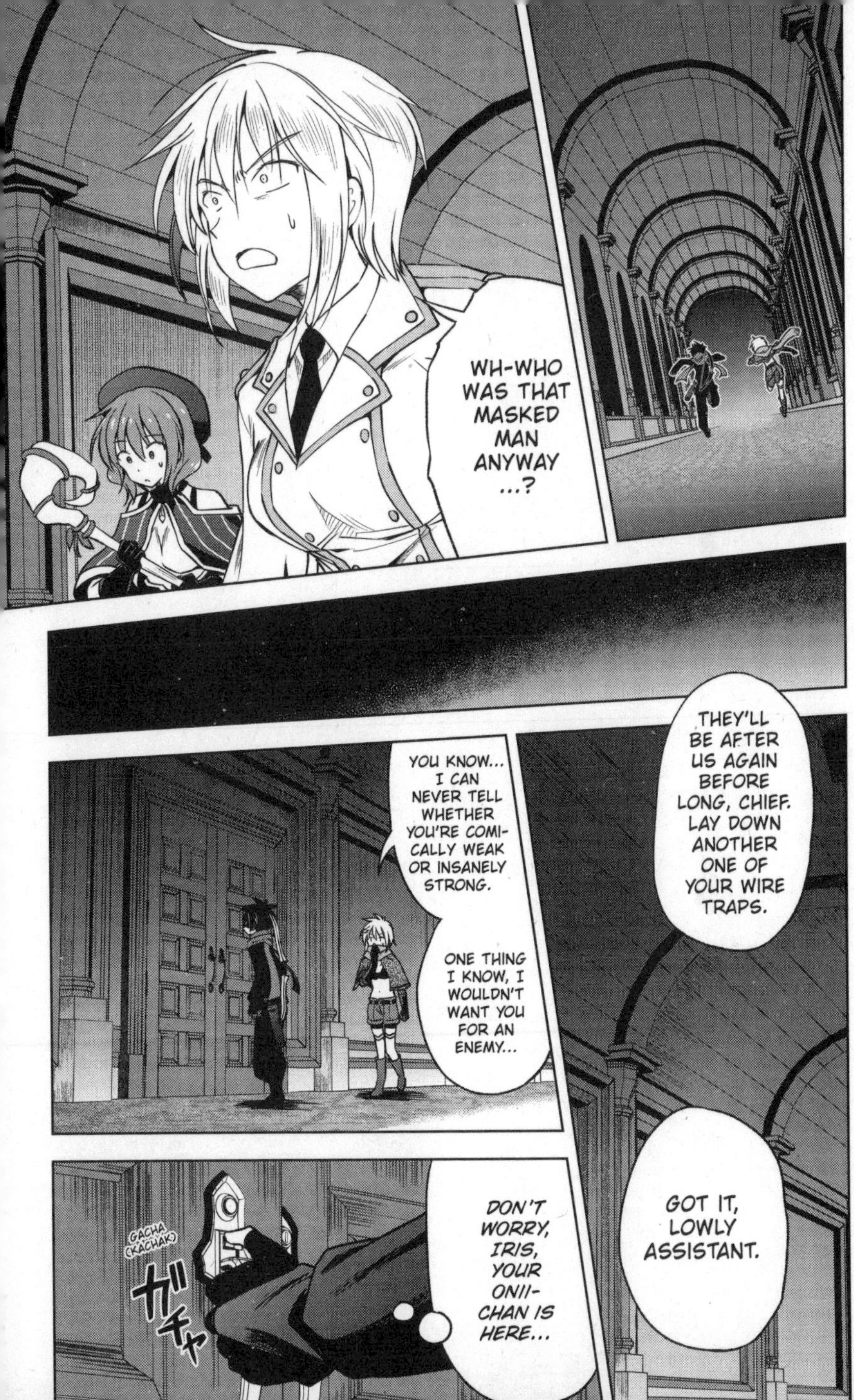
WH-WHO WAS THAT MASKED MAN ANYWAY ...?
THEY'LL BE AFTER US AGAIN BEFORE LONG, CHIEF. LAY DOWN ANOTHER ONE OF YOUR WIRE TRAPS.
GOT IT, LOWLY ASSISTANT.
YOU KNOW... I CAN NEVER TELL WHETHER YOU'RE COMI-CALLY WEAK OR INSANELY STRONG.
ONE THING I KNOW, I WOULDN'T WANT YOU FOR AN ENEMY...
DON'T WORRY, IRIS, YOUR ONII-CHAN IS HERE...
ガチャ
GACHA (KACHAK)

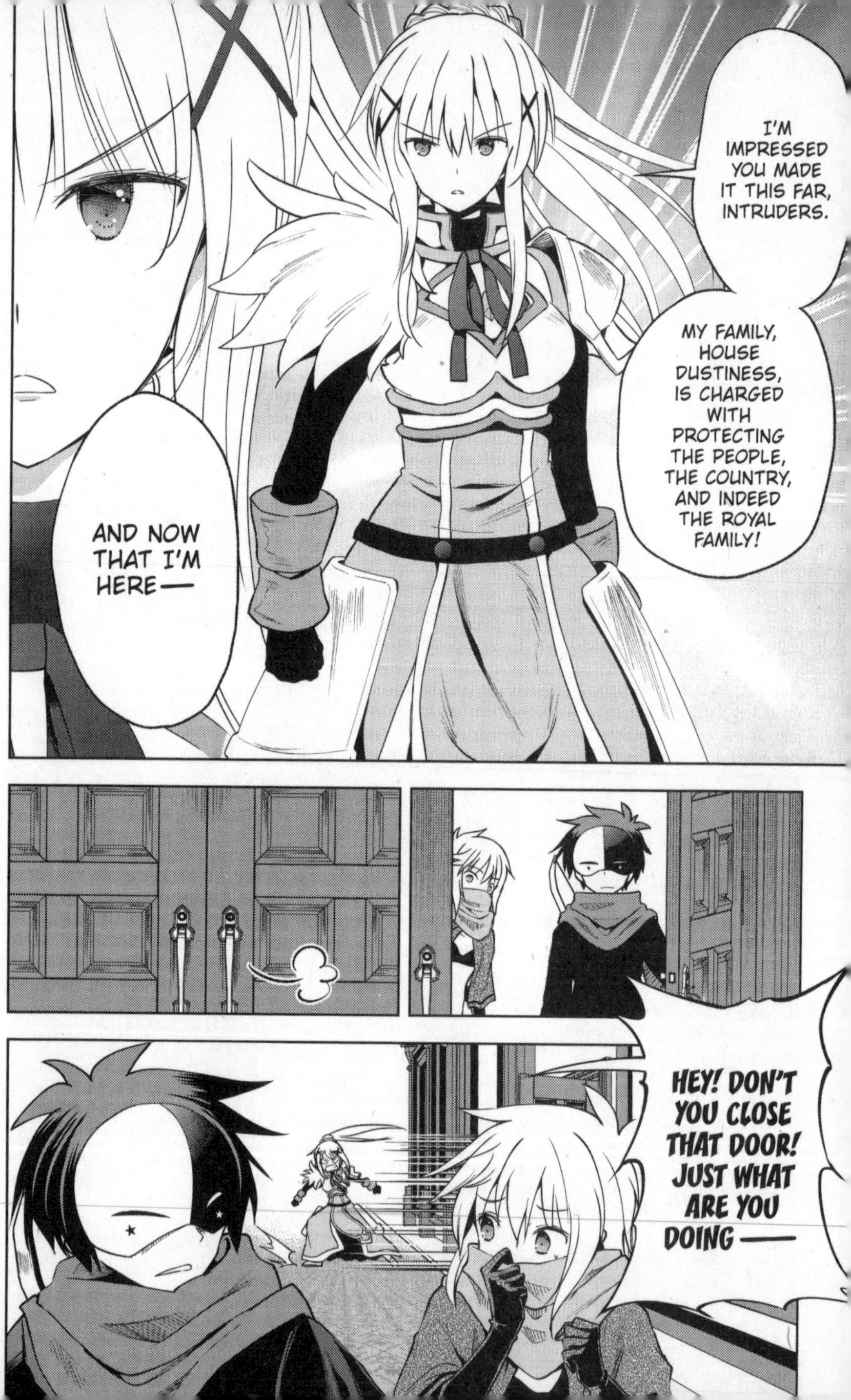
I'M IMPRESSED YOU MADE IT THIS FAR, INTRUDERS.
MY FAMILY, HOUSE DUSTINESS, IS CHARGED WITH PROTECTING THE PEOPLE, THE COUNTRY, AND INDEED THE ROYAL FAMILY!
AND NOW THAT I'M HERE—
HEY! DON'T YOU CLOSE THAT DOOR! JUST WHAT ARE YOU DOING—

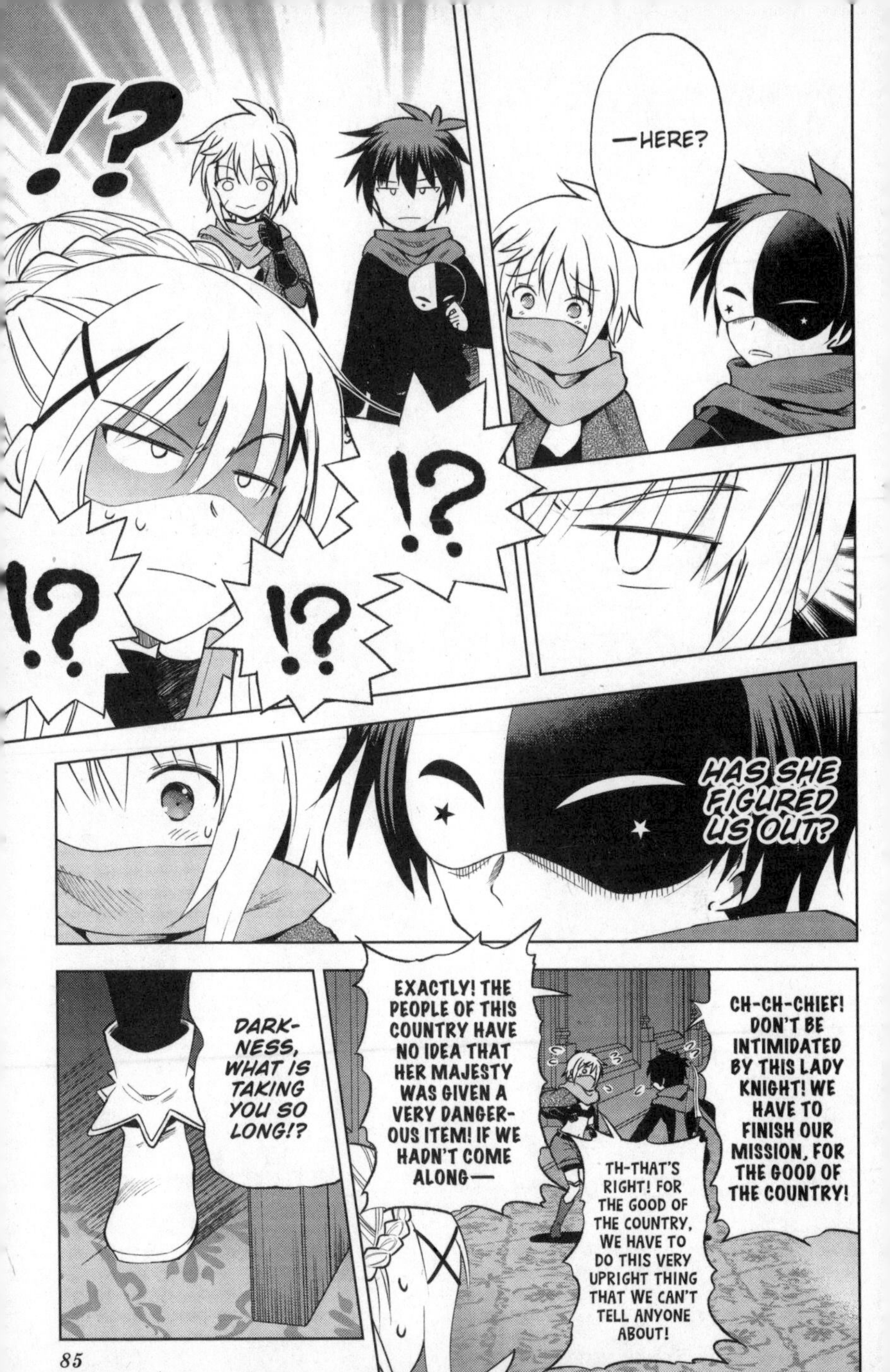
—HERE?
!?
!?
!?
!?
HAS SHE FIGURED US OUT?
CH-CH-CHIEF! DON'T BE INTIMIDATED BY THIS LADY KNIGHT! WE HAVE TO FINISH OUR MISSION, FOR THE GOOD OF THE COUNTRY!
TH-THAT'S RIGHT! FOR THE GOOD OF THE COUNTRY, WE HAVE TO DO THIS VERY UPRIGHT THING THAT WE CAN'T TELL ANYONE ABOUT!
EXACTLY! THE PEOPLE OF THIS COUNTRY HAVE NO IDEA THAT HER MAJESTY WAS GIVEN A VERY DANGEROUS ITEM! IF WE HADN'T COME ALONG—
DARKNESS, WHAT IS TAKING YOU SO LONG!?

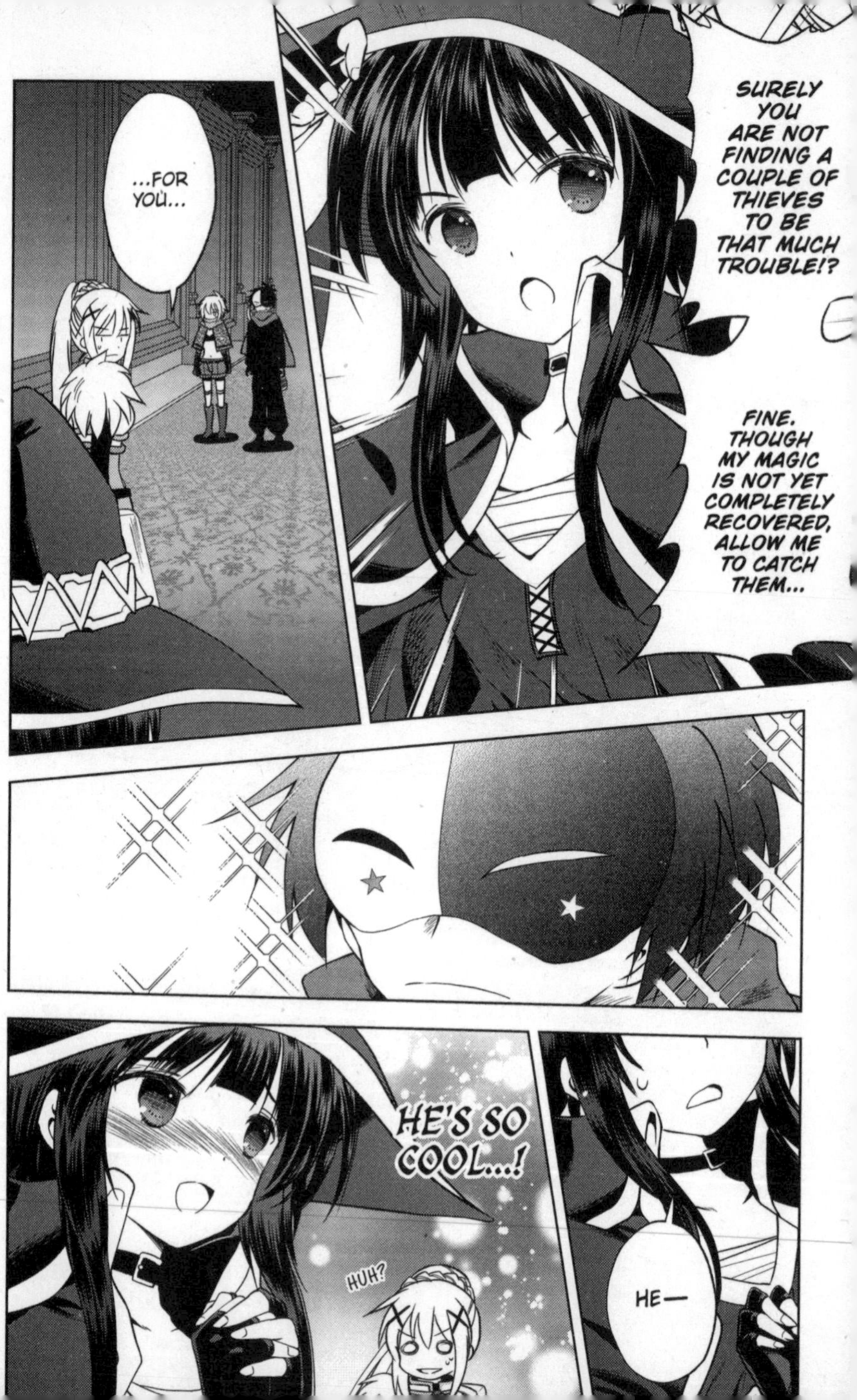
SURELY YOU ARE NOT FINDING A COUPLE OF THIEVES TO BE THAT MUCH TROUBLE!?
FINE. THOUGH MY MAGIC IS NOT YET COMPLETELY RECOVERED, ALLOW ME TO CATCH THEM...
...FOR YOU...
HE—
HE'S SO COOL...!
HUH?

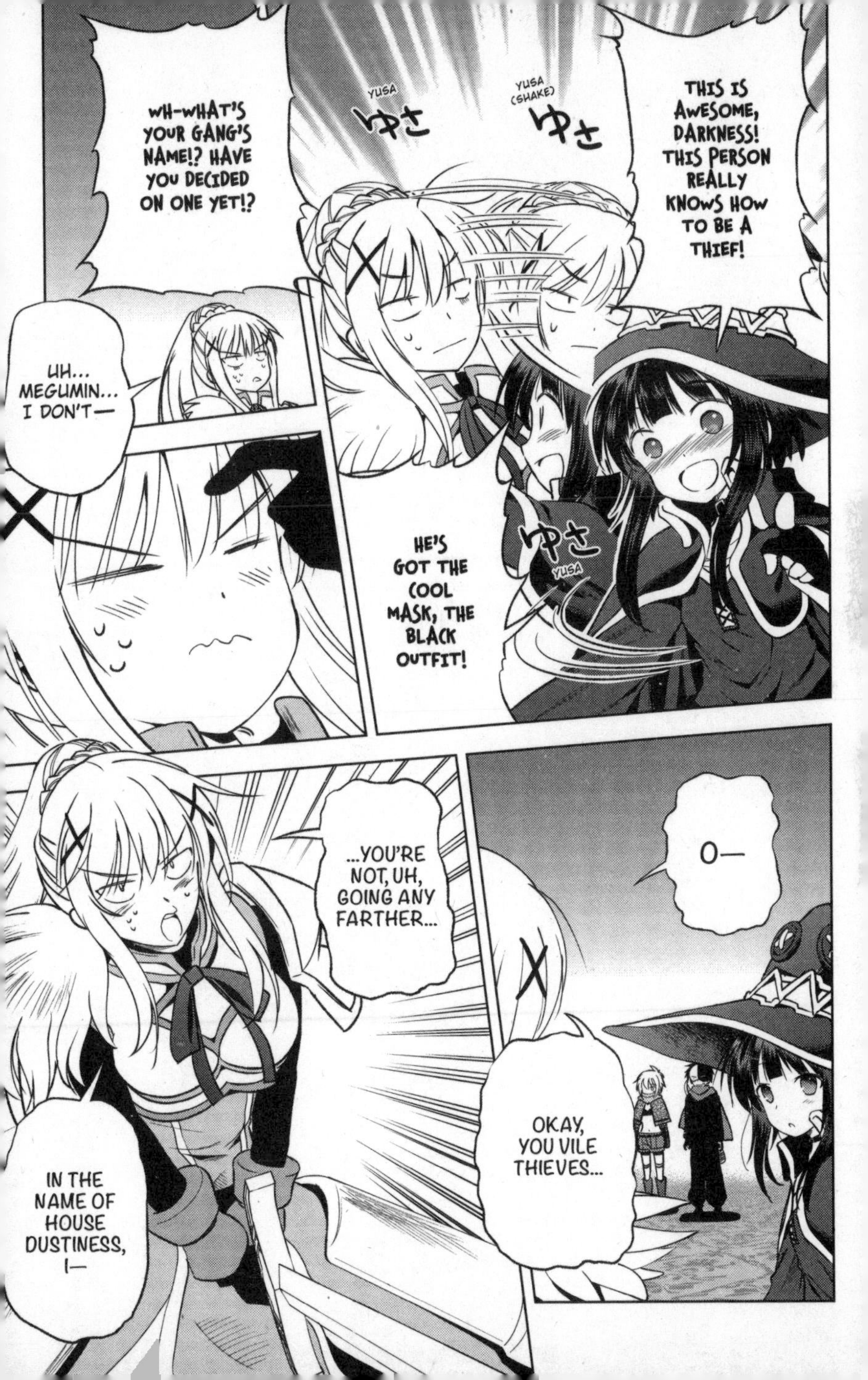
THIS IS AWESOME, DARKNESS! THIS PERSON REALLY KNOWS HOW TO BE A THIEF!
YUSA (SHAKE) ゆさ
YUSA ゆさ
WH-WHAT'S YOUR GANG'S NAME!? HAVE YOU DECIDED ON ONE YET!?
HE'S GOT THE COOL MASK, THE BLACK OUTFIT!
ゆさ YUSA
UH... MEGUMIN... I DON'T—
O—
OKAY, YOU VILE THIEVES...
...YOU'RE NOT, UH, GOING ANY FARTHER...
IN THE NAME OF HOUSE DUSTINESS, I—

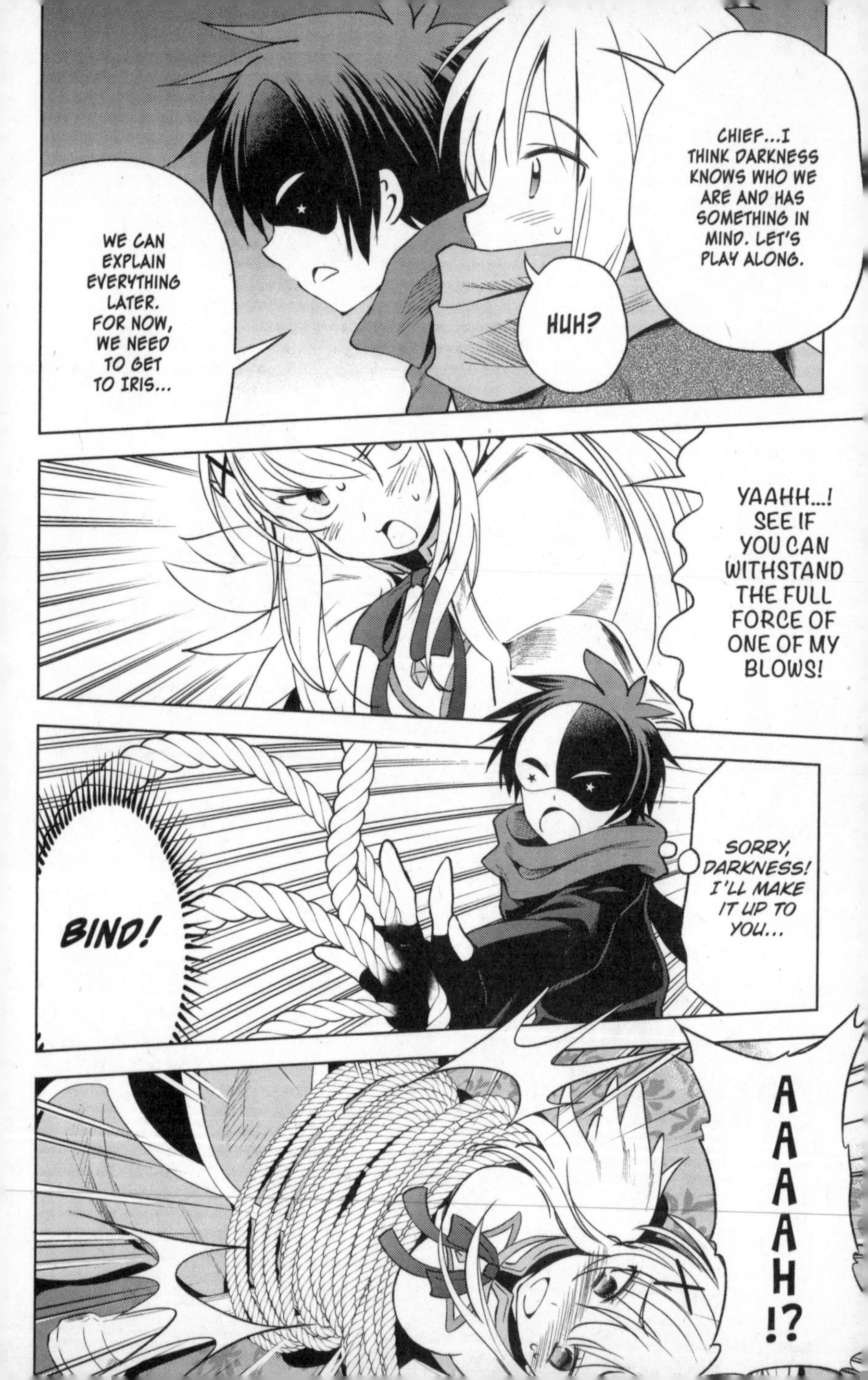
CHIEF...I THINK DARKNESS KNOWS WHO WE ARE AND HAS SOMETHING IN MIND. LET'S PLAY ALONG.
HUH?
WE CAN EXPLAIN EVERYTHING LATER. FOR NOW, WE NEED TO GET TO IRIS...
YAAHH...! SEE IF YOU CAN WITHSTAND THE FULL FORCE OF ONE OF MY BLOWS!
SORRY, DARKNESS! I'LL MAKE IT UP TO YOU...
BIND!
AAAAAH!?

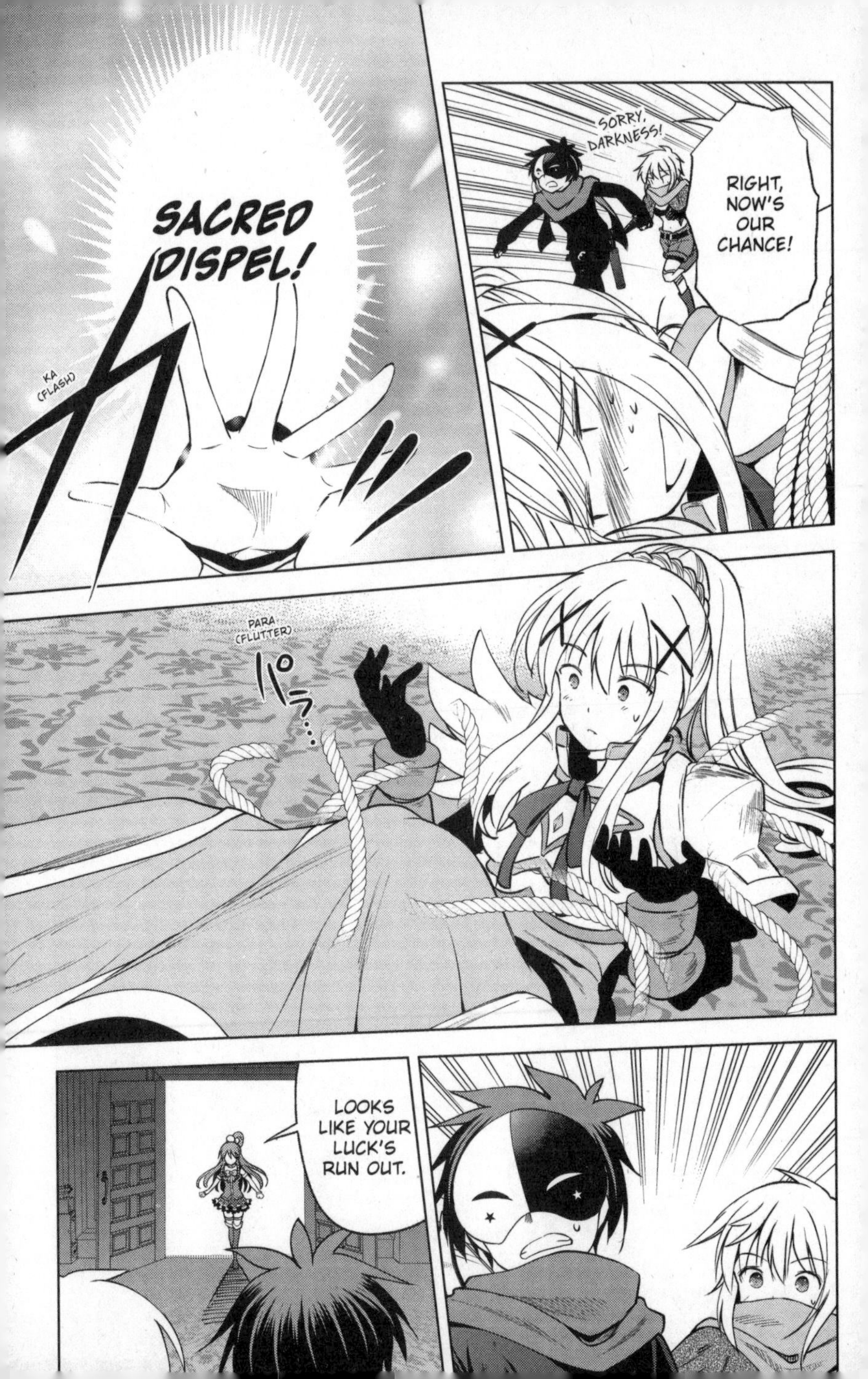
RIGHT, NOW'S OUR CHANCE!
SORRY, DARKNESS!
SACRED DISPEL!
KA (FLASH)
PARA (FLUTTER)
LOOKS LIKE YOUR LUCK'S RUN OUT.

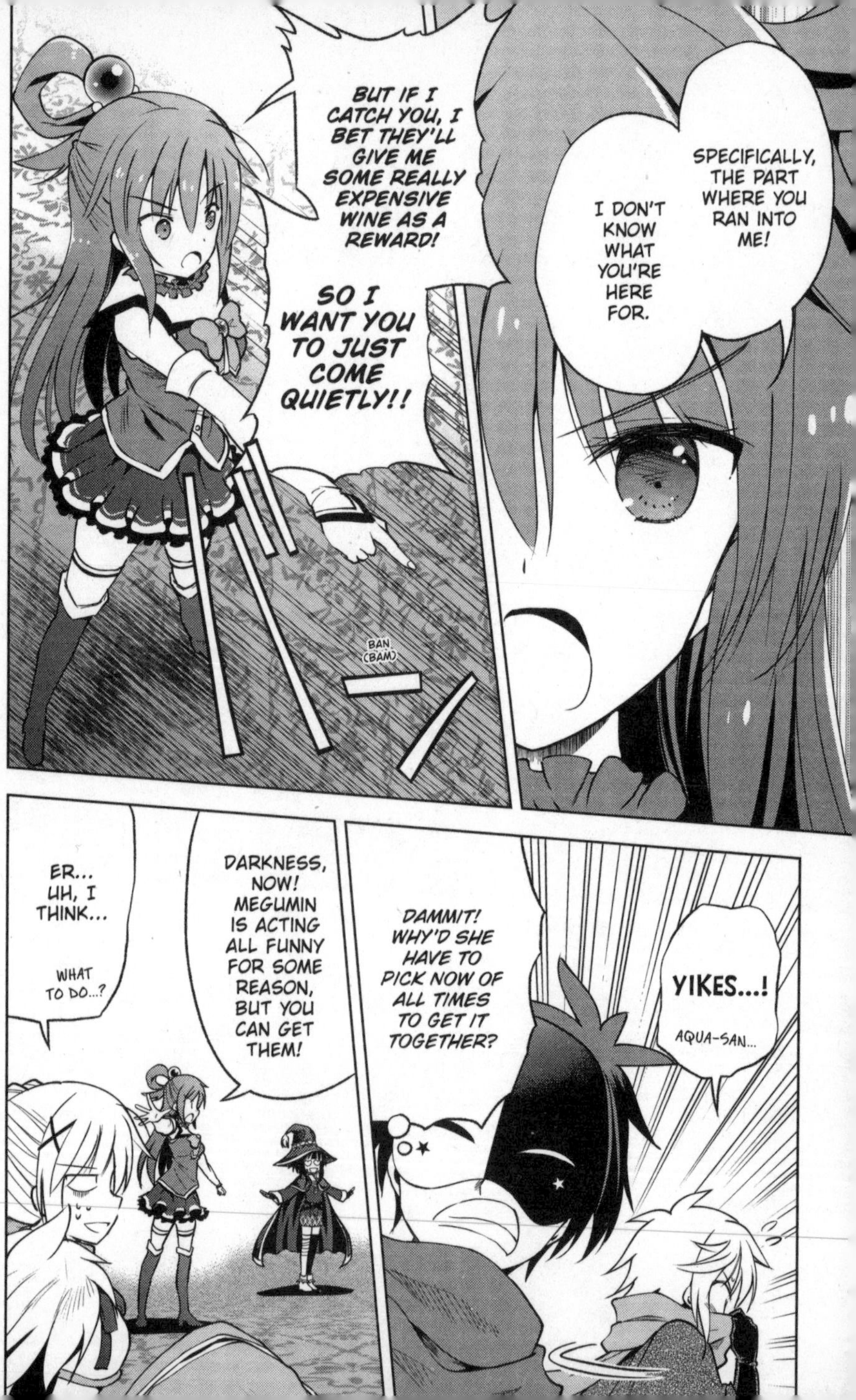
SPECIFICALLY, THE PART WHERE YOU RAN INTO ME!
I DON'T KNOW WHAT YOU'RE HERE FOR.
BUT IF I CATCH YOU, I BET THEY'LL GIVE ME SOME REALLY EXPENSIVE WINE AS A REWARD!
SO I WANT YOU TO JUST COME QUIETLY!!
BAN (BAM)
YIKES...!
AQUA-SAN...
DAMMIT! WHY'D SHE HAVE TO PICK NOW OF ALL TIMES TO GET IT TOGETHER?
DARKNESS, NOW! MEGUMIN IS ACTING ALL FUNNY FOR SOME REASON, BUT YOU CAN GET THEM!
ER... UH, I THINK...
WHAT TO DO...?

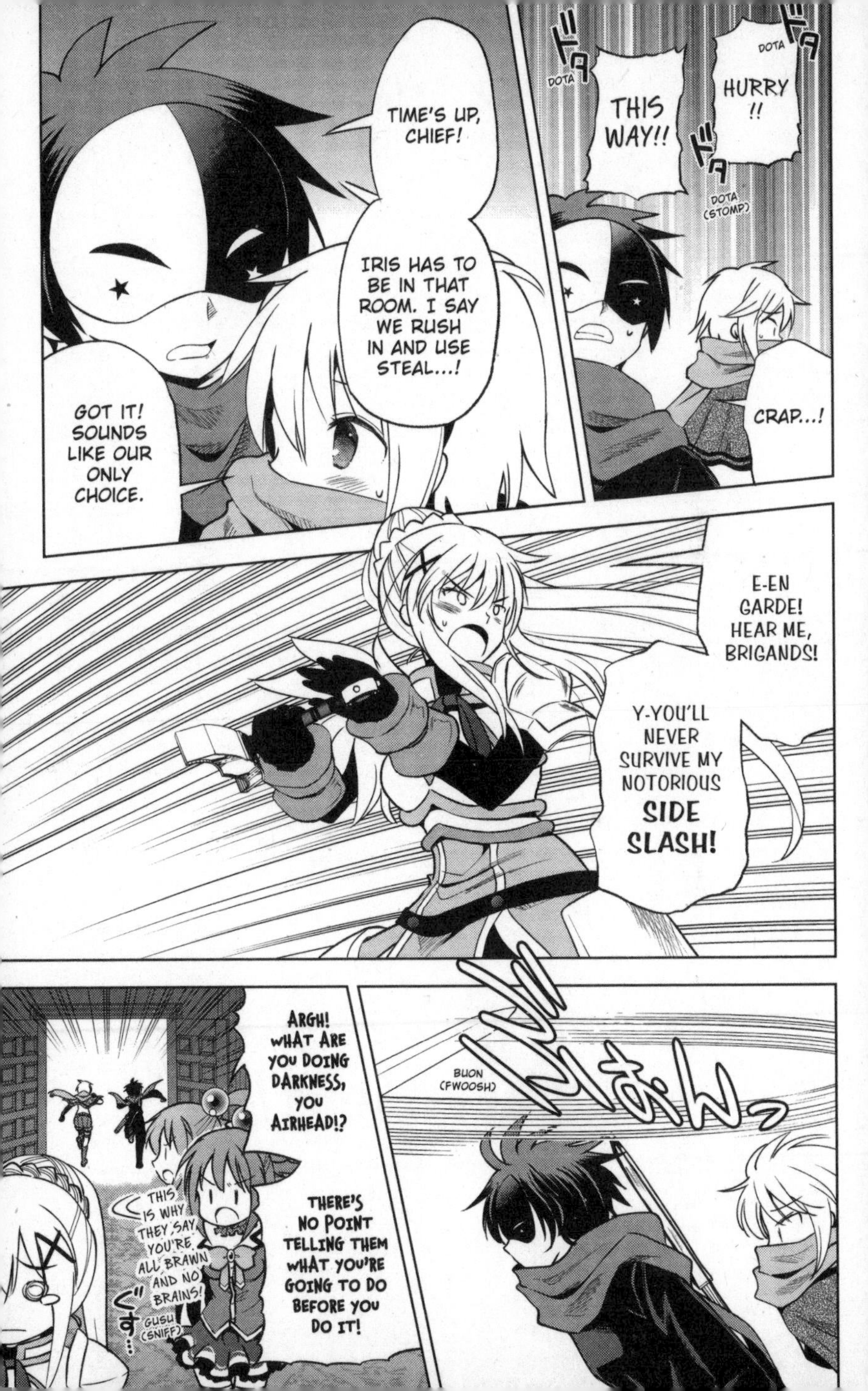

DOTA
HURRY!!
THIS WAY!!
DOTA
DOTA (STOMP)
CRAP...!
TIME'S UP, CHIEF!
IRIS HAS TO BE IN THAT ROOM. I SAY WE RUSH IN AND USE STEAL...!
GOT IT! SOUNDS LIKE OUR ONLY CHOICE.
E-EN GARDE! HEAR ME, BRIGANDS!
Y-YOU'LL NEVER SURVIVE MY NOTORIOUS SIDE SLASH!
BUON (FWOOSH)
ARGH! WHAT ARE YOU DOING DARKNESS, YOU AIRHEAD!?
THERE'S NO POINT TELLING THEM WHAT YOU'RE GOING TO DO BEFORE YOU DO IT!
THIS IS WHY THEY SAY YOU'RE ALL BRAWN AND NO BRAINS!
GUSU (SNIFF)

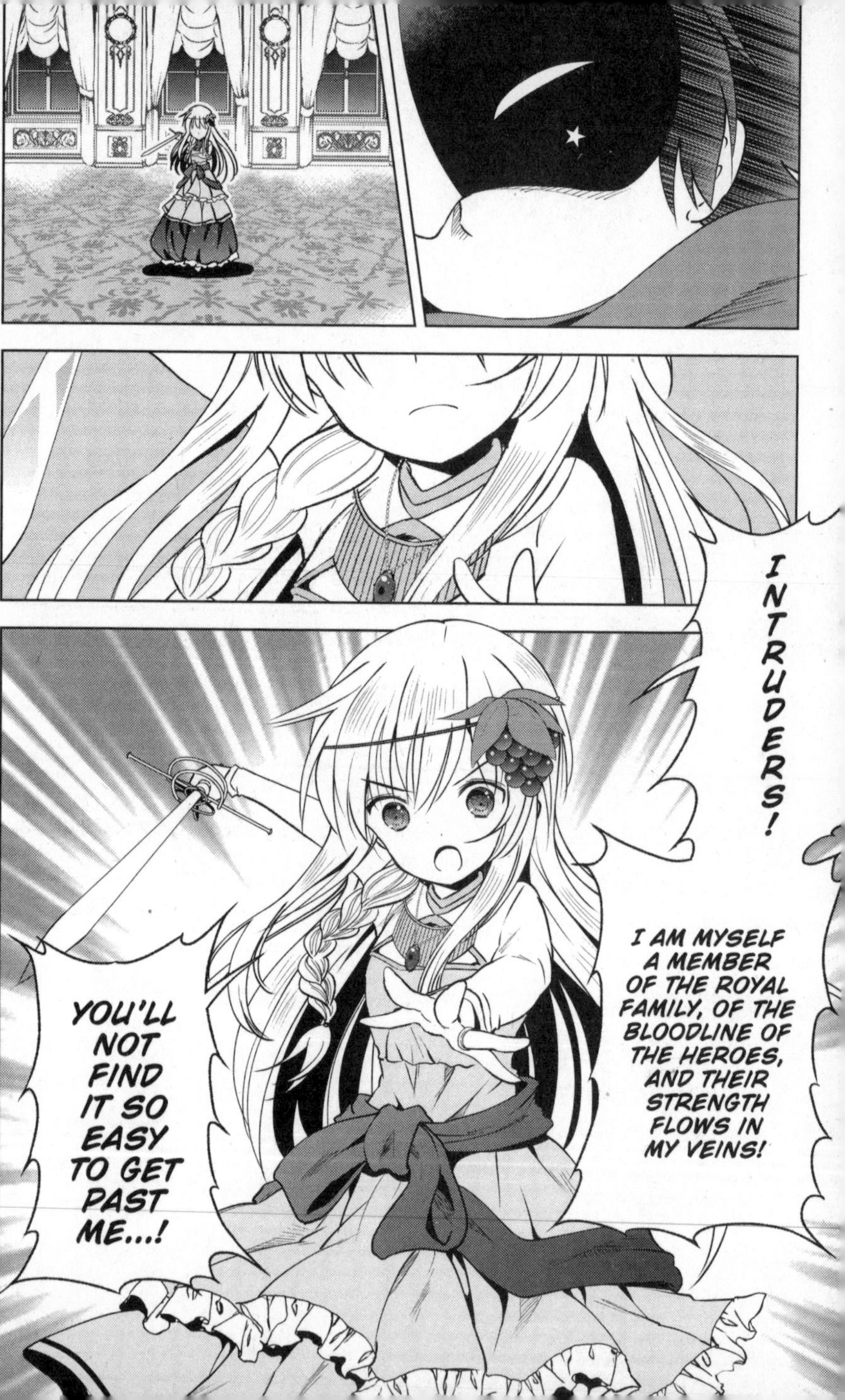
INTRUDERS!
I AM MYSELF A MEMBER OF THE ROYAL FAMILY, OF THE BLOODLINE OF THE HEROES, AND THEIR STRENGTH FLOWS IN MY VEINS!
YOU'LL NOT FIND IT SO EASY TO GET PAST ME...!

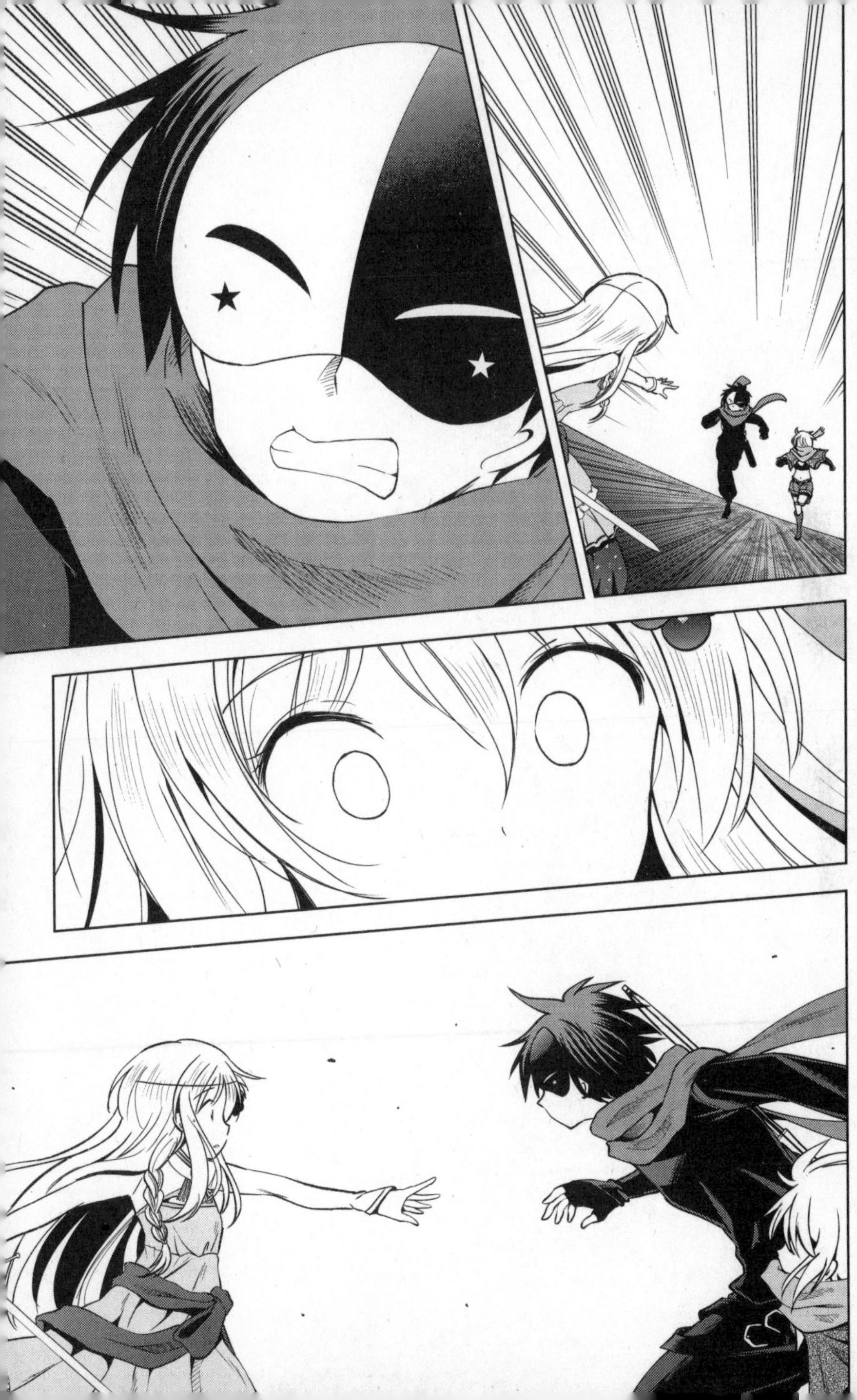

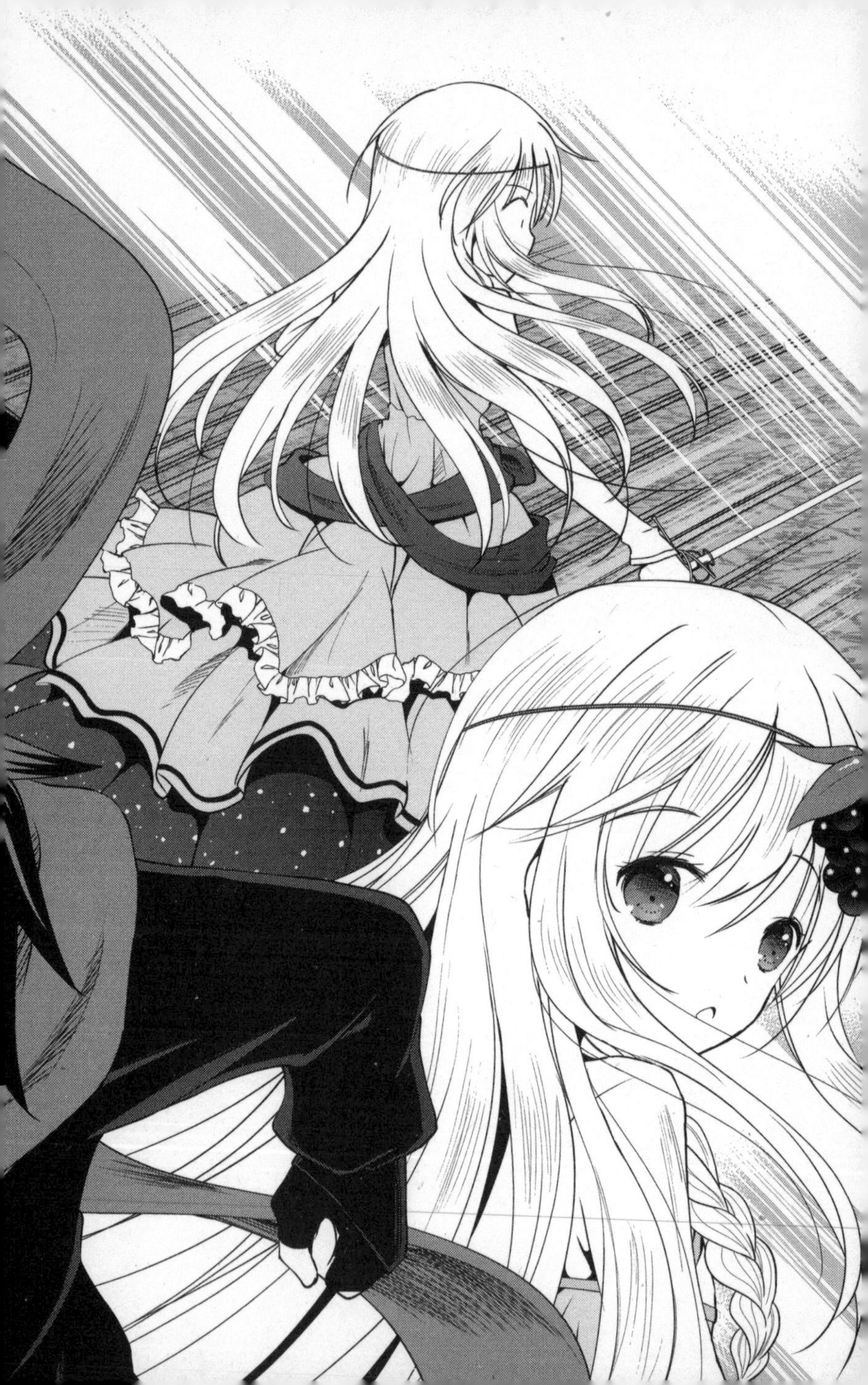

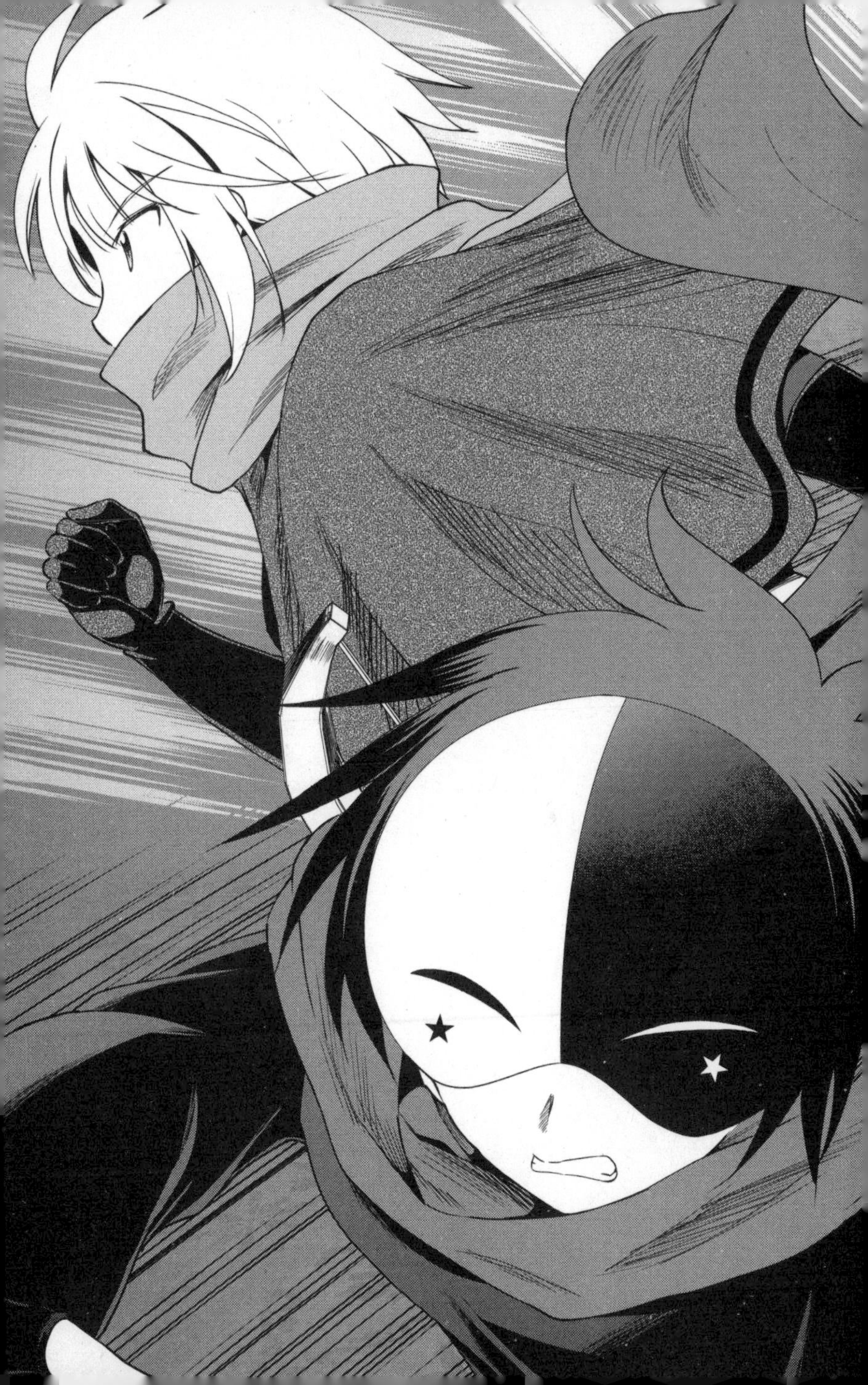

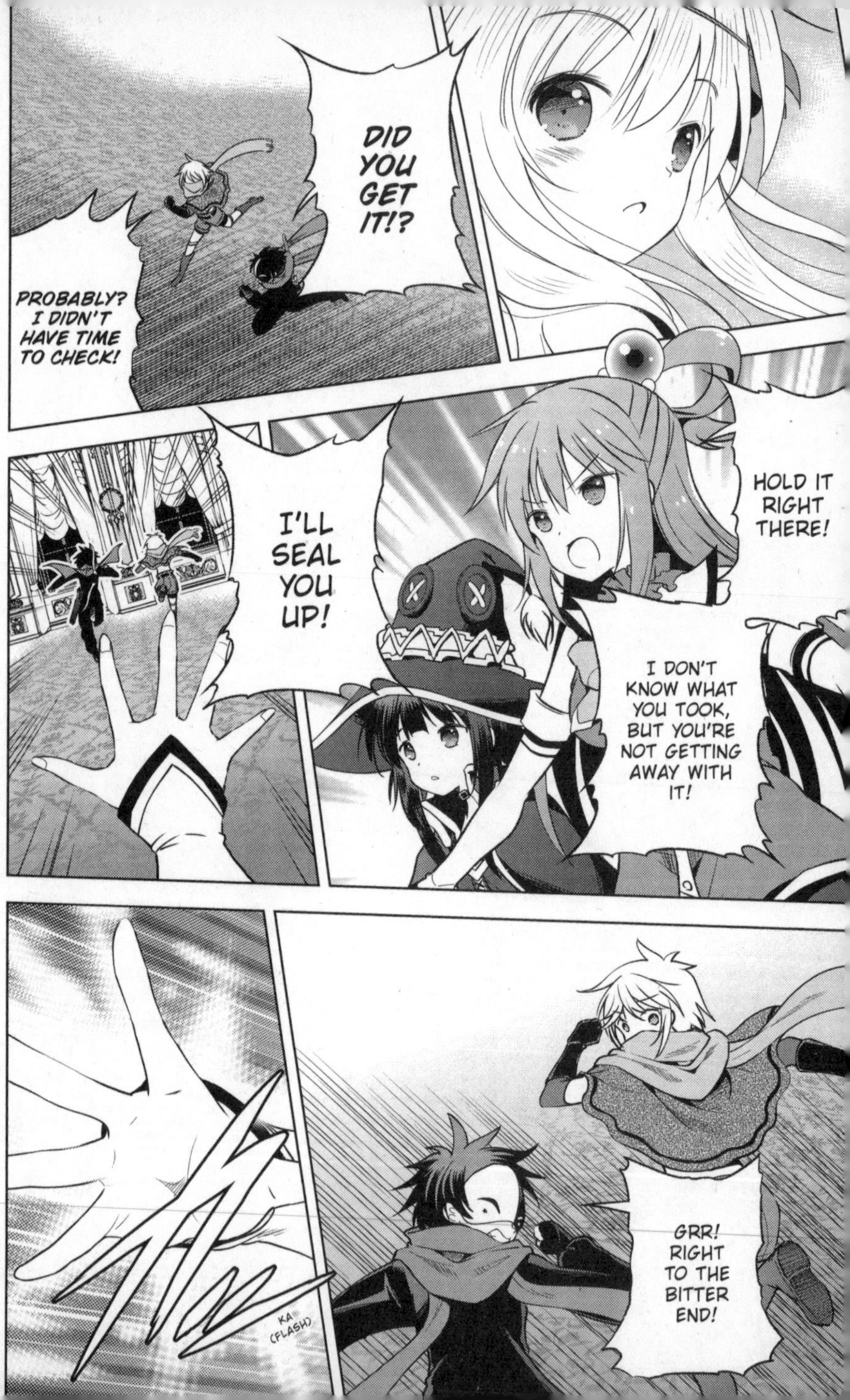
DID YOU GET IT!?
PROBABLY? I DIDN'T HAVE TIME TO CHECK!
HOLD IT RIGHT THERE!
I DON'T KNOW WHAT YOU TOOK, BUT YOU'RE NOT GETTING AWAY WITH IT!
I'LL SEAL YOU UP!
GRR! RIGHT TO THE BITTER END!
KA (FLASH)

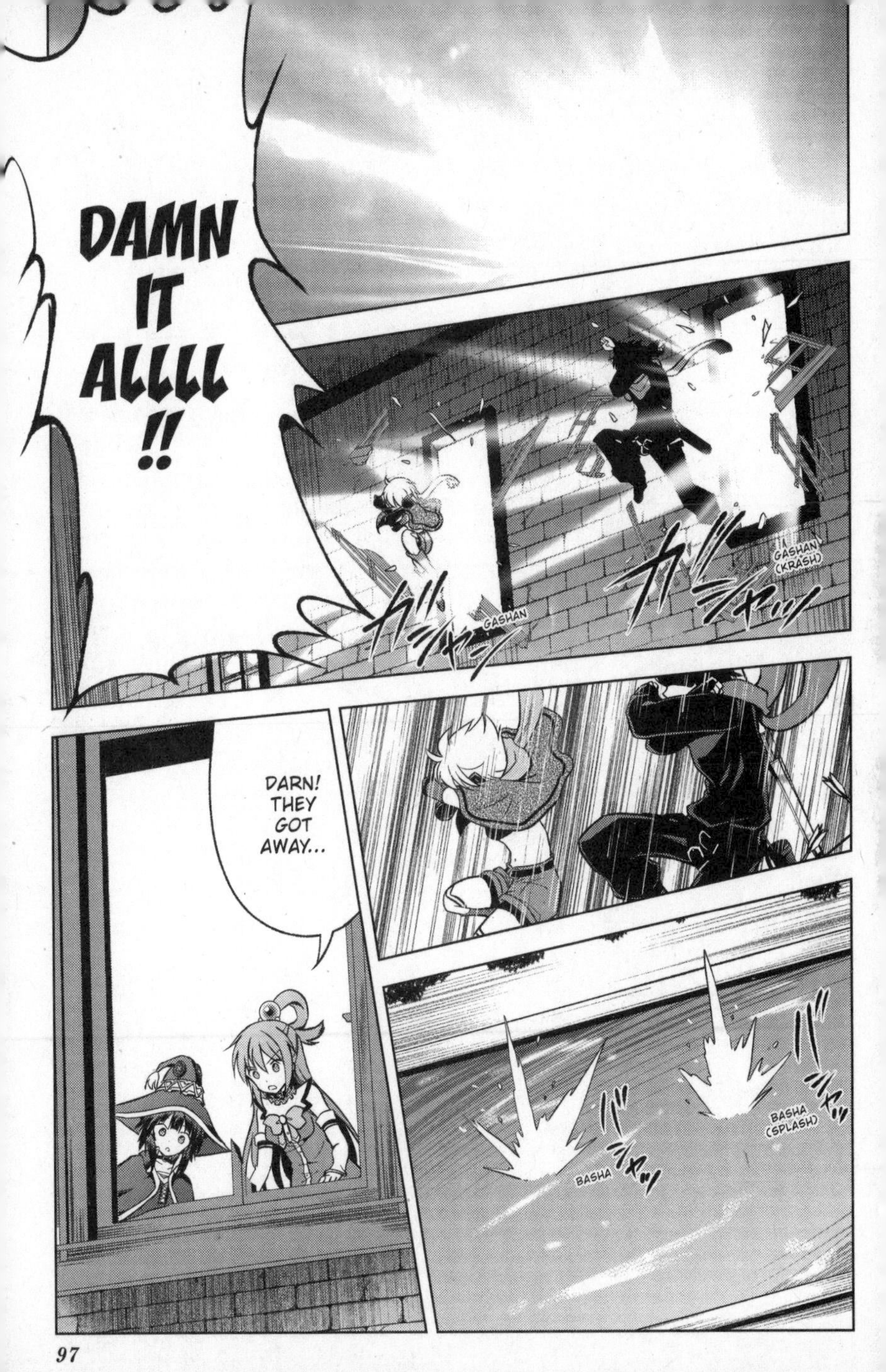
DAMN IT ALLLL!!
GASHAN (KRASH)
GASHAN
BASHA (SPLASH)
BASHA
DARN! THEY GOT AWAY...

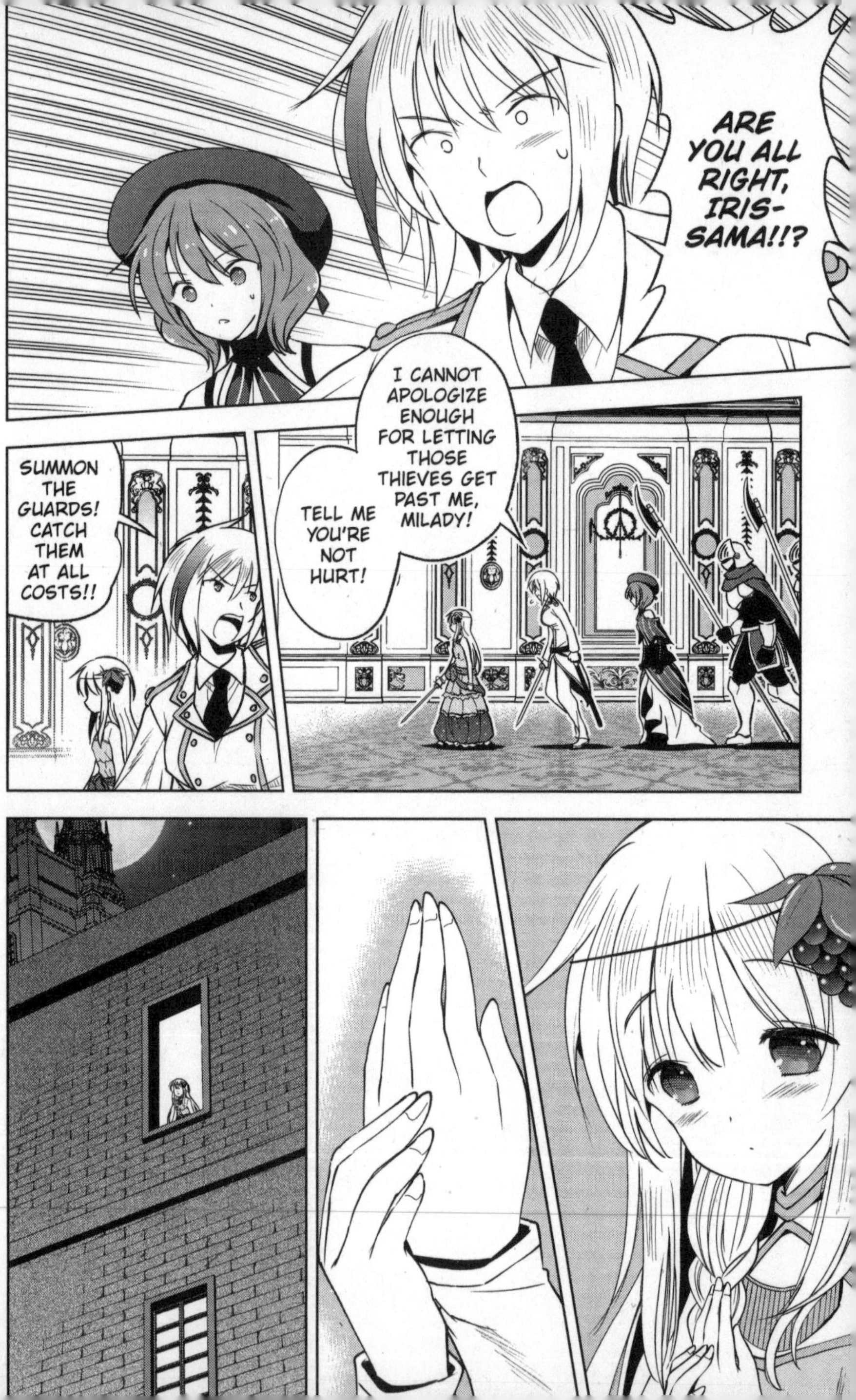
ARE YOU ALL RIGHT, IRIS-SAMA!!?
I CANNOT APOLOGIZE ENOUGH FOR LETTING THOSE THIEVES GET PAST ME, MILADY!
TELL ME YOU'RE NOT HURT!
SUMMON THE GUARDS! CATCH THEM AT ALL COSTS!!

GOD'S
BLESSING
ON THIS
WONDERFUL
WORLD!

11

11

GOD'S
BLESSING
ON THIS
WONDERFUL
WORLD!

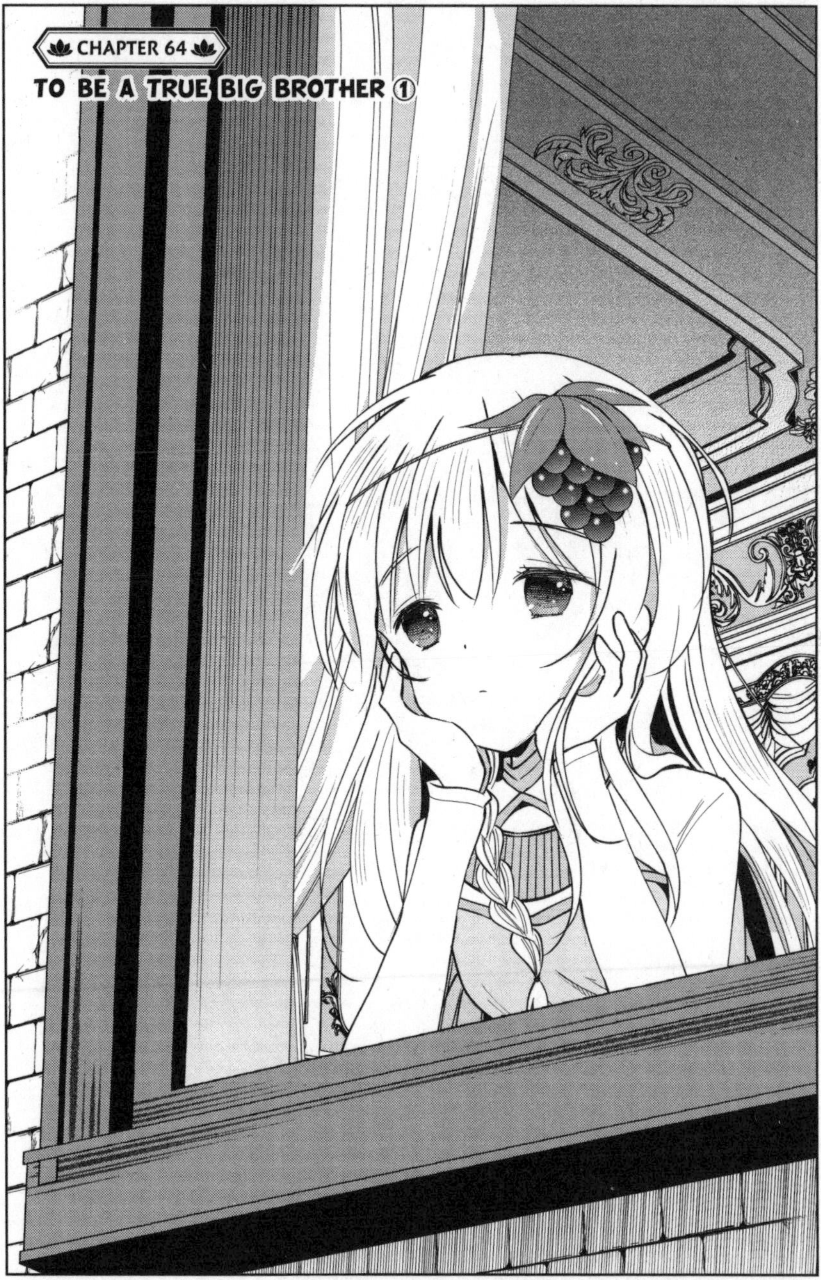
CHAPTER 64
TO BE A TRUE BIG BROTHER ①

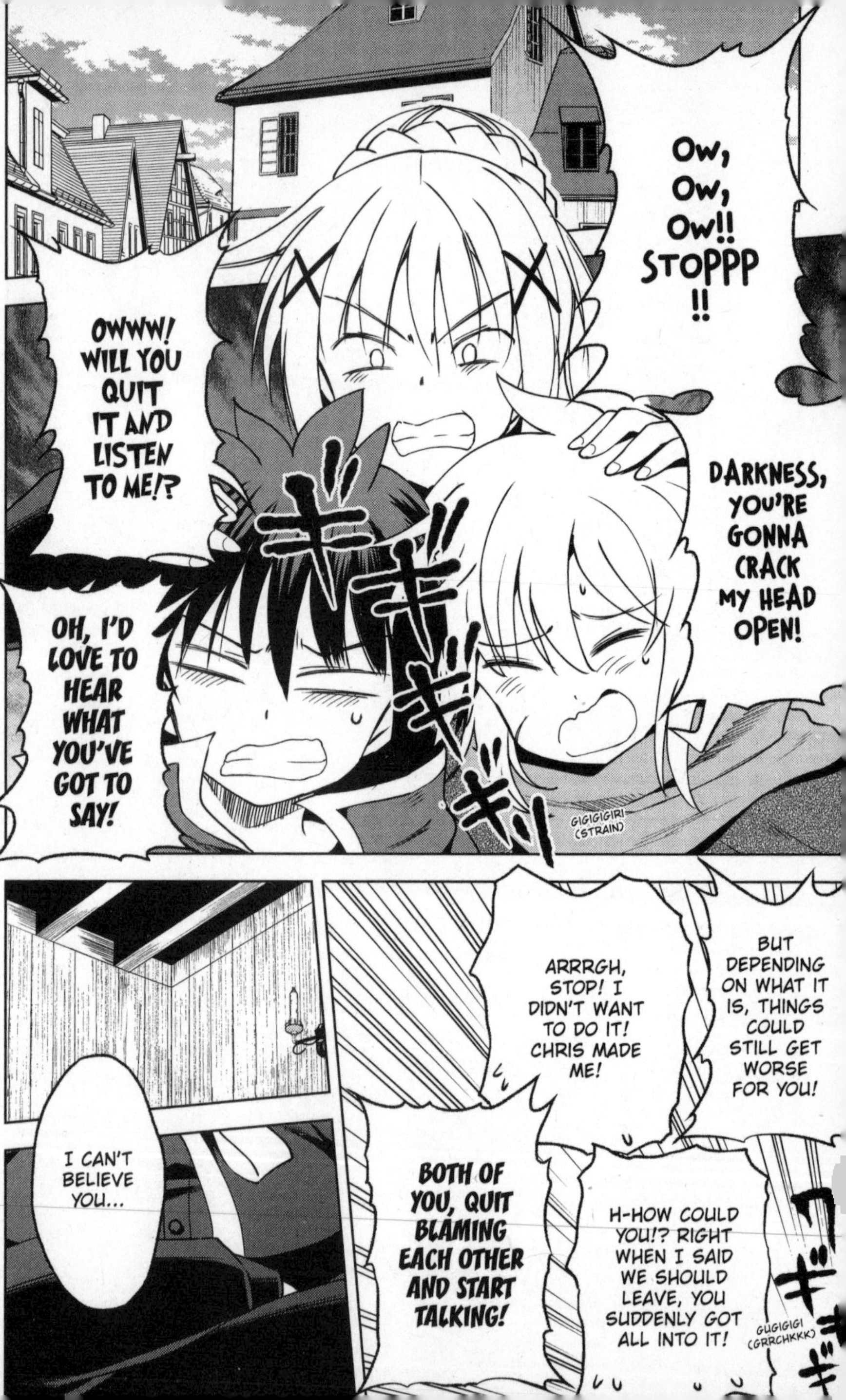
Ow, Ow, Ow!! STOPPP !!
DARKNESS, YOU'RE GONNA CRACK MY HEAD OPEN!
OWWW! WILL YOU QUIT IT AND LISTEN TO ME!?
OH, I'D LOVE TO HEAR WHAT YOU'VE GOT TO SAY!
GIGIGIGIRI (STRAIN)
BUT DEPENDING ON WHAT IT IS, THINGS COULD STILL GET WORSE FOR YOU!
ARRRGH, STOP! I DIDN'T WANT TO DO IT! CHRIS MADE ME!
GUGIGIGI (GRRCHKKK)
H-HOW COULD YOU!? RIGHT WHEN I SAID WE SHOULD LEAVE, YOU SUDDENLY GOT ALL INTO IT!
BOTH OF YOU, QUIT BLAMING EACH OTHER AND START TALKING!
I CAN'T BELIEVE YOU...

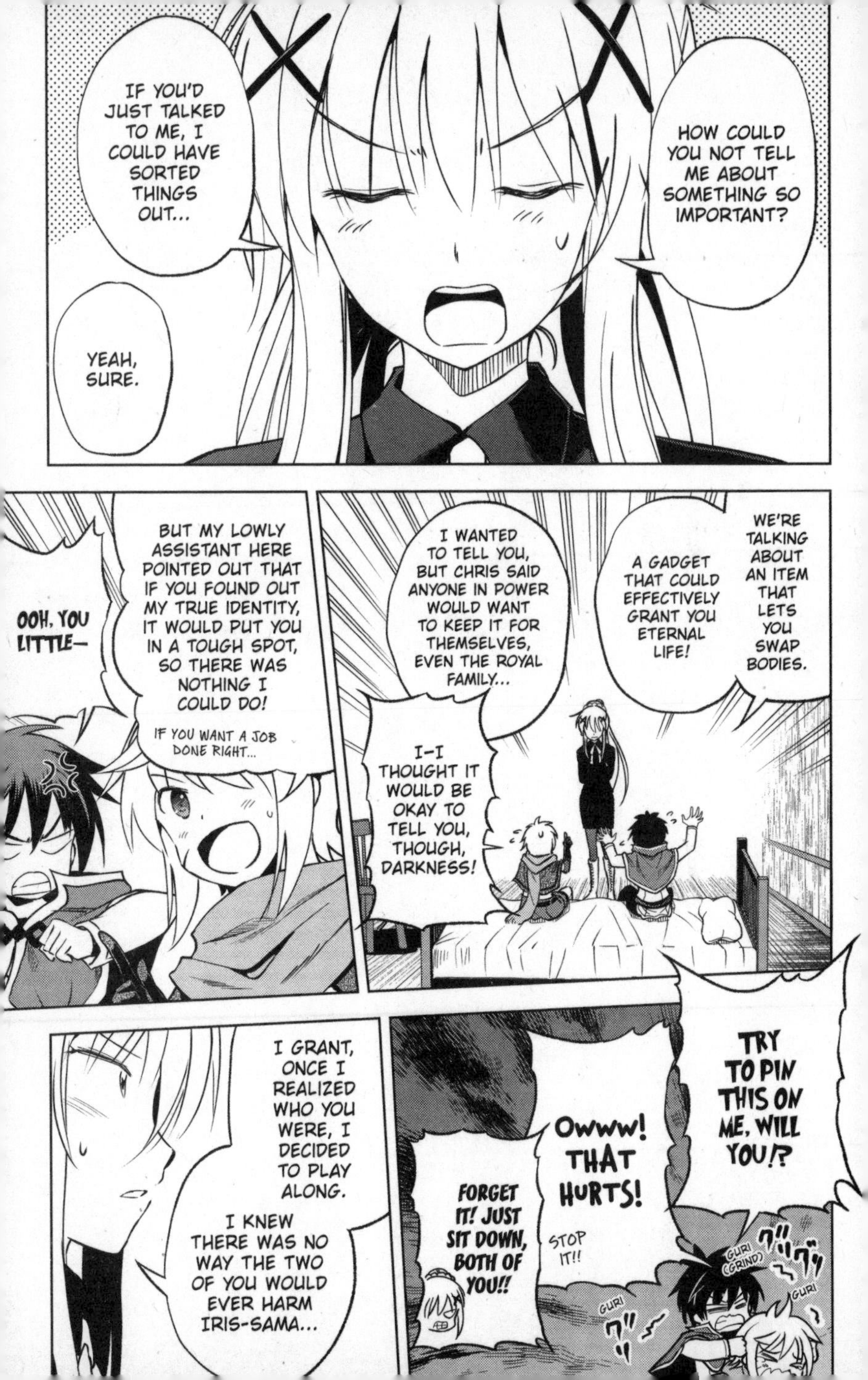
HOW COULD YOU NOT TELL ME ABOUT SOMETHING SO IMPORTANT?
IF YOU'D JUST TALKED TO ME, I COULD HAVE SORTED THINGS OUT...
YEAH, SURE.
WE'RE TALKING ABOUT AN ITEM THAT LETS YOU SWAP BODIES.
A GADGET THAT COULD EFFECTIVELY GRANT YOU ETERNAL LIFE!
I WANTED TO TELL YOU, BUT CHRIS SAID ANYONE IN POWER WOULD WANT TO KEEP IT FOR THEMSELVES, EVEN THE ROYAL FAMILY...
I-I THOUGHT IT WOULD BE OKAY TO TELL YOU, THOUGH, DARKNESS!
BUT MY LOWLY ASSISTANT HERE POINTED OUT THAT IF YOU FOUND OUT MY TRUE IDENTITY, IT WOULD PUT YOU IN A TOUGH SPOT, SO THERE WAS NOTHING I COULD DO!
IF YOU WANT A JOB DONE RIGHT...
OOH, YOU LITTLE—
TRY TO PIN THIS ON ME, WILL YOU!?
Owww! THAT HURTS!
FORGET IT! JUST SIT DOWN, BOTH OF YOU!!
STOP IT!!
GURI (GRIND)
GURI
GURI
I GRANT, ONCE I REALIZED WHO YOU WERE, I DECIDED TO PLAY ALONG.
I KNEW THERE WAS NO WAY THE TWO OF YOU WOULD EVER HARM IRIS-SAMA...

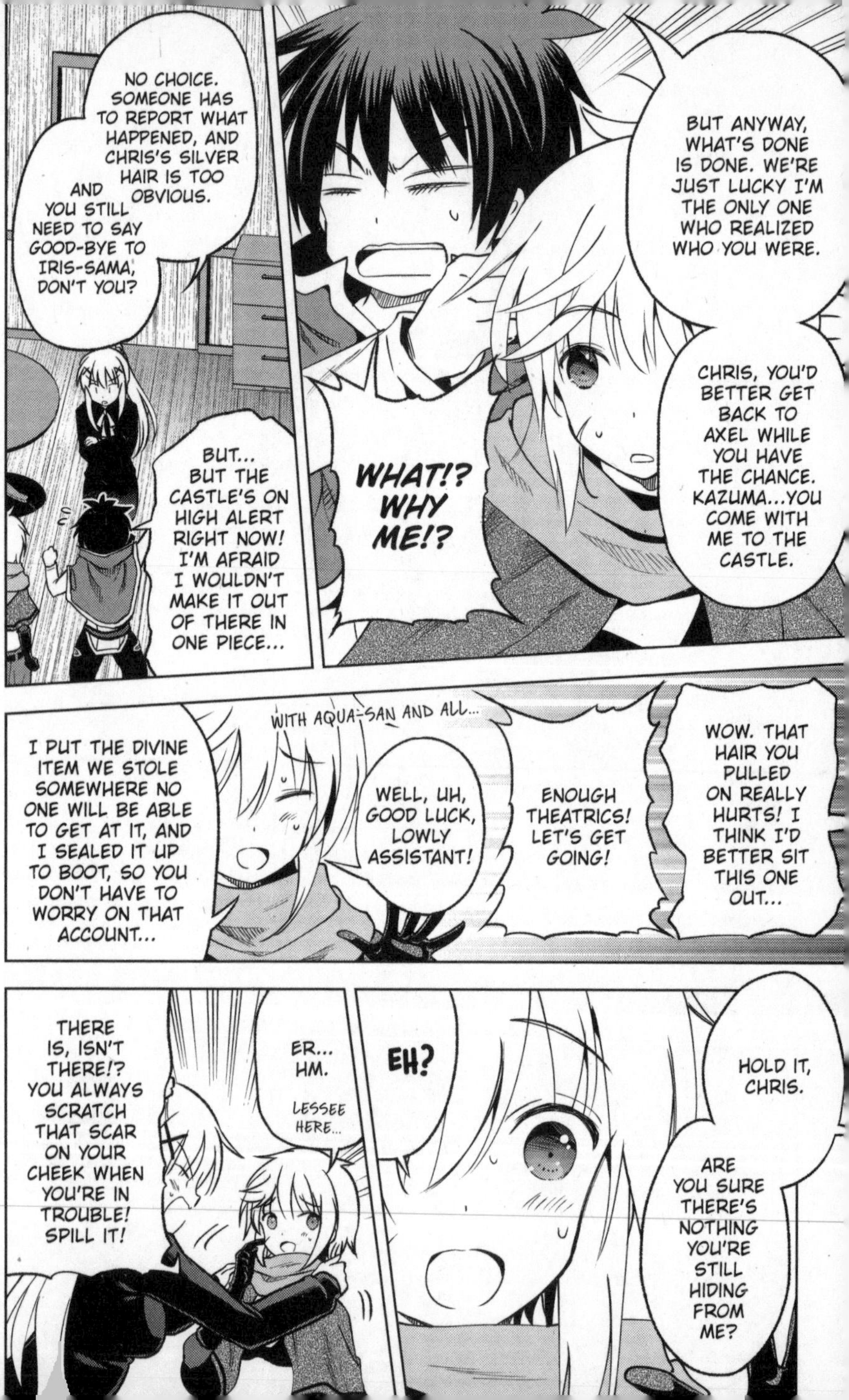
BUT ANYWAY, WHAT'S DONE IS DONE. WE'RE JUST LUCKY I'M THE ONLY ONE WHO REALIZED WHO YOU WERE.
CHRIS, YOU'D BETTER GET BACK TO AXEL WHILE YOU HAVE THE CHANCE. KAZUMA...YOU COME WITH ME TO THE CASTLE.
WHAT!? WHY ME!?
NO CHOICE. SOMEONE HAS TO REPORT WHAT HAPPENED, AND CHRIS'S SILVER HAIR IS TOO OBVIOUS.
AND YOU STILL NEED TO SAY GOOD-BYE TO IRIS-SAMA, DON'T YOU?
BUT... BUT THE CASTLE'S ON HIGH ALERT RIGHT NOW! I'M AFRAID I WOULDN'T MAKE IT OUT OF THERE IN ONE PIECE...
WOW. THAT HAIR YOU PULLED ON REALLY HURTS! I THINK I'D BETTER SIT THIS ONE OUT...
ENOUGH THEATRICS! LET'S GET GOING!
WITH AQUA-SAN AND ALL...
WELL, UH, GOOD LUCK, LOWLY ASSISTANT!
I PUT THE DIVINE ITEM WE STOLE SOMEWHERE NO ONE WILL BE ABLE TO GET AT IT, AND I SEALED IT UP TO BOOT, SO YOU DON'T HAVE TO WORRY ON THAT ACCOUNT...
HOLD IT, CHRIS.
ARE YOU SURE THERE'S NOTHING YOU'RE STILL HIDING FROM ME?
EH?
ER... HM.
LESSEE HERE...
THERE IS, ISN'T THERE!? YOU ALWAYS SCRATCH THAT SCAR ON YOUR CHEEK WHEN YOU'RE IN TROUBLE! SPILL IT!

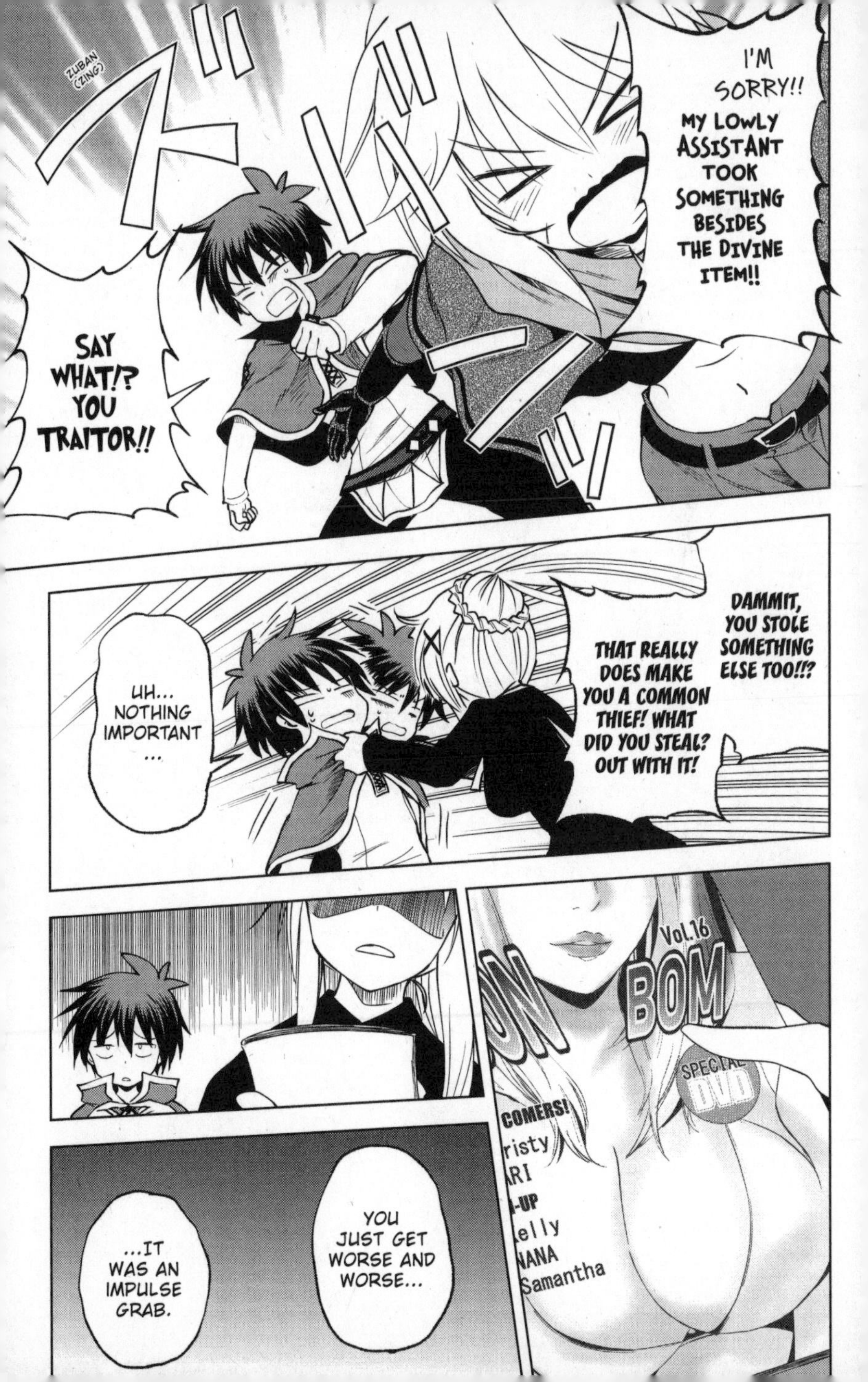
I'M SORRY!!
MY LOWLY ASSISTANT TOOK SOMETHING BESIDES THE DIVINE ITEM!!
ZUBAN (ZING)
SAY WHAT!? YOU TRAITOR!!
DAMMIT, YOU STOLE SOMETHING ELSE TOO!!?
THAT REALLY DOES MAKE YOU A COMMON THIEF! WHAT DID YOU STEAL? OUT WITH IT!
UH... NOTHING IMPORTANT ...
Vol.16
BOM
SPECIAL DVD
COMERS!
risty
ARI
A-UP
Kelly
NANA
Samantha
YOU JUST GET WORSE AND WORSE...
...IT WAS AN IMPULSE GRAB.

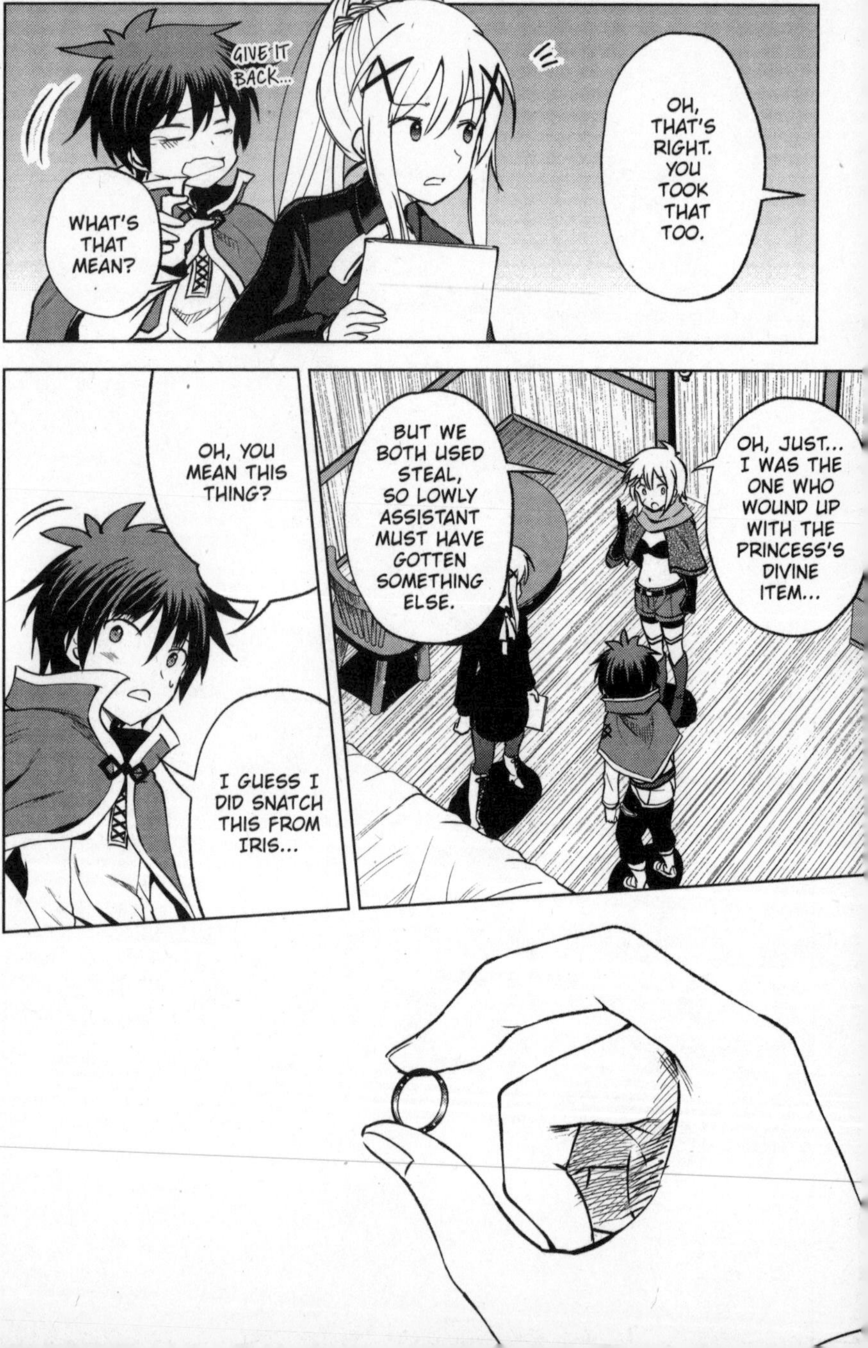
OH, THAT'S RIGHT. YOU TOOK THAT TOO.
GIVE IT BACK...
WHAT'S THAT MEAN?
OH, JUST... I WAS THE ONE WHO WOUND UP WITH THE PRINCESS'S DIVINE ITEM...
BUT WE BOTH USED STEAL, SO LOWLY ASSISTANT MUST HAVE GOTTEN SOMETHING ELSE.
OH, YOU MEAN THIS THING?
I GUESS I DID SNATCH THIS FROM IRIS...

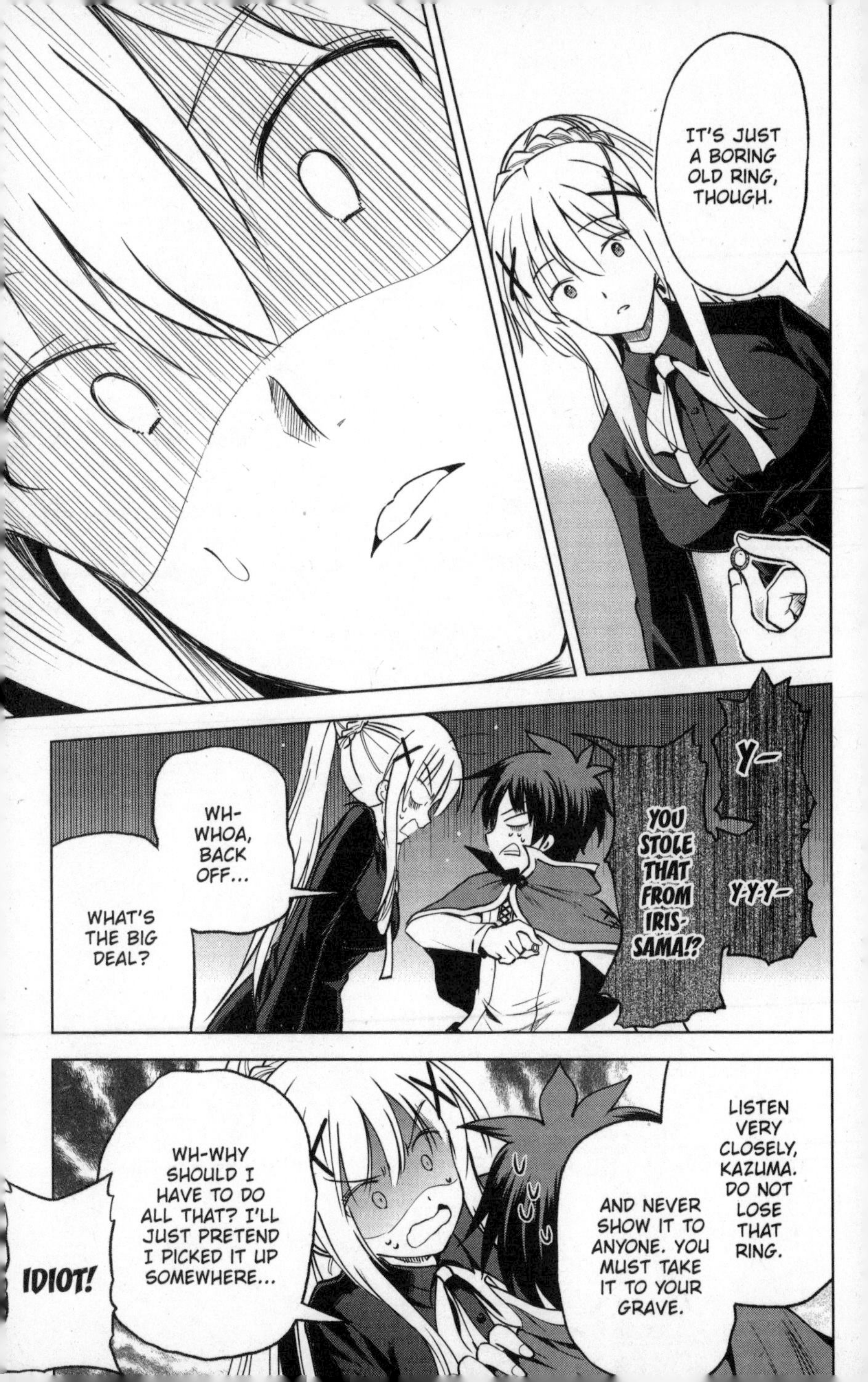
IT'S JUST A BORING OLD RING, THOUGH.
Y-
Y-Y-Y-
YOU STOLE THAT FROM IRIS-SAMA!?
WH-WHOA, BACK OFF...
WHAT'S THE BIG DEAL?
LISTEN VERY CLOSELY, KAZUMA. DO NOT LOSE THAT RING.
AND NEVER SHOW IT TO ANYONE. YOU MUST TAKE IT TO YOUR GRAVE.
WH-WHY SHOULD I HAVE TO DO ALL THAT? I'LL JUST PRETEND I PICKED IT UP SOMEWHERE...
IDIOT!

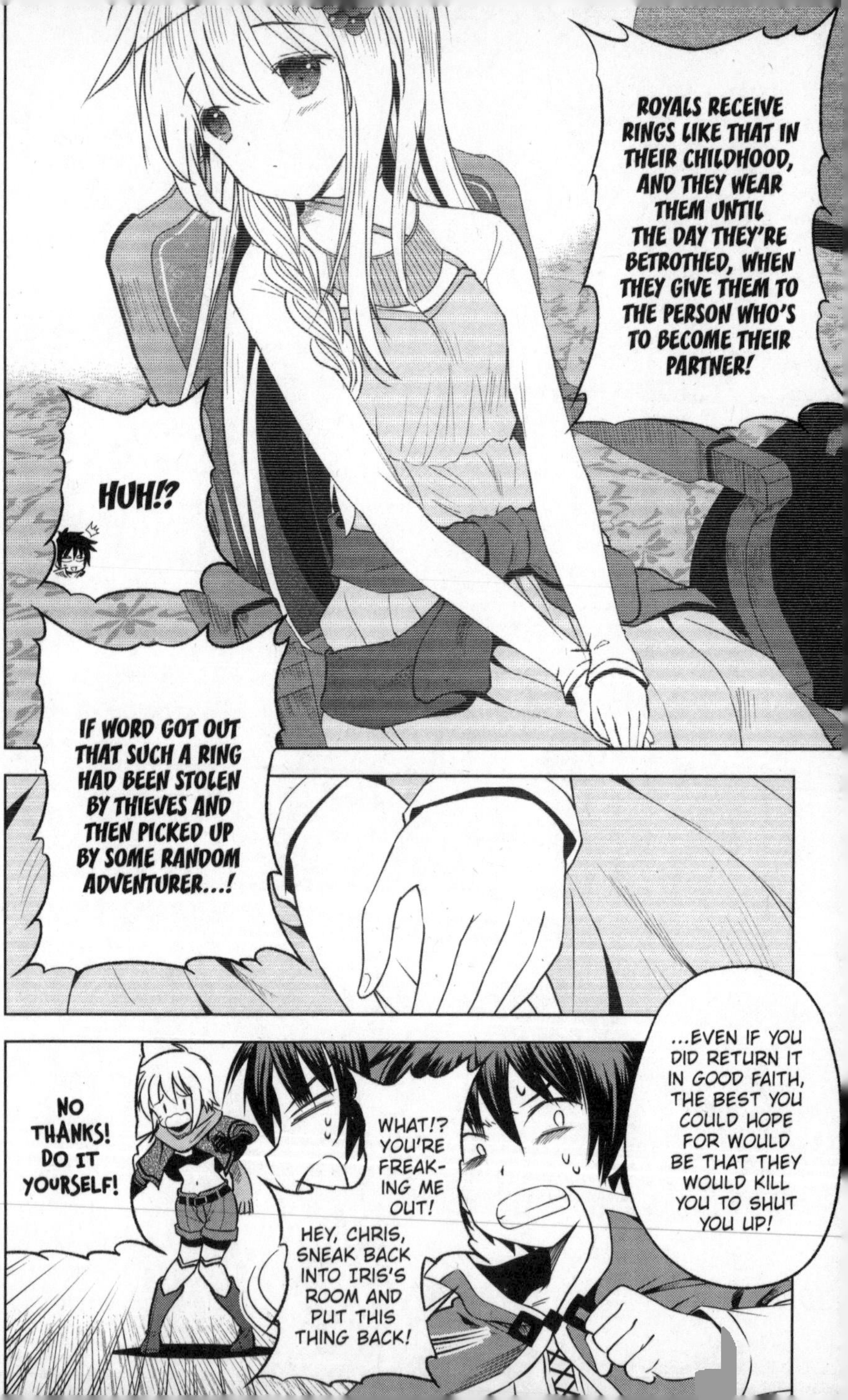
ROYALS RECEIVE RINGS LIKE THAT IN THEIR CHILDHOOD, AND THEY WEAR THEM UNTIL THE DAY THEY'RE BETROTHED, WHEN THEY GIVE THEM TO THE PERSON WHO'S TO BECOME THEIR PARTNER!
HUH!?
IF WORD GOT OUT THAT SUCH A RING HAD BEEN STOLEN BY THIEVES AND THEN PICKED UP BY SOME RANDOM ADVENTURER...!
...EVEN IF YOU DID RETURN IT IN GOOD FAITH, THE BEST YOU COULD HOPE FOR WOULD BE THAT THEY WOULD KILL YOU TO SHUT YOU UP!
WHAT!? YOU'RE FREAK-ING ME OUT!
HEY, CHRIS, SNEAK BACK INTO IRIS'S ROOM AND PUT THIS THING BACK!
NO THANKS! DO IT YOURSELF!

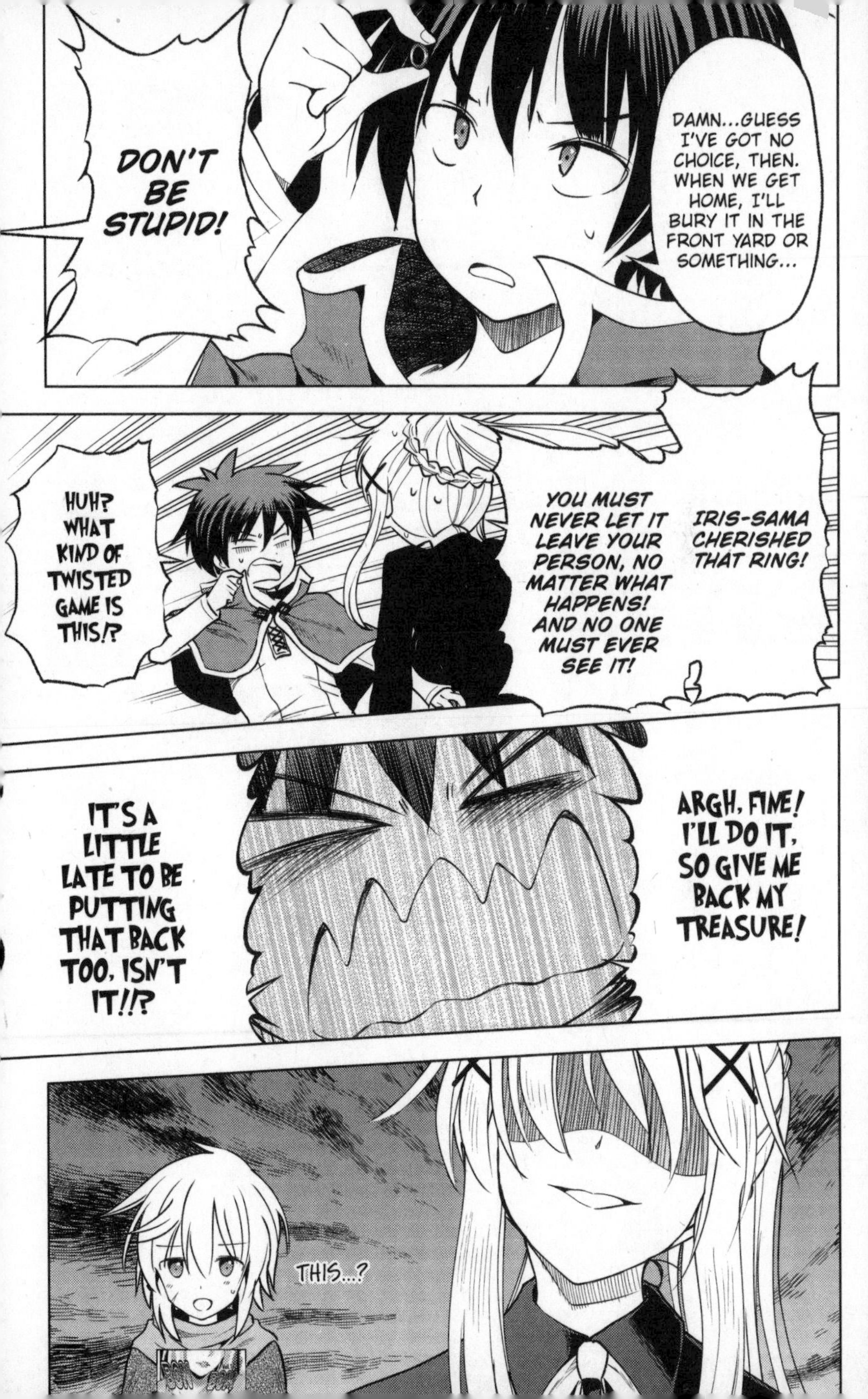

DAMN...GUESS I'VE GOT NO CHOICE, THEN. WHEN WE GET HOME, I'LL BURY IT IN THE FRONT YARD OR SOMETHING...
DON'T BE STUPID!
IRIS-SAMA CHERISHED THAT RING!
YOU MUST NEVER LET IT LEAVE YOUR PERSON, NO MATTER WHAT HAPPENS! AND NO ONE MUST EVER SEE IT!
HUH? WHAT KIND OF TWISTED GAME IS THIS!?
ARGH, FINE! I'LL DO IT, SO GIVE ME BACK MY TREASURE!
IT'S A LITTLE LATE TO BE PUTTING THAT BACK TOO, ISN'T IT!!?
THIS...?

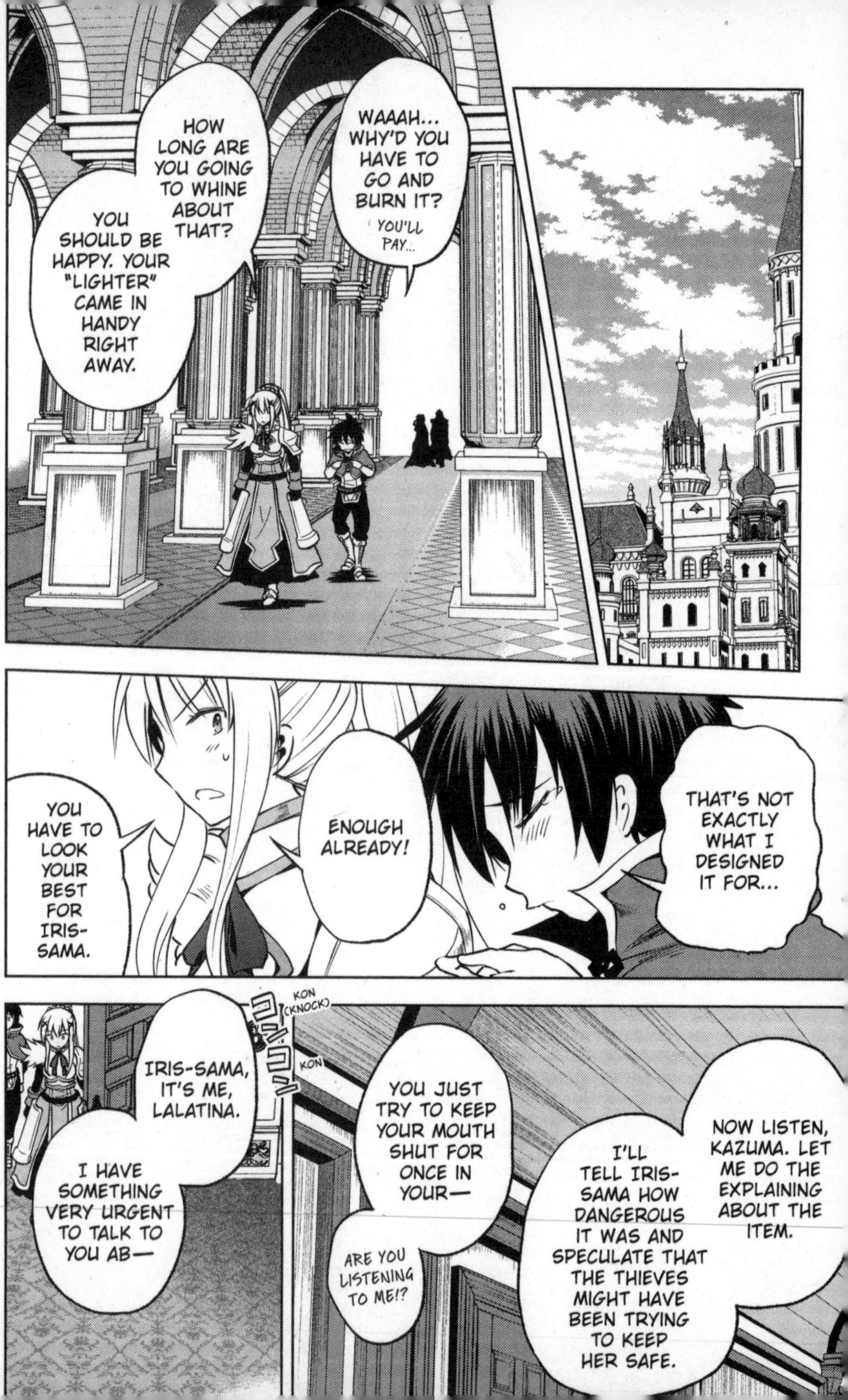
WAAAH... WHY'D YOU HAVE TO GO AND BURN IT?
YOU'LL PAY...
HOW LONG ARE YOU GOING TO WHINE ABOUT THAT?
YOU SHOULD BE HAPPY. YOUR "LIGHTER" CAME IN HANDY RIGHT AWAY.
THAT'S NOT EXACTLY WHAT I DESIGNED IT FOR...
ENOUGH ALREADY!
YOU HAVE TO LOOK YOUR BEST FOR IRIS-SAMA.
NOW LISTEN, KAZUMA. LET ME DO THE EXPLAINING ABOUT THE ITEM.
I'LL TELL IRIS-SAMA HOW DANGEROUS IT WAS AND SPECULATE THAT THE THIEVES MIGHT HAVE BEEN TRYING TO KEEP HER SAFE.
YOU JUST TRY TO KEEP YOUR MOUTH SHUT FOR ONCE IN YOUR—
ARE YOU LISTENING TO ME!?
KON (KNOCK)
KON
IRIS-SAMA, IT'S ME, LALATINA.
I HAVE SOMETHING VERY URGENT TO TALK TO YOU AB—

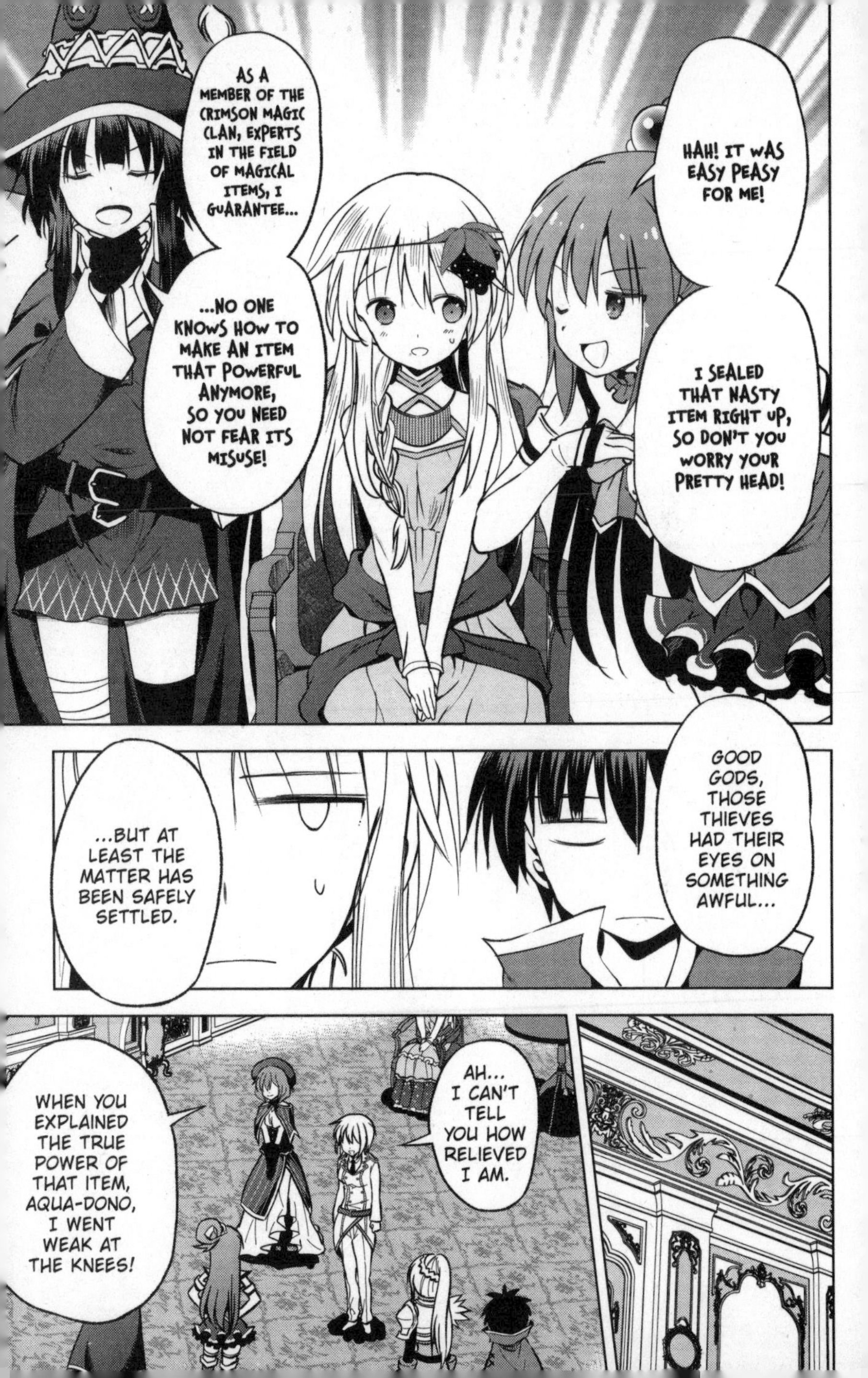
HAH! IT WAS EASY PEASY FOR ME!
I SEALED THAT NASTY ITEM RIGHT UP, SO DON'T YOU WORRY YOUR PRETTY HEAD!
AS A MEMBER OF THE CRIMSON MAGIC CLAN, EXPERTS IN THE FIELD OF MAGICAL ITEMS, I GUARANTEE...
...NO ONE KNOWS HOW TO MAKE AN ITEM THAT POWERFUL ANYMORE, SO YOU NEED NOT FEAR ITS MISUSE!
GOOD GODS, THOSE THIEVES HAD THEIR EYES ON SOMETHING AWFUL...
...BUT AT LEAST THE MATTER HAS BEEN SAFELY SETTLED.
AH... I CAN'T TELL YOU HOW RELIEVED I AM.
WHEN YOU EXPLAINED THE TRUE POWER OF THAT ITEM, AQUA-DONO, I WENT WEAK AT THE KNEES!

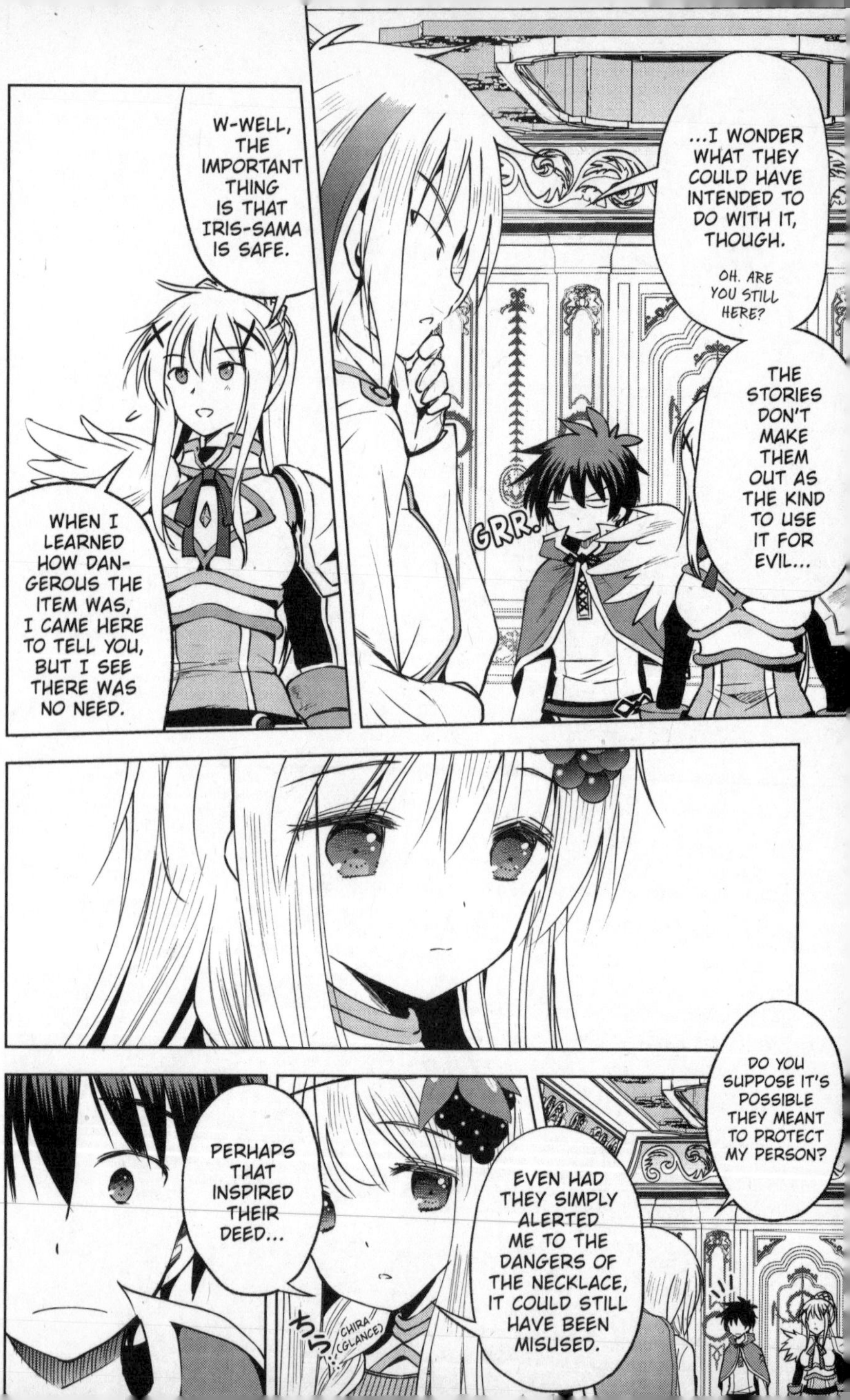
...I WONDER WHAT THEY COULD HAVE INTENDED TO DO WITH IT, THOUGH.
OH. ARE YOU STILL HERE?
THE STORIES DON'T MAKE THEM OUT AS THE KIND TO USE IT FOR EVIL...
GRR.
W-WELL, THE IMPORTANT THING IS THAT IRIS-SAMA IS SAFE.
WHEN I LEARNED HOW DAN-GEROUS THE ITEM WAS, I CAME HERE TO TELL YOU, BUT I SEE THERE WAS NO NEED.
DO YOU SUPPOSE IT'S POSSIBLE THEY MEANT TO PROTECT MY PERSON?
EVEN HAD THEY SIMPLY ALERTED ME TO THE DANGERS OF THE NECKLACE, IT COULD STILL HAVE BEEN MISUSED.
PERHAPS THAT INSPIRED THEIR DEED...
ちら CHIRA (GLANCE)

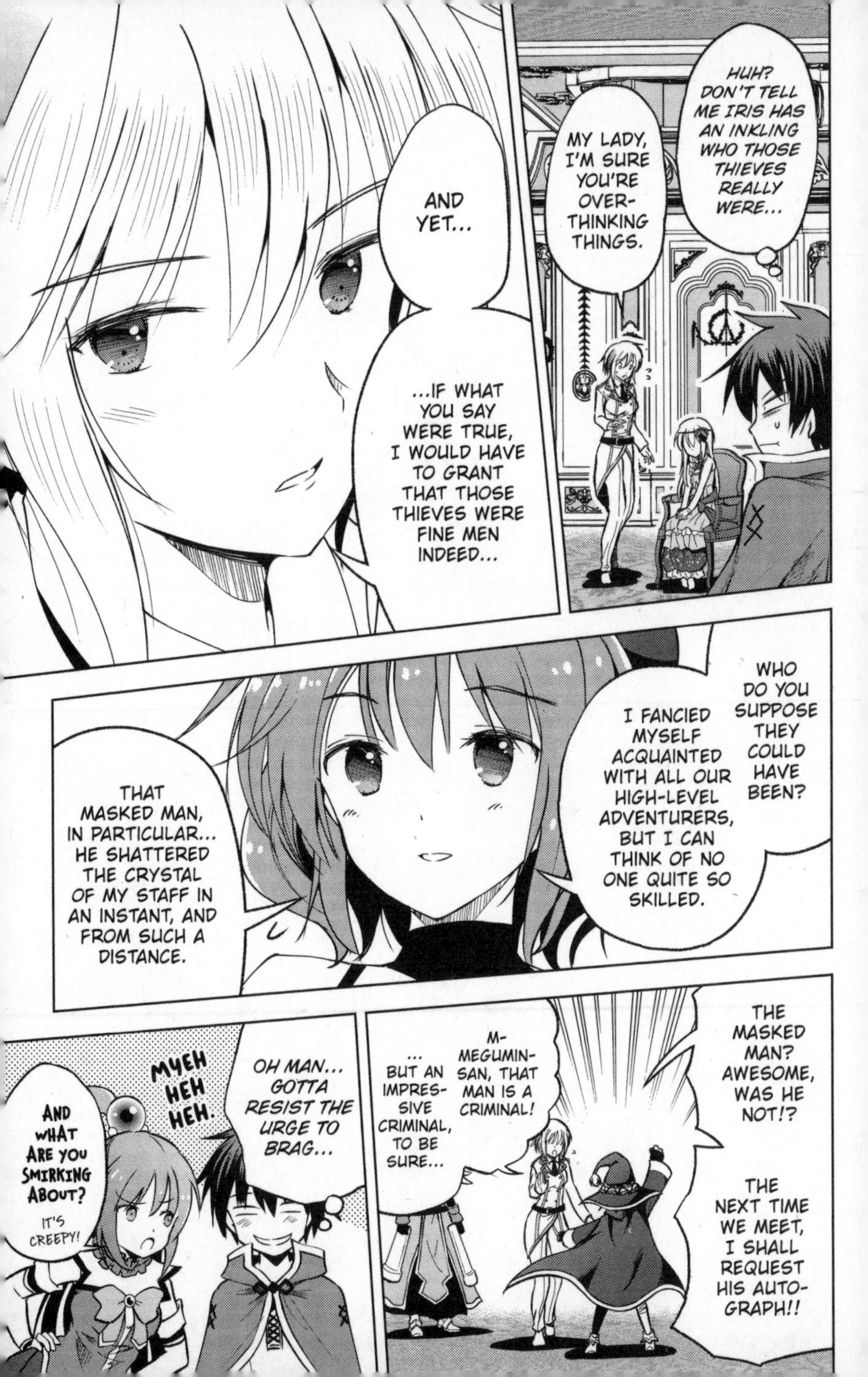
HUH? DON'T TELL ME IRIS HAS AN INKLING WHO THOSE THIEVES REALLY WERE...
MY LADY, I'M SURE YOU'RE OVER-THINKING THINGS.
AND YET...
...IF WHAT YOU SAY WERE TRUE, I WOULD HAVE TO GRANT THAT THOSE THIEVES WERE FINE MEN INDEED...
WHO DO YOU SUPPOSE THEY COULD HAVE BEEN?
I FANCIED MYSELF ACQUAINTED WITH ALL OUR HIGH-LEVEL ADVENTURERS, BUT I CAN THINK OF NO ONE QUITE SO SKILLED.
THAT MASKED MAN, IN PARTICULAR... HE SHATTERED THE CRYSTAL OF MY STAFF IN AN INSTANT, AND FROM SUCH A DISTANCE.
THE MASKED MAN? AWESOME, WAS HE NOT!?
THE NEXT TIME WE MEET, I SHALL REQUEST HIS AUTO-GRAPH!!
M-MEGUMIN-SAN, THAT MAN IS A CRIMINAL!
... BUT AN IMPRES-SIVE CRIMINAL, TO BE SURE...
OH MAN... GOTTA RESIST THE URGE TO BRAG...
MYEH HEH HEH.
AND WHAT ARE YOU SMIRKING ABOUT?
IT'S CREEPY!

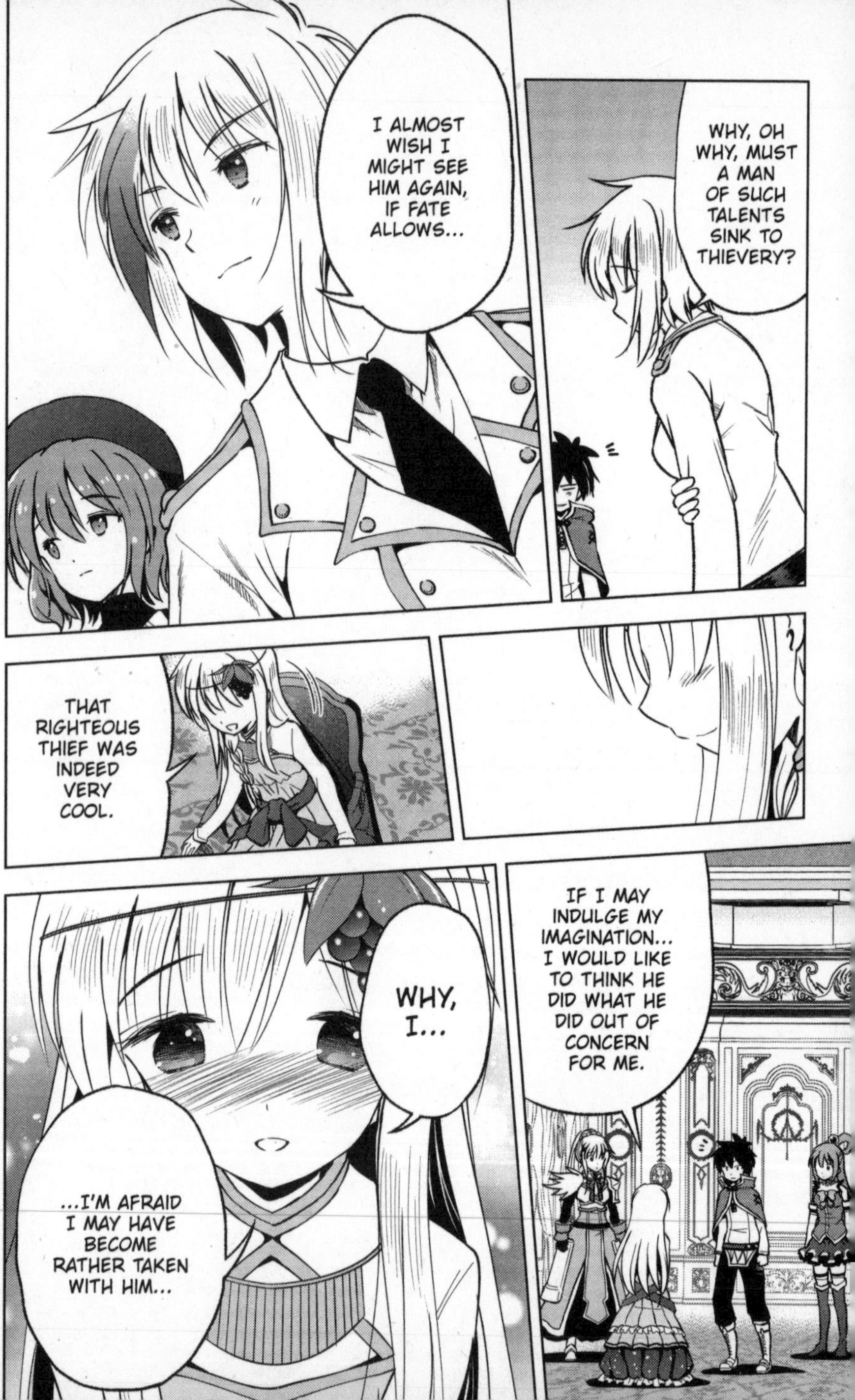
WHY, OH WHY, MUST A MAN OF SUCH TALENTS SINK TO THIEVERY?
I ALMOST WISH I MIGHT SEE HIM AGAIN, IF FATE ALLOWS...
THAT RIGHTEOUS THIEF WAS INDEED VERY COOL.
IF I MAY INDULGE MY IMAGINATION... I WOULD LIKE TO THINK HE DID WHAT HE DID OUT OF CONCERN FOR ME.
WHY, I...
...I'M AFRAID I MAY HAVE BECOME RATHER TAKEN WITH HIM...

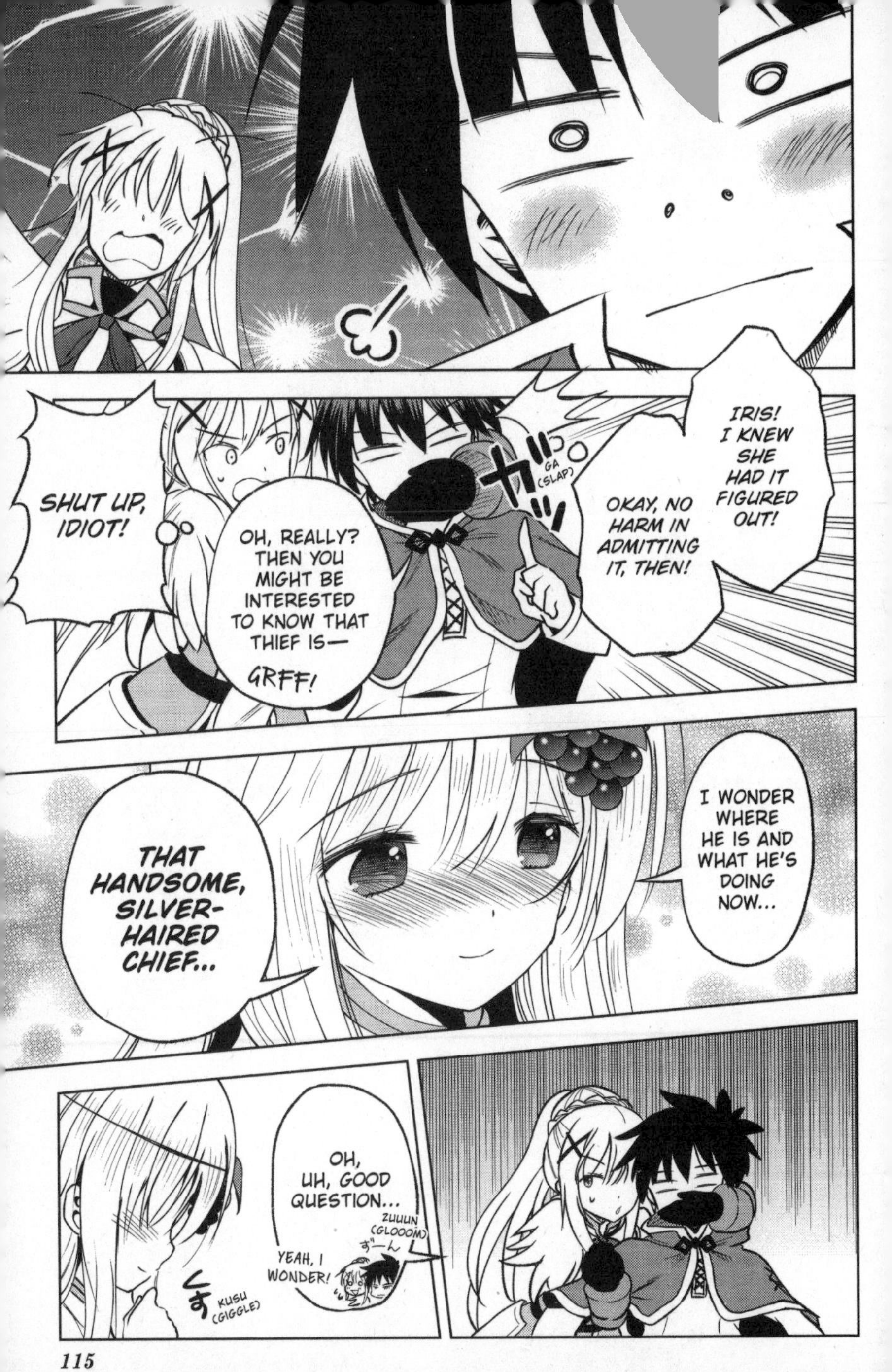

IRIS! I KNEW SHE HAD IT FIGURED OUT!
OKAY, NO HARM IN ADMITTING IT, THEN!
ガッ
GA (SLAP)
OH, REALLY? THEN YOU MIGHT BE INTERESTED TO KNOW THAT THIEF IS—
GRFF!
SHUT UP, IDIOT!
I WONDER WHERE HE IS AND WHAT HE'S DOING NOW...
THAT HANDSOME, SILVER-HAIRED CHIEF...
OH, UH, GOOD QUESTION...
ずーん
ZUUUN (GLOOOM)
YEAH, I WONDER!
くす
KUSU (GIGGLE)

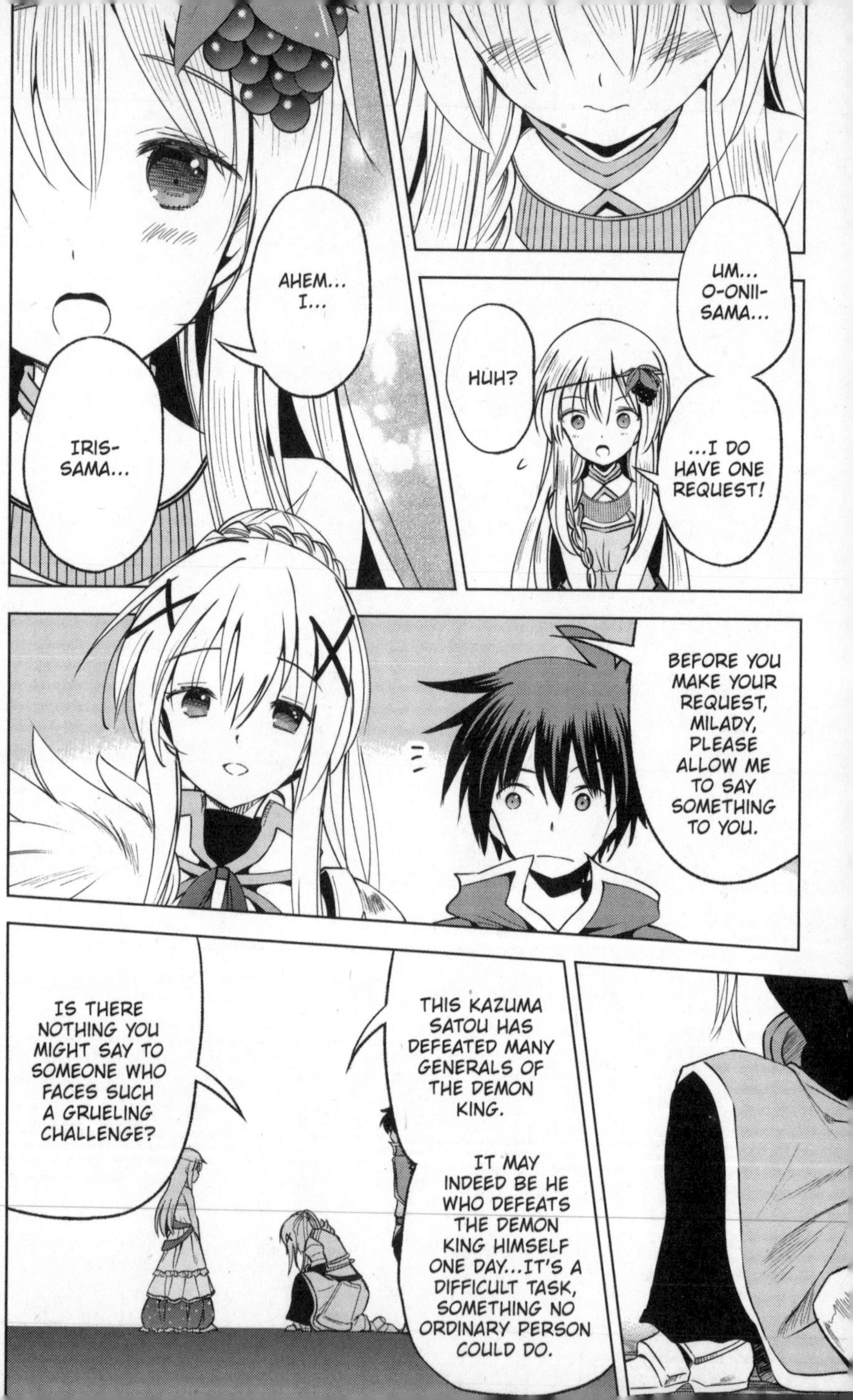
UM... O-ONII-SAMA...
HUH?
...I DO HAVE ONE REQUEST!
AHEM... I...
IRIS-SAMA...
BEFORE YOU MAKE YOUR REQUEST, MILADY, PLEASE ALLOW ME TO SAY SOMETHING TO YOU.
THIS KAZUMA SATOU HAS DEFEATED MANY GENERALS OF THE DEMON KING.
IT MAY INDEED BE HE WHO DEFEATS THE DEMON KING HIMSELF ONE DAY...IT'S A DIFFICULT TASK, SOMETHING NO ORDINARY PERSON COULD DO.
IS THERE NOTHING YOU MIGHT SAY TO SOMEONE WHO FACES SUCH A GRUELING CHALLENGE?

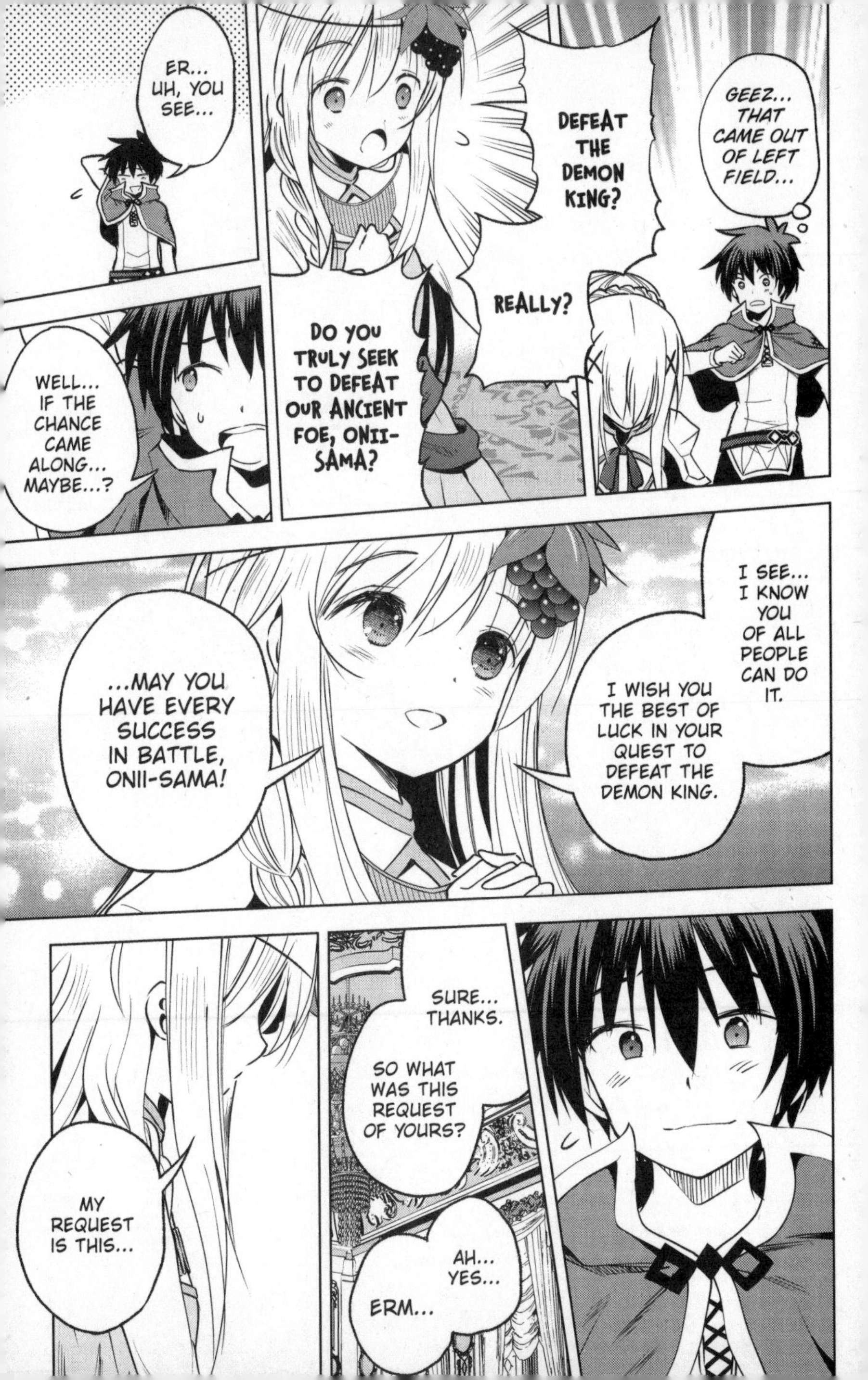
GEEZ... THAT CAME OUT OF LEFT FIELD...
DEFEAT THE DEMON KING?
REALLY?
DO YOU TRULY SEEK TO DEFEAT OUR ANCIENT FOE, ONII-SAMA?
ER... UH, YOU SEE...
WELL... IF THE CHANCE CAME ALONG... MAYBE...?
I SEE... I KNOW YOU OF ALL PEOPLE CAN DO IT.
I WISH YOU THE BEST OF LUCK IN YOUR QUEST TO DEFEAT THE DEMON KING.
...MAY YOU HAVE EVERY SUCCESS IN BATTLE, ONII-SAMA!
SURE... THANKS.
SO WHAT WAS THIS REQUEST OF YOURS?
AH... YES...
ERM...
MY REQUEST IS THIS...

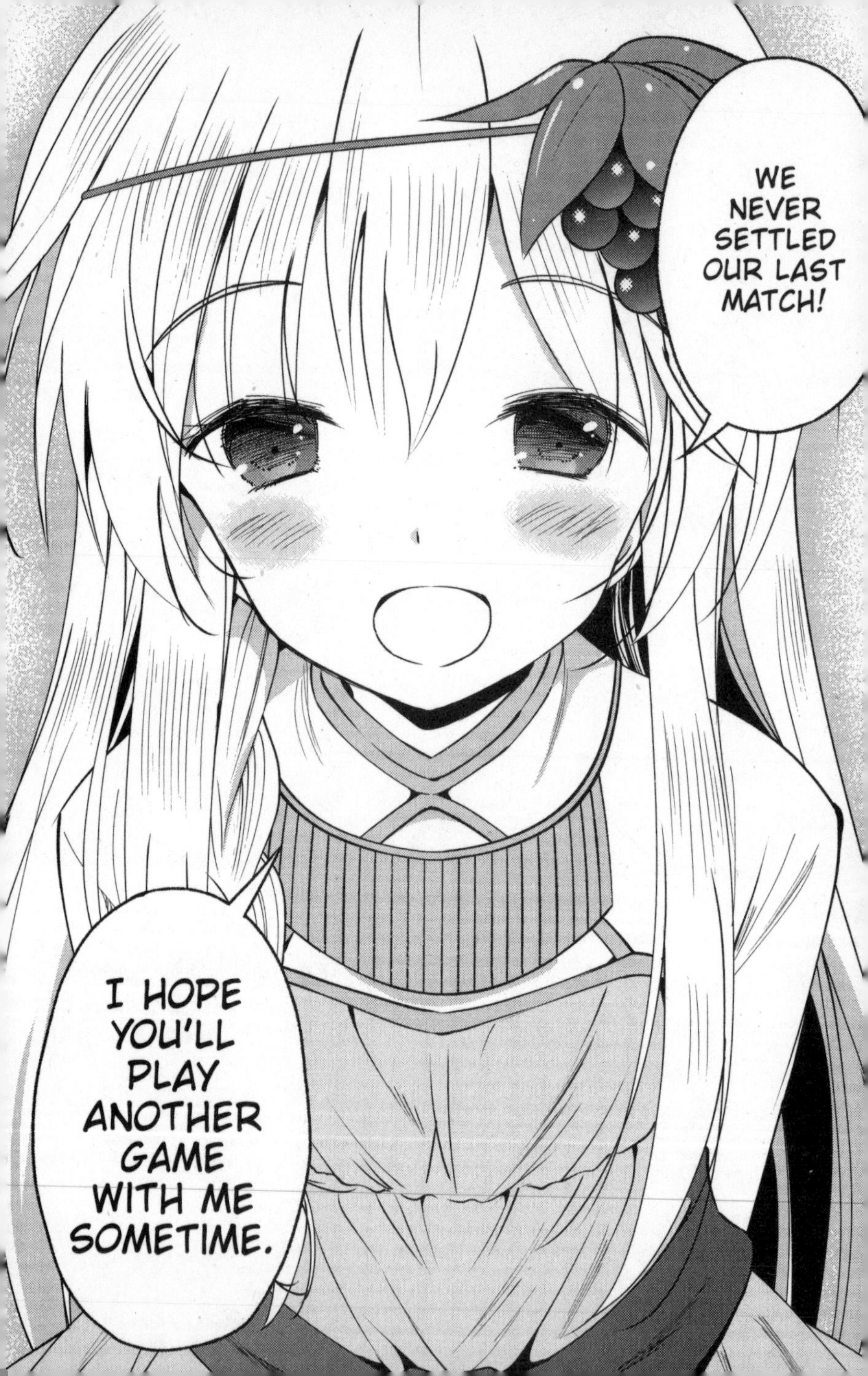
WE NEVER SETTLED OUR LAST MATCH!
I HOPE YOU'LL PLAY ANOTHER GAME WITH ME SOMETIME.

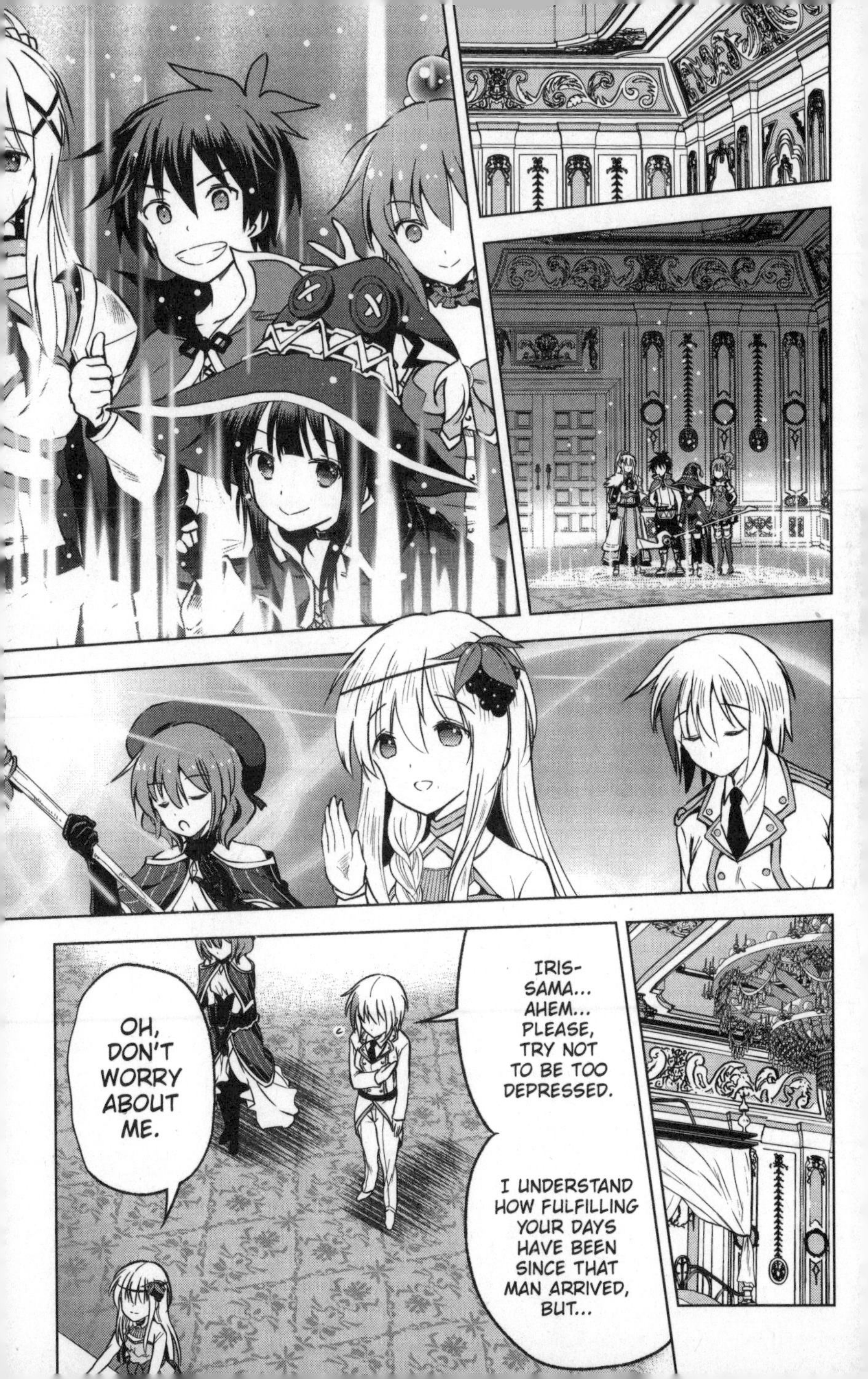

IRIS-SAMA... AHEM... PLEASE, TRY NOT TO BE TOO DEPRESSED.
I UNDERSTAND HOW FULFILLING YOUR DAYS HAVE BEEN SINCE THAT MAN ARRIVED, BUT...
OH, DON'T WORRY ABOUT ME.

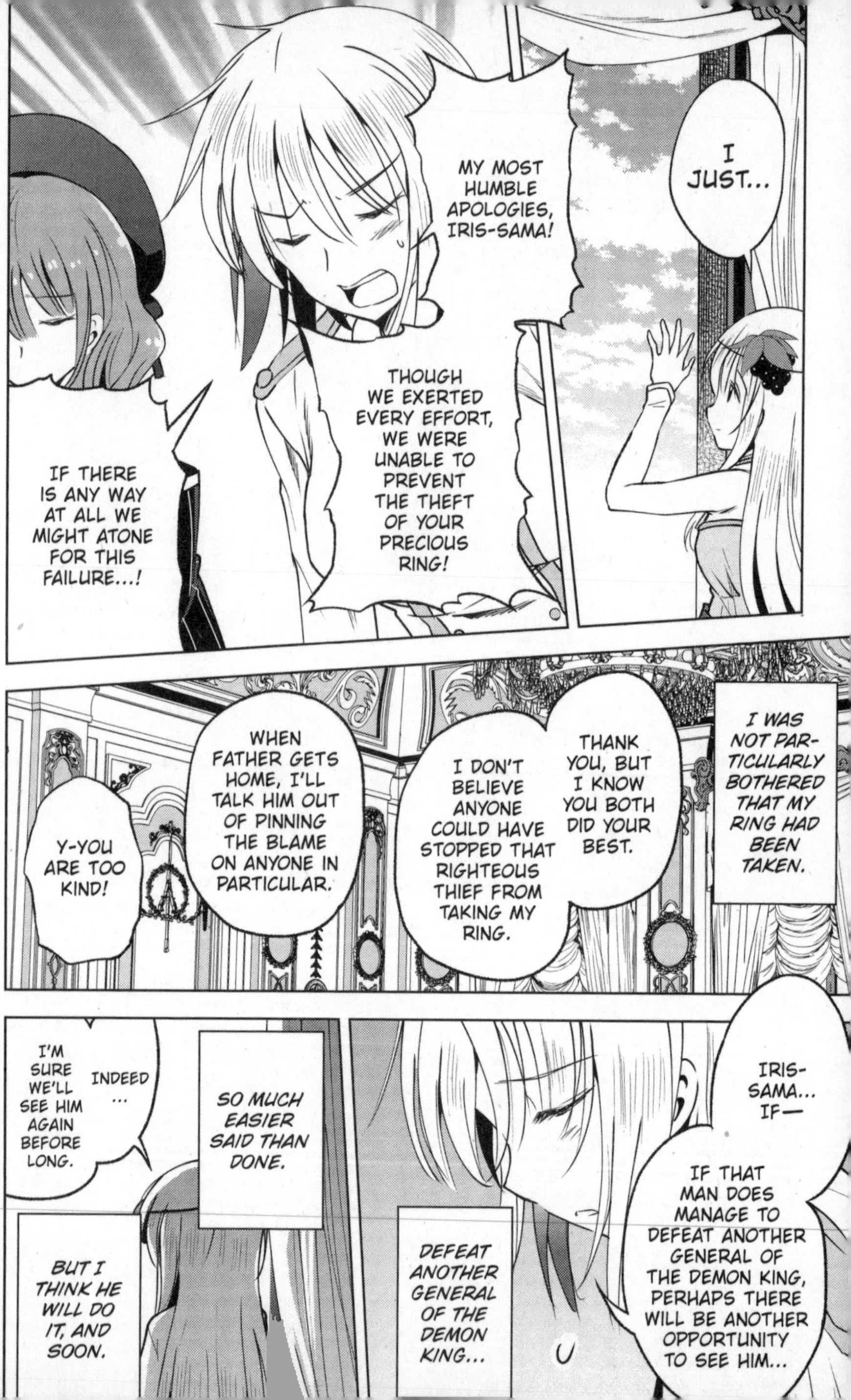
I JUST...
MY MOST HUMBLE APOLOGIES, IRIS-SAMA!
THOUGH WE EXERTED EVERY EFFORT, WE WERE UNABLE TO PREVENT THE THEFT OF YOUR PRECIOUS RING!
IF THERE IS ANY WAY AT ALL WE MIGHT ATONE FOR THIS FAILURE...!
I WAS NOT PARTICULARLY BOTHERED THAT MY RING HAD BEEN TAKEN.
THANK YOU, BUT I KNOW YOU BOTH DID YOUR BEST.
I DON'T BELIEVE ANYONE COULD HAVE STOPPED THAT RIGHTEOUS THIEF FROM TAKING MY RING.
WHEN FATHER GETS HOME, I'LL TALK HIM OUT OF PINNING THE BLAME ON ANYONE IN PARTICULAR.
Y-YOU ARE TOO KIND!
IRIS-SAMA... IF—
IF THAT MAN DOES MANAGE TO DEFEAT ANOTHER GENERAL OF THE DEMON KING, PERHAPS THERE WILL BE ANOTHER OPPORTUNITY TO SEE HIM...
DEFEAT ANOTHER GENERAL OF THE DEMON KING...
SO MUCH EASIER SAID THAN DONE.
INDEED...
I'M SURE WE'LL SEE HIM AGAIN BEFORE LONG.
BUT I THINK HE WILL DO IT, AND SOON.

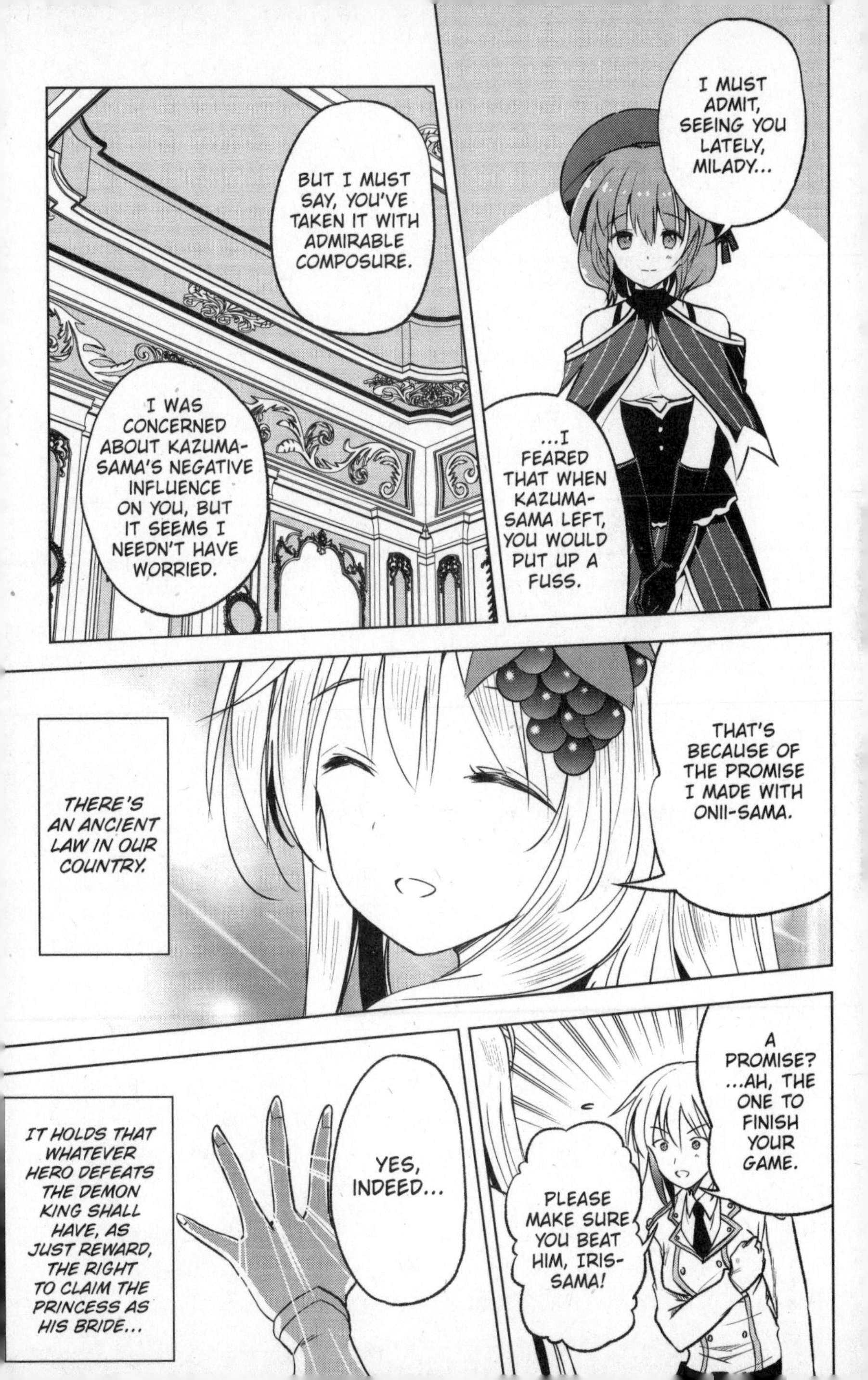
I MUST ADMIT, SEEING YOU LATELY, MILADY...
...I FEARED THAT WHEN KAZUMA-SAMA LEFT, YOU WOULD PUT UP A FUSS.
BUT I MUST SAY, YOU'VE TAKEN IT WITH ADMIRABLE COMPOSURE.
I WAS CONCERNED ABOUT KAZUMA-SAMA'S NEGATIVE INFLUENCE ON YOU, BUT IT SEEMS I NEEDN'T HAVE WORRIED.
THAT'S BECAUSE OF THE PROMISE I MADE WITH ONII-SAMA.
THERE'S AN ANCIENT LAW IN OUR COUNTRY.
A PROMISE? ...AH, THE ONE TO FINISH YOUR GAME.
PLEASE MAKE SURE YOU BEAT HIM, IRIS-SAMA!
YES, INDEED...
IT HOLDS THAT WHATEVER HERO DEFEATS THE DEMON KING SHALL HAVE, AS JUST REWARD, THE RIGHT TO CLAIM THE PRINCESS AS HIS BRIDE...

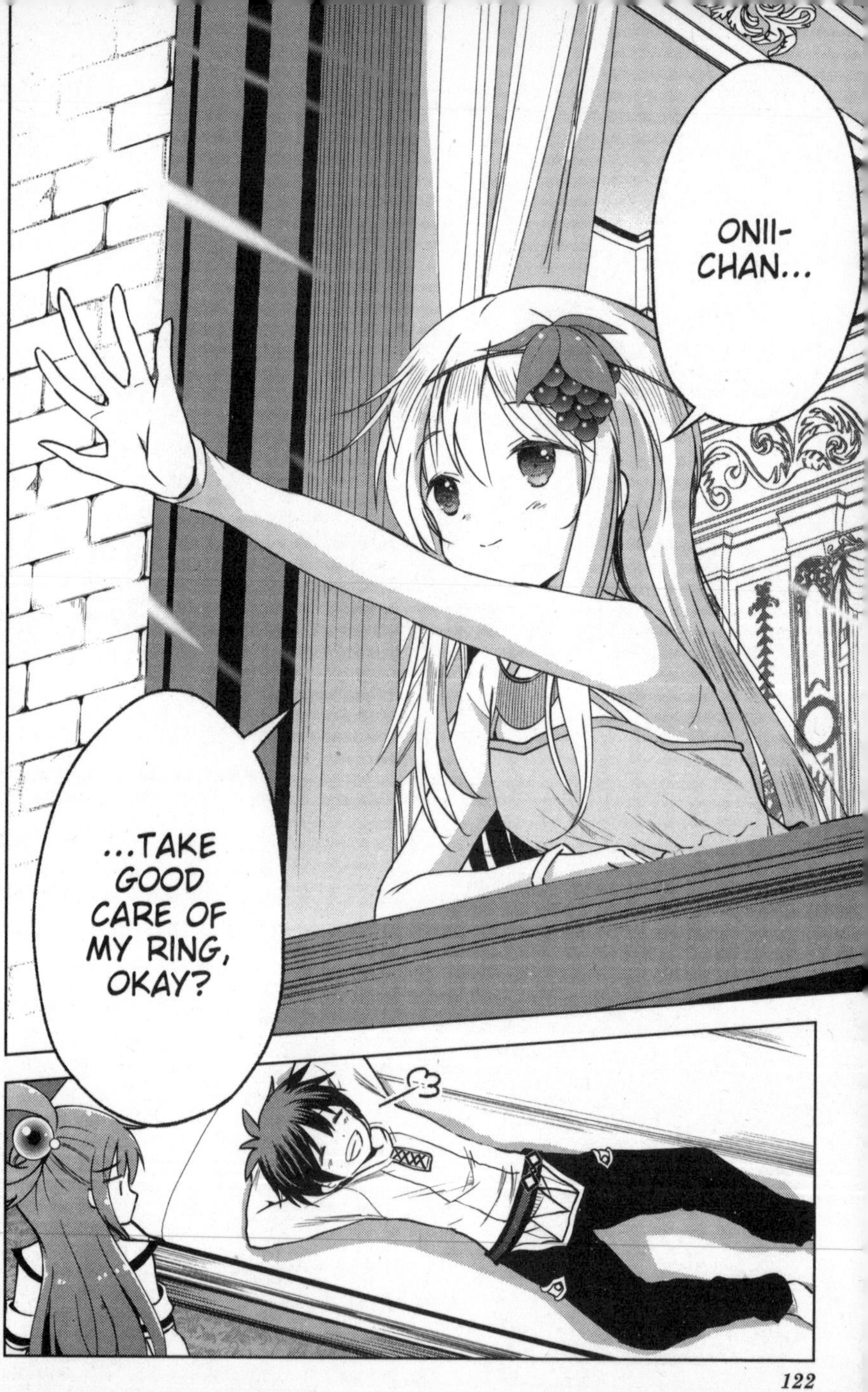
ONII-CHAN...
...TAKE GOOD CARE OF MY RING, OKAY?

GOD'S
BLESSING
ON THIS
WONDERFUL
WORLD!

11

11

GOD'S
BLESSING
ON THIS
WONDERFUL
WORLD!

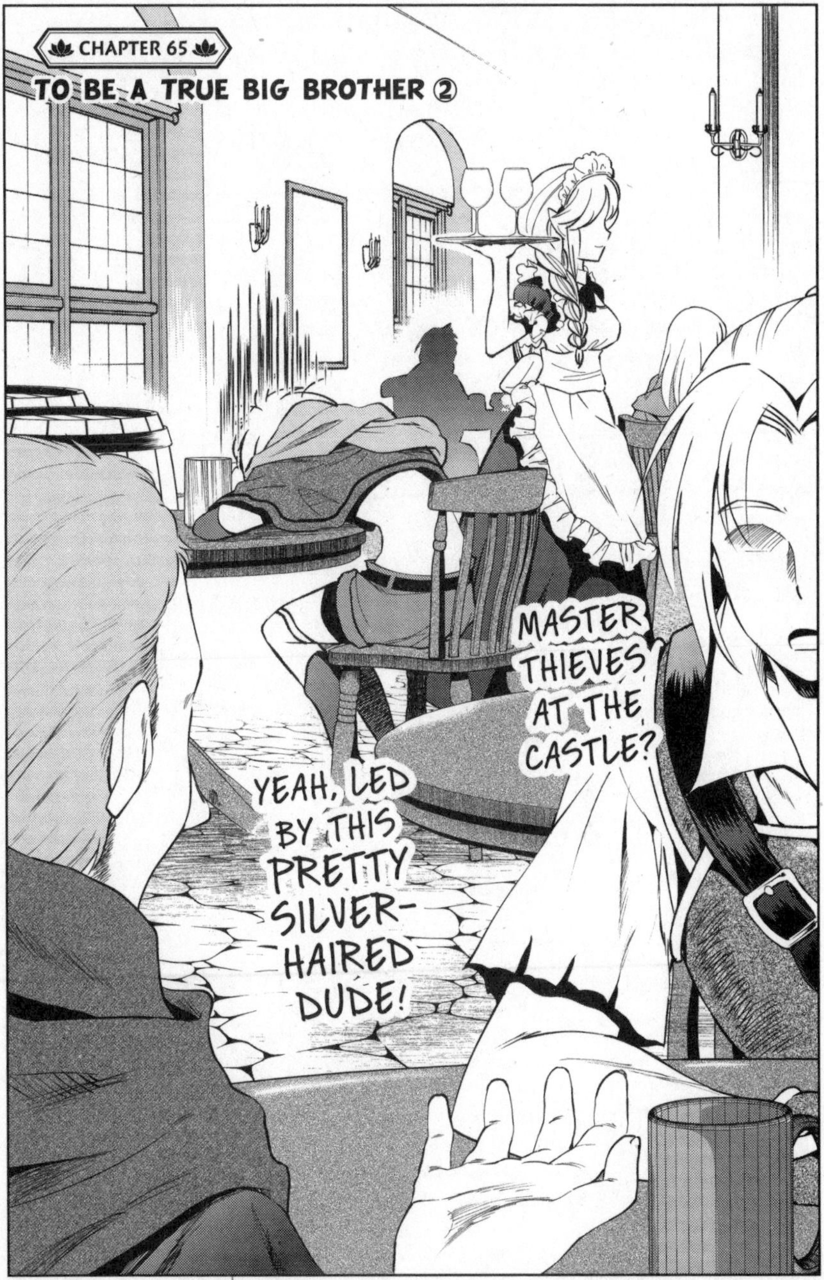
CHAPTER 65
TO BE A TRUE BIG BROTHER ②
MASTER THIEVES AT THE CASTLE?
YEAH, LED BY THIS PRETTY SILVER-HAIRED DUDE!

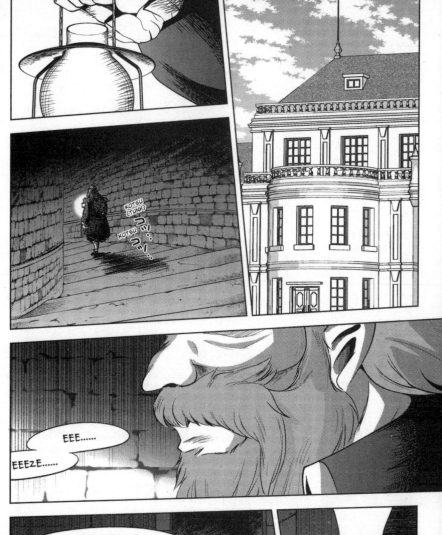

KOTSU
GYUN!

KOTSU
GYUN!...

EEE......

EEEZE......

WHEEEEEEZE...

WHEEZE...

WHEEEZE......

WHEEEEEEEZE......

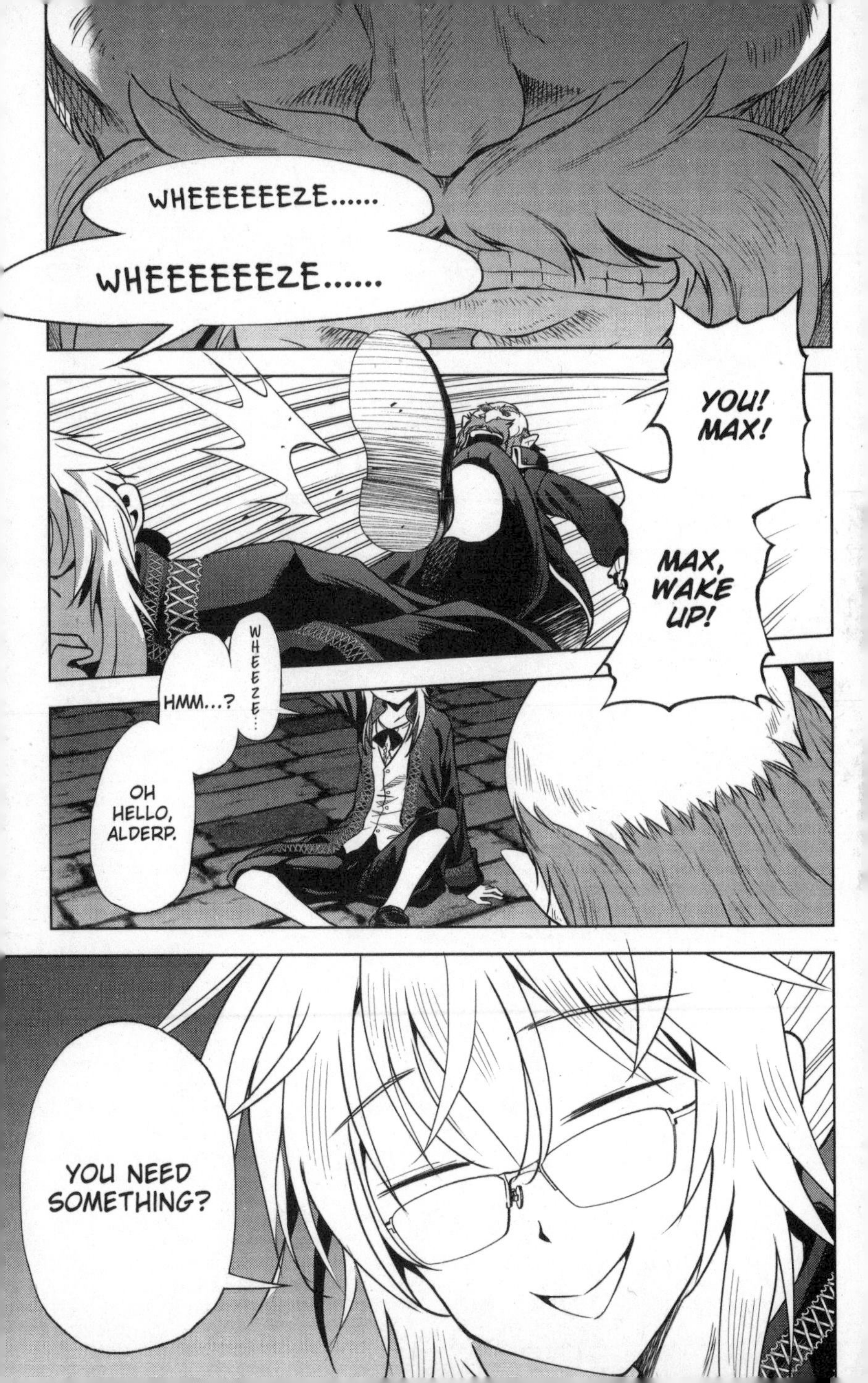
WHEEEEEEEZE......
WHEEEEEEEZE......
YOU! MAX!
MAX, WAKE UP!
WHEEZE...
HMM...?
OH HELLO, ALDERP.
YOU NEED SOMETHING?

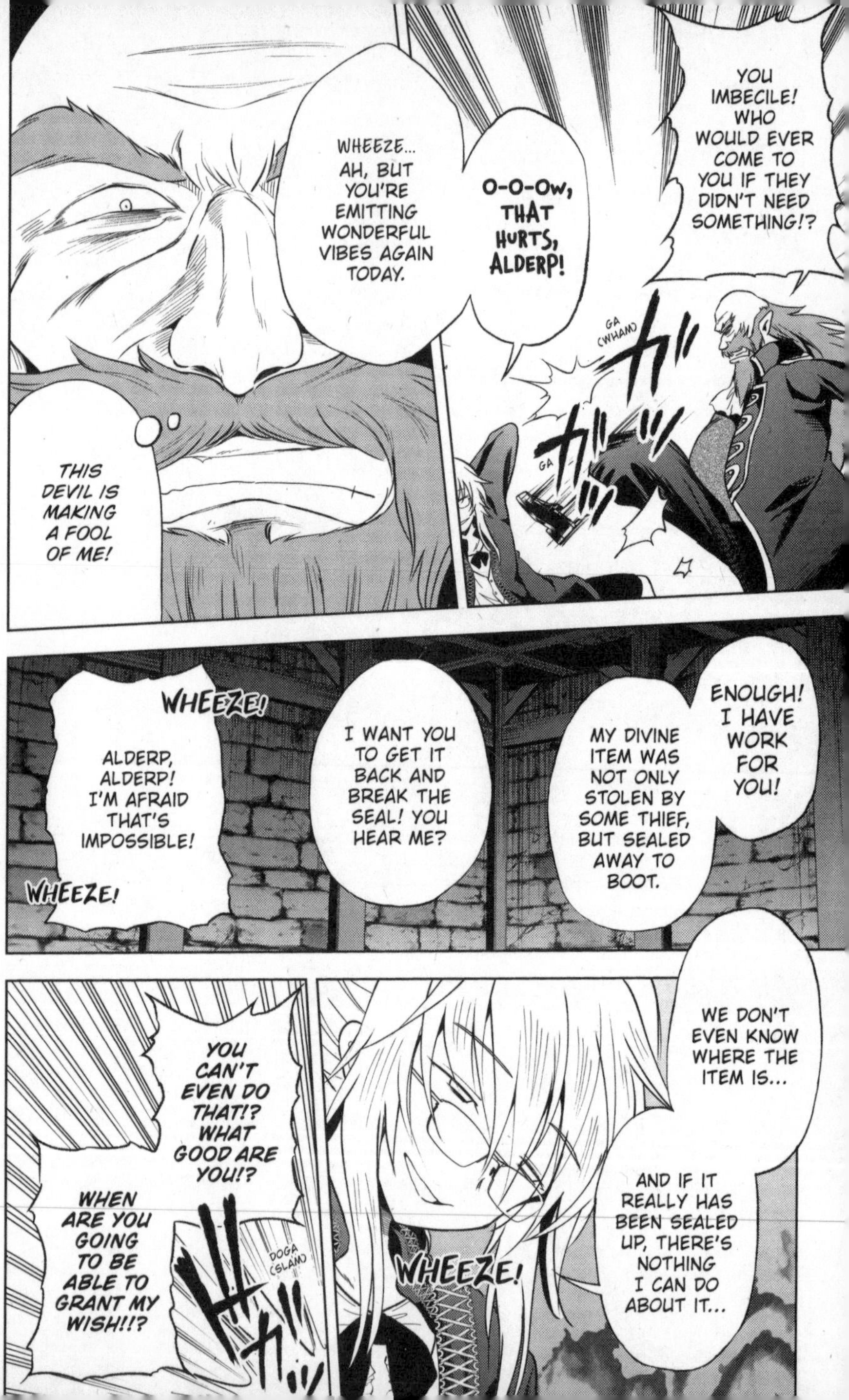
YOU IMBECILE! WHO WOULD EVER COME TO YOU IF THEY DIDN'T NEED SOMETHING!?
O-O-OW, THAT HURTS, ALDERP!
WHEEZE... AH, BUT YOU'RE EMITTING WONDERFUL VIBES AGAIN TODAY.
GA (WHAM)
GA
THIS DEVIL IS MAKING A FOOL OF ME!
ENOUGH! I HAVE WORK FOR YOU!
MY DIVINE ITEM WAS NOT ONLY STOLEN BY SOME THIEF, BUT SEALED AWAY TO BOOT.
I WANT YOU TO GET IT BACK AND BREAK THE SEAL! YOU HEAR ME?
WHEEZE!
ALDERP, ALDERP! I'M AFRAID THAT'S IMPOSSIBLE!
WHEEZE!
WE DON'T EVEN KNOW WHERE THE ITEM IS...
AND IF IT REALLY HAS BEEN SEALED UP, THERE'S NOTHING I CAN DO ABOUT IT...
WHEEZE!
YOU CAN'T EVEN DO THAT!? WHAT GOOD ARE YOU!?
WHEN ARE YOU GOING TO BE ABLE TO GRANT MY WISH!!?
DOGA (SLAM)

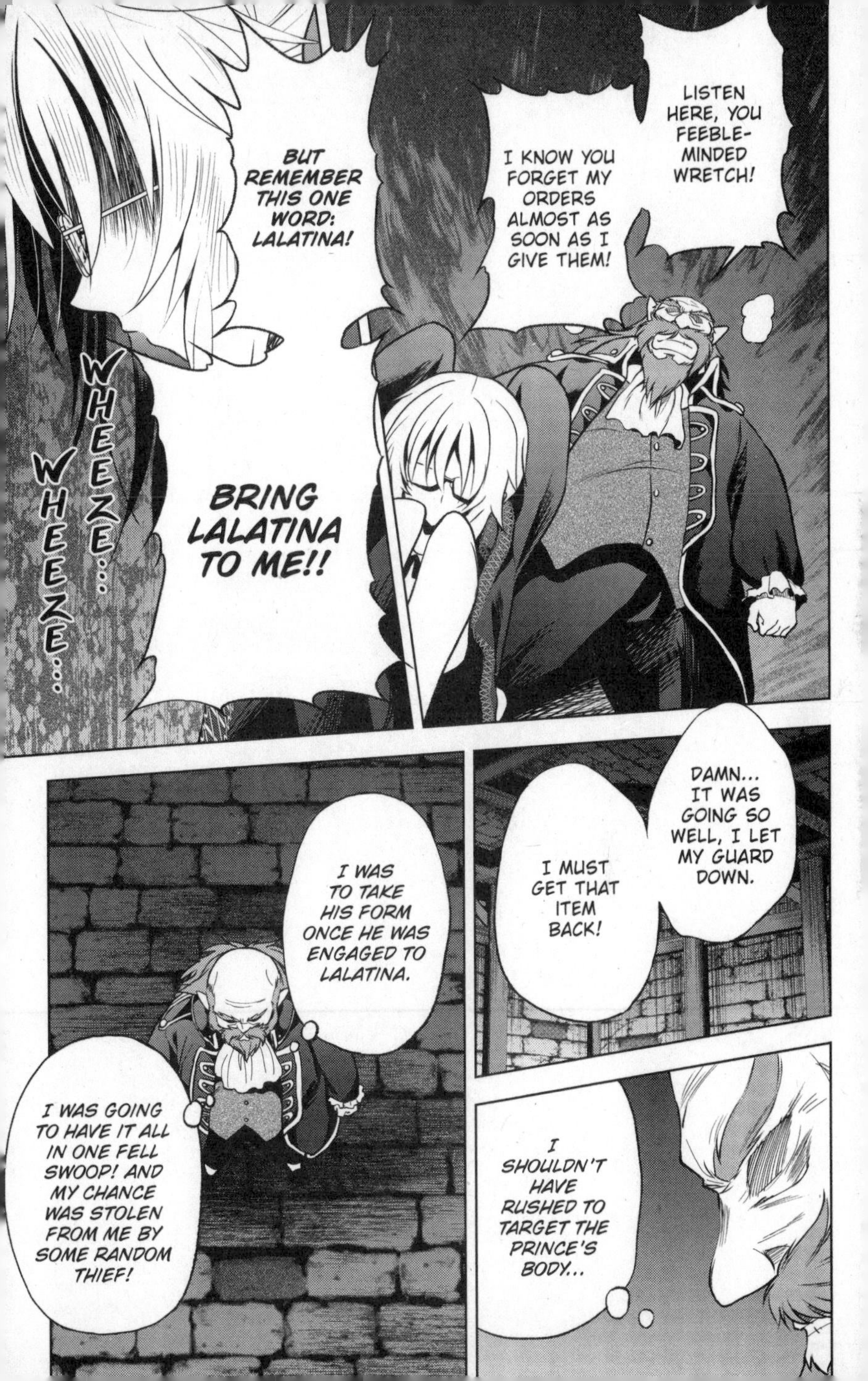
LISTEN HERE, YOU FEEBLE-MINDED WRETCH!
I KNOW YOU FORGET MY ORDERS ALMOST AS SOON AS I GIVE THEM!
BUT REMEMBER THIS ONE WORD: LALATINA!
BRING LALATINA TO ME!!
WHEEZE... WHEEZE...
DAMN... IT WAS GOING SO WELL, I LET MY GUARD DOWN.
I MUST GET THAT ITEM BACK!
I SHOULDN'T HAVE RUSHED TO TARGET THE PRINCE'S BODY...
I WAS TO TAKE HIS FORM ONCE HE WAS ENGAGED TO LALATINA.
I WAS GOING TO HAVE IT ALL IN ONE FELL SWOOP! AND MY CHANCE WAS STOLEN FROM ME BY SOME RANDOM THIEF!

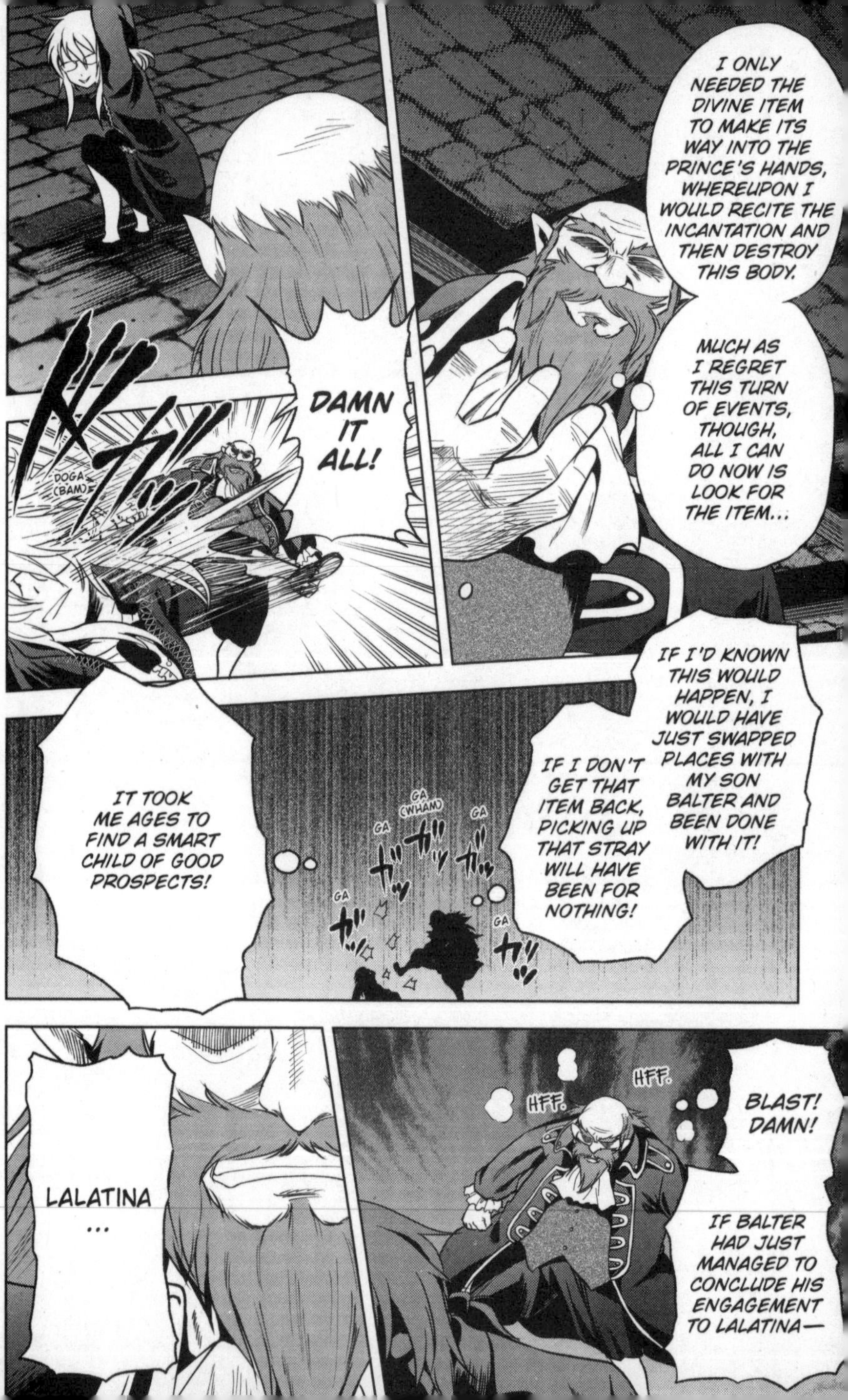

I ONLY NEEDED THE DIVINE ITEM TO MAKE ITS WAY INTO THE PRINCE'S HANDS, WHEREUPON I WOULD RECITE THE INCANTATION AND THEN DESTROY THIS BODY.
MUCH AS I REGRET THIS TURN OF EVENTS, THOUGH, ALL I CAN DO NOW IS LOOK FOR THE ITEM...
DAMN IT ALL!
DOGA (BAM)
IF I'D KNOWN THIS WOULD HAPPEN, I WOULD HAVE JUST SWAPPED PLACES WITH MY SON BALTER AND BEEN DONE WITH IT!
IF I DON'T GET THAT ITEM BACK, PICKING UP THAT STRAY WILL HAVE BEEN FOR NOTHING!
GA (WHAM)
GA
GA
GA
GA
IT TOOK ME AGES TO FIND A SMART CHILD OF GOOD PROSPECTS!
BLAST! DAMN!
HFF.
HFF.
IF BALTER HAD JUST MANAGED TO CONCLUDE HIS ENGAGEMENT TO LALATINA—
LALATINA ...

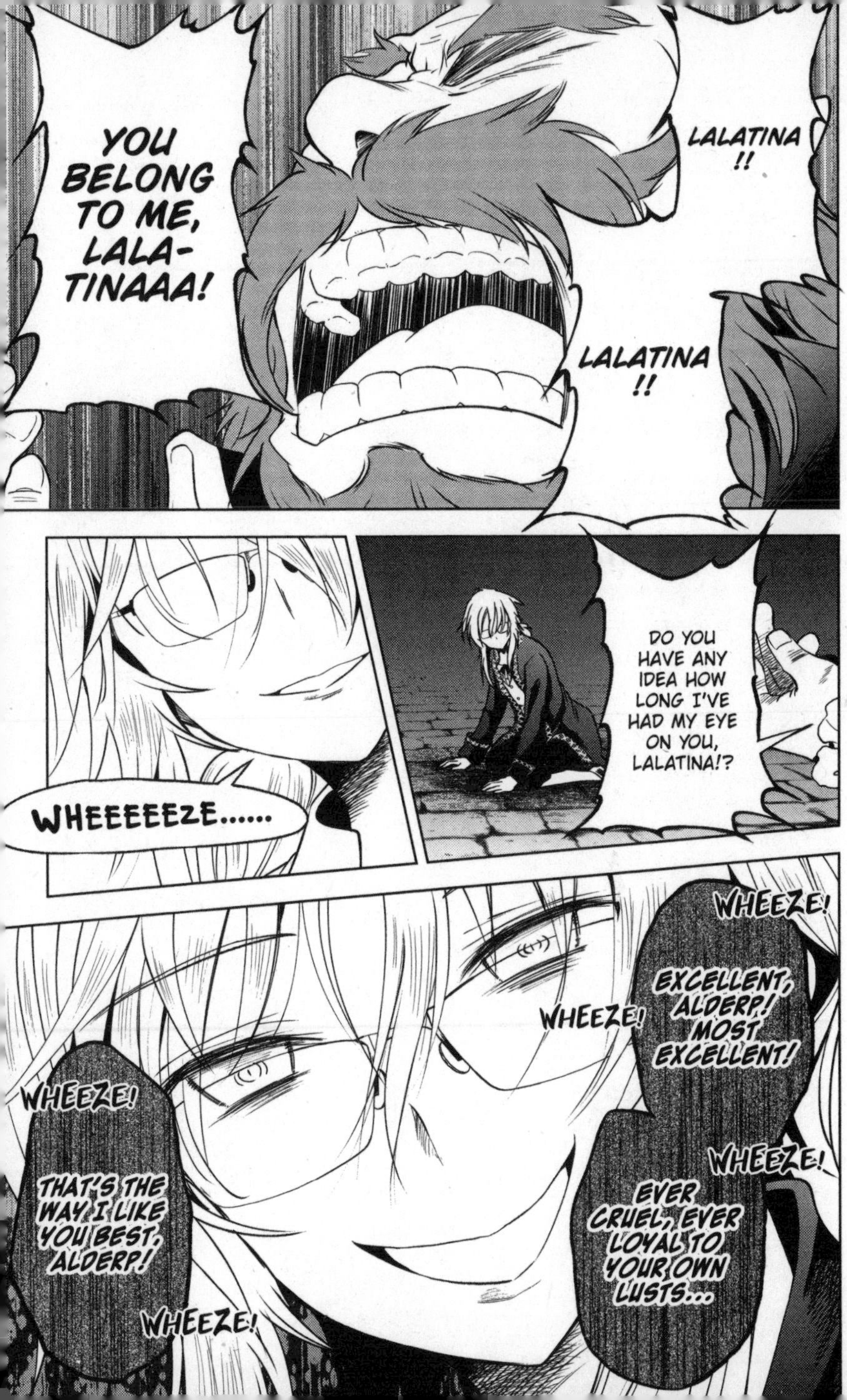
LALATINA !!
LALATINA !!
YOU BELONG TO ME, LALA-TINAAA!
DO YOU HAVE ANY IDEA HOW LONG I'VE HAD MY EYE ON YOU, LALATINA!?
WHEEEEEZE......
WHEEZE!
EXCELLENT, ALDERP! MOST EXCELLENT!
WHEEZE!
WHEEZE!
EVER CRUEL, EVER LOYAL TO YOUR OWN LUSTS...
WHEEZE!
THAT'S THE WAY I LIKE YOU BEST, ALDERP!
WHEEZE!

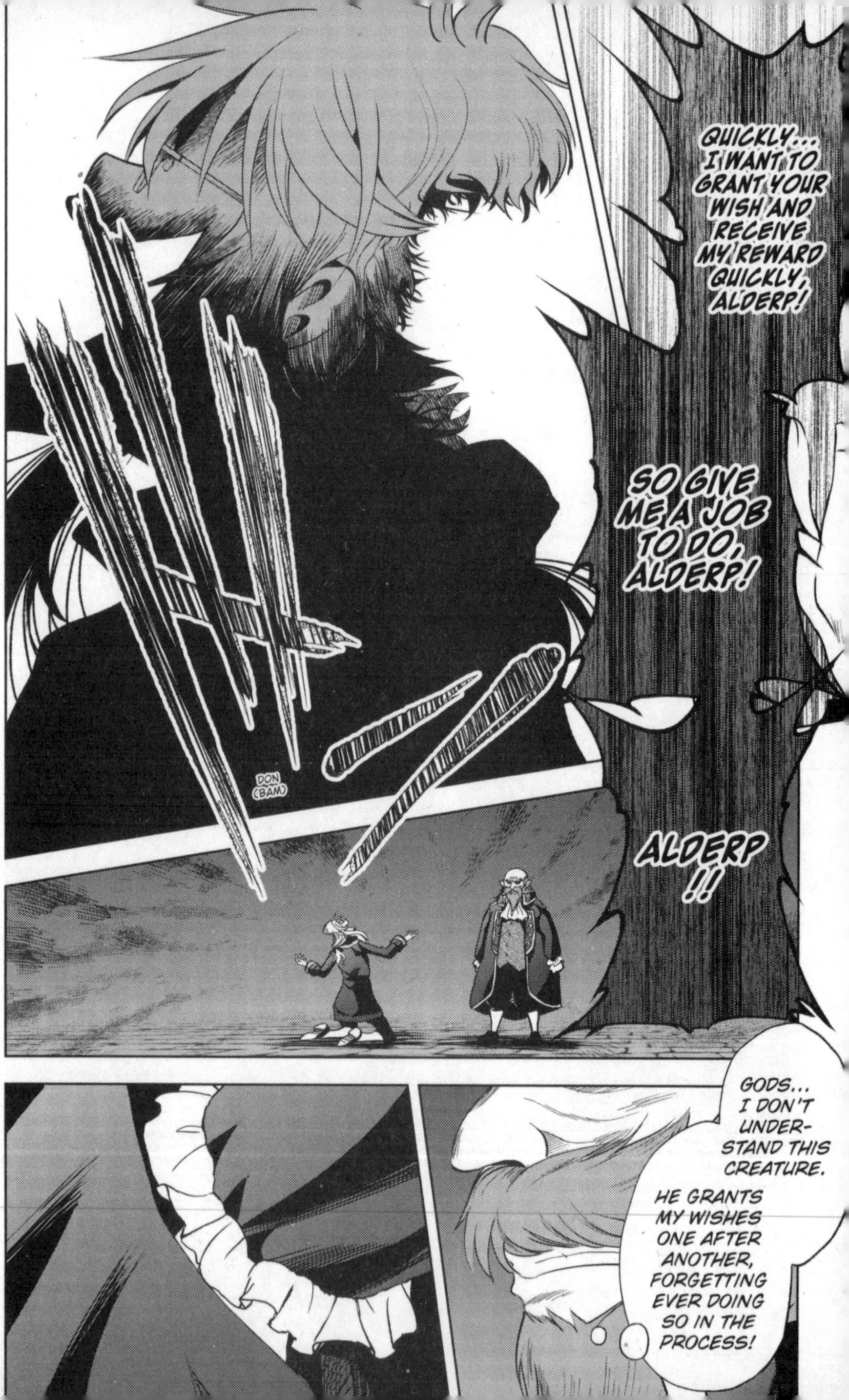
QUICKLY... I WANT TO GRANT YOUR WISH AND RECEIVE MY REWARD QUICKLY, ALDERP!
SO GIVE ME A JOB TO DO, ALDERP!
ALDERP!!
DON (BAM)
GODS... I DON'T UNDER-STAND THIS CREATURE.
HE GRANTS MY WISHES ONE AFTER ANOTHER, FORGETTING EVER DOING SO IN THE PROCESS!

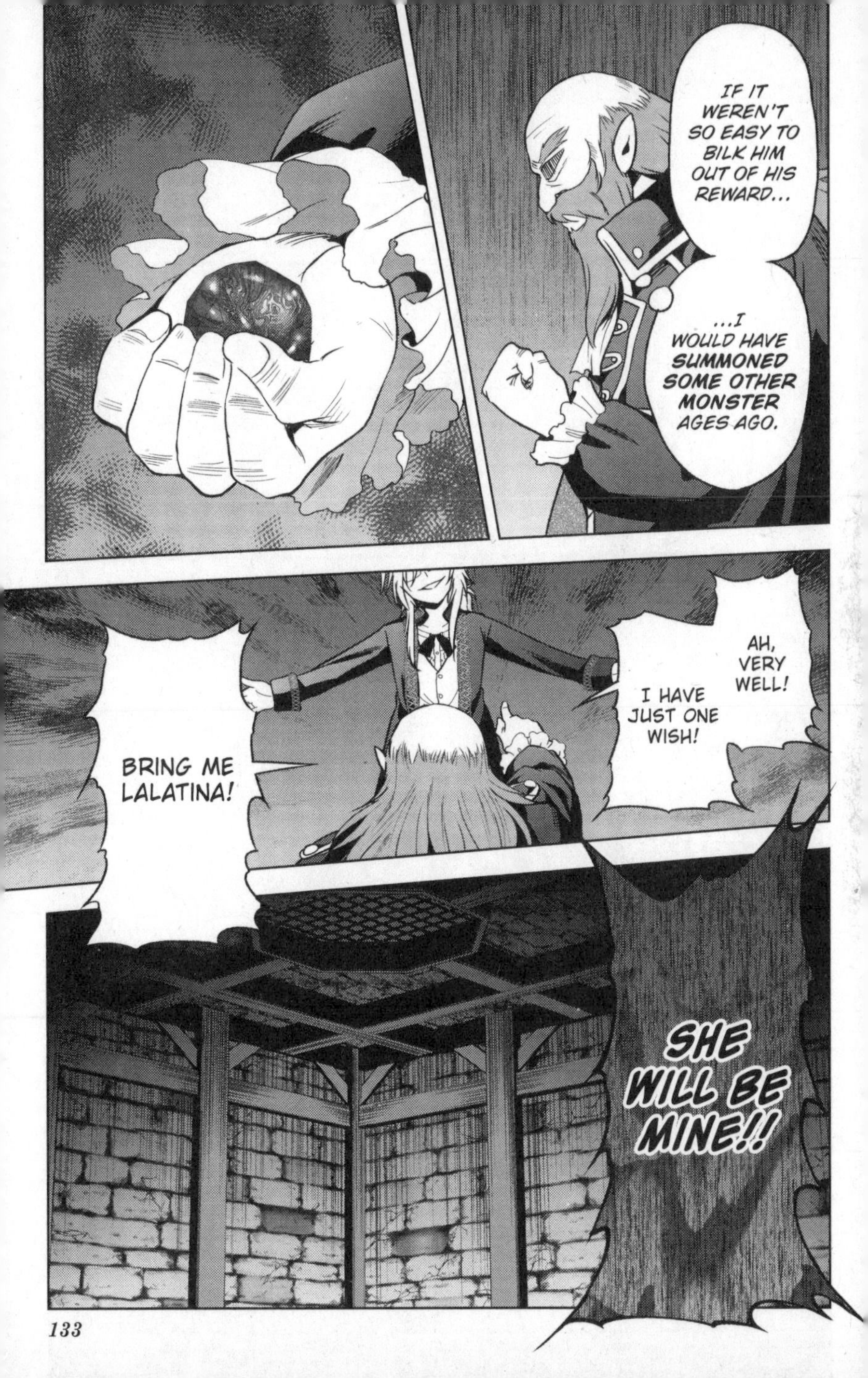
IF IT WEREN'T SO EASY TO BILK HIM OUT OF HIS REWARD...
...I WOULD HAVE SUMMONED SOME OTHER MONSTER AGES AGO.
AH, VERY WELL!
I HAVE JUST ONE WISH!
BRING ME LALATINA!
SHE WILL BE MINE!!

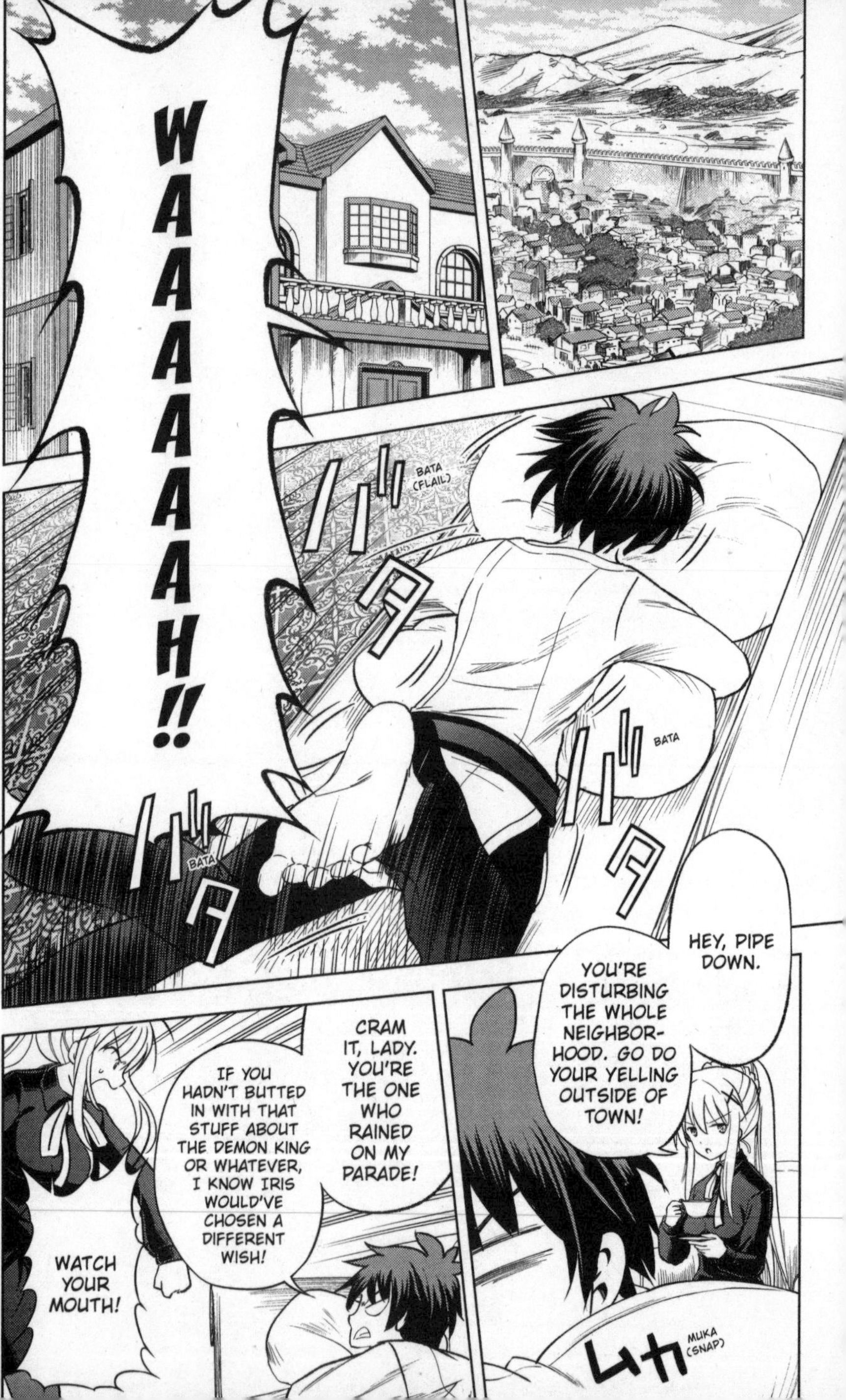
WAAAAAAAH!!
BATA (FLAIL)
BATA
BATA
HEY, PIPE DOWN.
YOU'RE DISTURBING THE WHOLE NEIGHBOR-HOOD. GO DO YOUR YELLING OUTSIDE OF TOWN!
MUKA (SNAP)
CRAM IT, LADY. YOU'RE THE ONE WHO RAINED ON MY PARADE!
IF YOU HADN'T BUTTED IN WITH THAT STUFF ABOUT THE DEMON KING OR WHATEVER, I KNOW IRIS WOULD'VE CHOSEN A DIFFERENT WISH!
WATCH YOUR MOUTH!

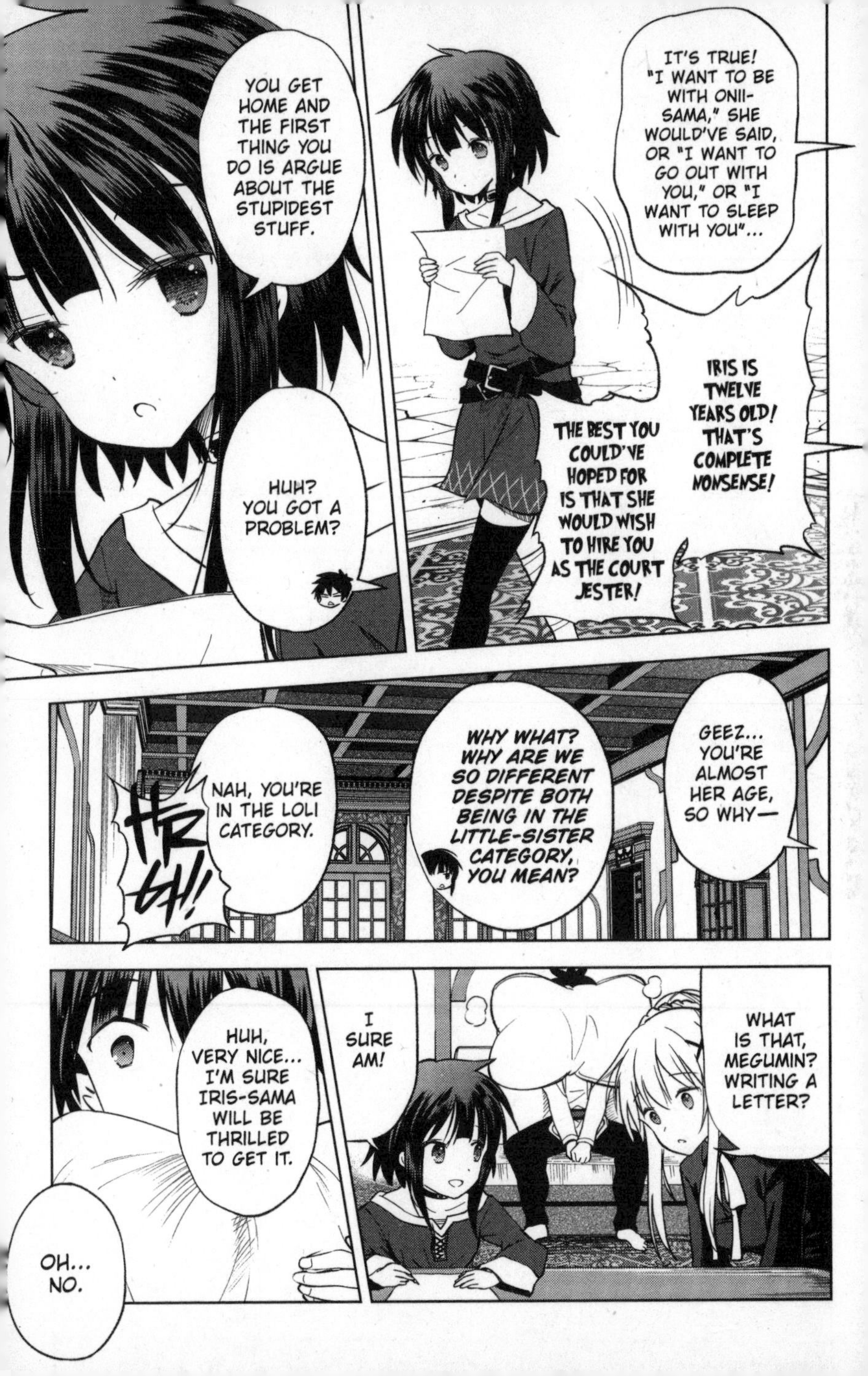
IT'S TRUE! "I WANT TO BE WITH ONII-SAMA," SHE WOULD'VE SAID, OR "I WANT TO GO OUT WITH YOU," OR "I WANT TO SLEEP WITH YOU"...
IRIS IS TWELVE YEARS OLD! THAT'S COMPLETE NONSENSE!
THE BEST YOU COULD'VE HOPED FOR IS THAT SHE WOULD WISH TO HIRE YOU AS THE COURT JESTER!
YOU GET HOME AND THE FIRST THING YOU DO IS ARGUE ABOUT THE STUPIDEST STUFF.
HUH? YOU GOT A PROBLEM?
GEEZ... YOU'RE ALMOST HER AGE, SO WHY—
WHY WHAT? WHY ARE WE SO DIFFERENT DESPITE BOTH BEING IN THE LITTLE-SISTER CATEGORY, YOU MEAN?
HRSH!
NAH, YOU'RE IN THE LOLI CATEGORY.
WHAT IS THAT, MEGUMIN? WRITING A LETTER?
I SURE AM!
HUH, VERY NICE... I'M SURE IRIS-SAMA WILL BE THRILLED TO GET IT.
OH... NO.

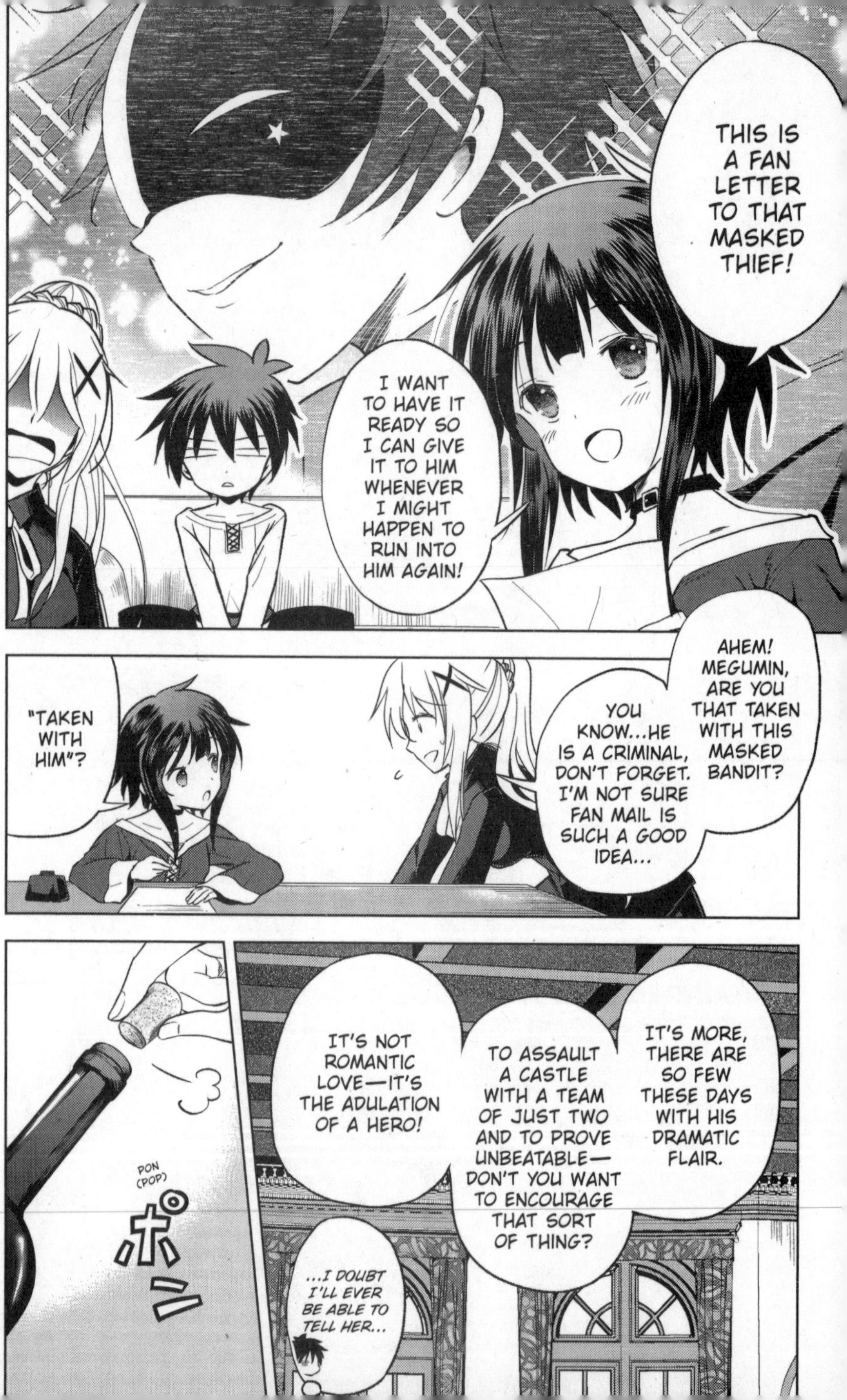

THIS IS A FAN LETTER TO THAT MASKED THIEF!
I WANT TO HAVE IT READY SO I CAN GIVE IT TO HIM WHENEVER I MIGHT HAPPEN TO RUN INTO HIM AGAIN!
AHEM! MEGUMIN, ARE YOU THAT TAKEN WITH THIS MASKED BANDIT?
YOU KNOW...HE IS A CRIMINAL, DON'T FORGET. I'M NOT SURE FAN MAIL IS SUCH A GOOD IDEA...
"TAKEN WITH HIM"?
IT'S MORE, THERE ARE SO FEW THESE DAYS WITH HIS DRAMATIC FLAIR.
TO ASSAULT A CASTLE WITH A TEAM OF JUST TWO AND TO PROVE UNBEATABLE—DON'T YOU WANT TO ENCOURAGE THAT SORT OF THING?
IT'S NOT ROMANTIC LOVE—IT'S THE ADULATION OF A HERO!
...I DOUBT I'LL EVER BE ABLE TO TELL HER...
PON (POP)
ポン

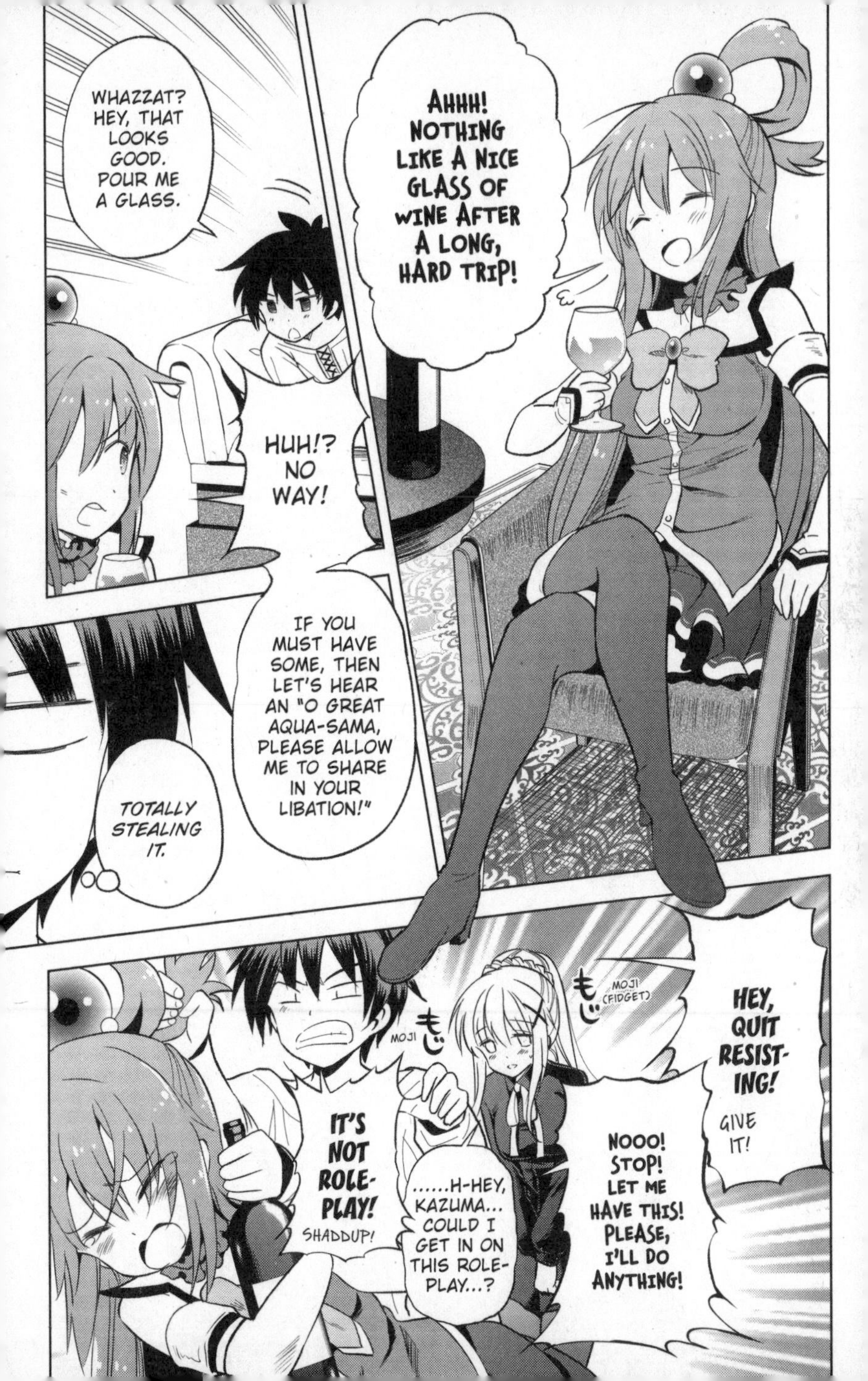
AHHH! NOTHING LIKE A NICE GLASS OF WINE AFTER A LONG, HARD TRIP!
WHAZZAT? HEY, THAT LOOKS GOOD. POUR ME A GLASS.
HUH!? NO WAY!
IF YOU MUST HAVE SOME, THEN LET'S HEAR AN "O GREAT AQUA-SAMA, PLEASE ALLOW ME TO SHARE IN YOUR LIBATION!"
TOTALLY STEALING IT.
HEY, QUIT RESISTING!
GIVE IT!
NOOO! STOP! LET ME HAVE THIS! PLEASE, I'LL DO ANYTHING!
もじ
MOJI (FIDGET)
もじ
MOJI
......H-HEY, KAZUMA... COULD I GET IN ON THIS ROLE-PLAY...?
IT'S NOT ROLE-PLAY!
SHADDUP!

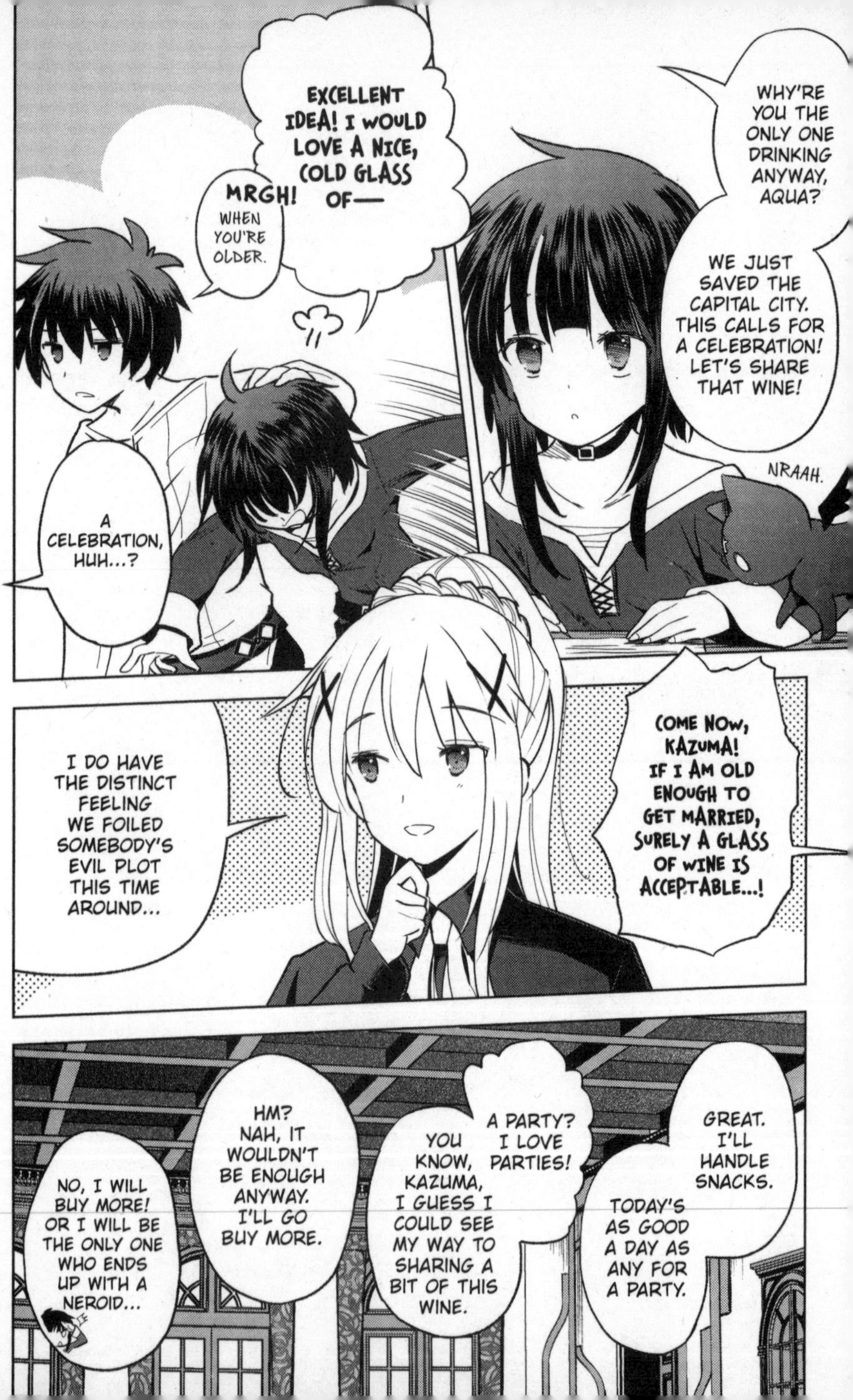
WHY'RE YOU THE ONLY ONE DRINKING ANYWAY, AQUA?
WE JUST SAVED THE CAPITAL CITY. THIS CALLS FOR A CELEBRATION! LET'S SHARE THAT WINE!
NRAAH.
EXCELLENT IDEA! I WOULD LOVE A NICE, COLD GLASS OF—
MRGH!
WHEN YOU'RE OLDER.
A CELEBRATION, HUH...?
COME NOW, KAZUMA! IF I AM OLD ENOUGH TO GET MARRIED, SURELY A GLASS OF WINE IS ACCEPTABLE...!
I DO HAVE THE DISTINCT FEELING WE FOILED SOMEBODY'S EVIL PLOT THIS TIME AROUND...
GREAT. I'LL HANDLE SNACKS.
TODAY'S AS GOOD A DAY AS ANY FOR A PARTY.
A PARTY? I LOVE PARTIES!
YOU KNOW, KAZUMA, I GUESS I COULD SEE MY WAY TO SHARING A BIT OF THIS WINE.
HM? NAH, IT WOULDN'T BE ENOUGH ANYWAY. I'LL GO BUY MORE.
NO, I WILL BUY MORE! OR I WILL BE THE ONLY ONE WHO ENDS UP WITH A NEROID...

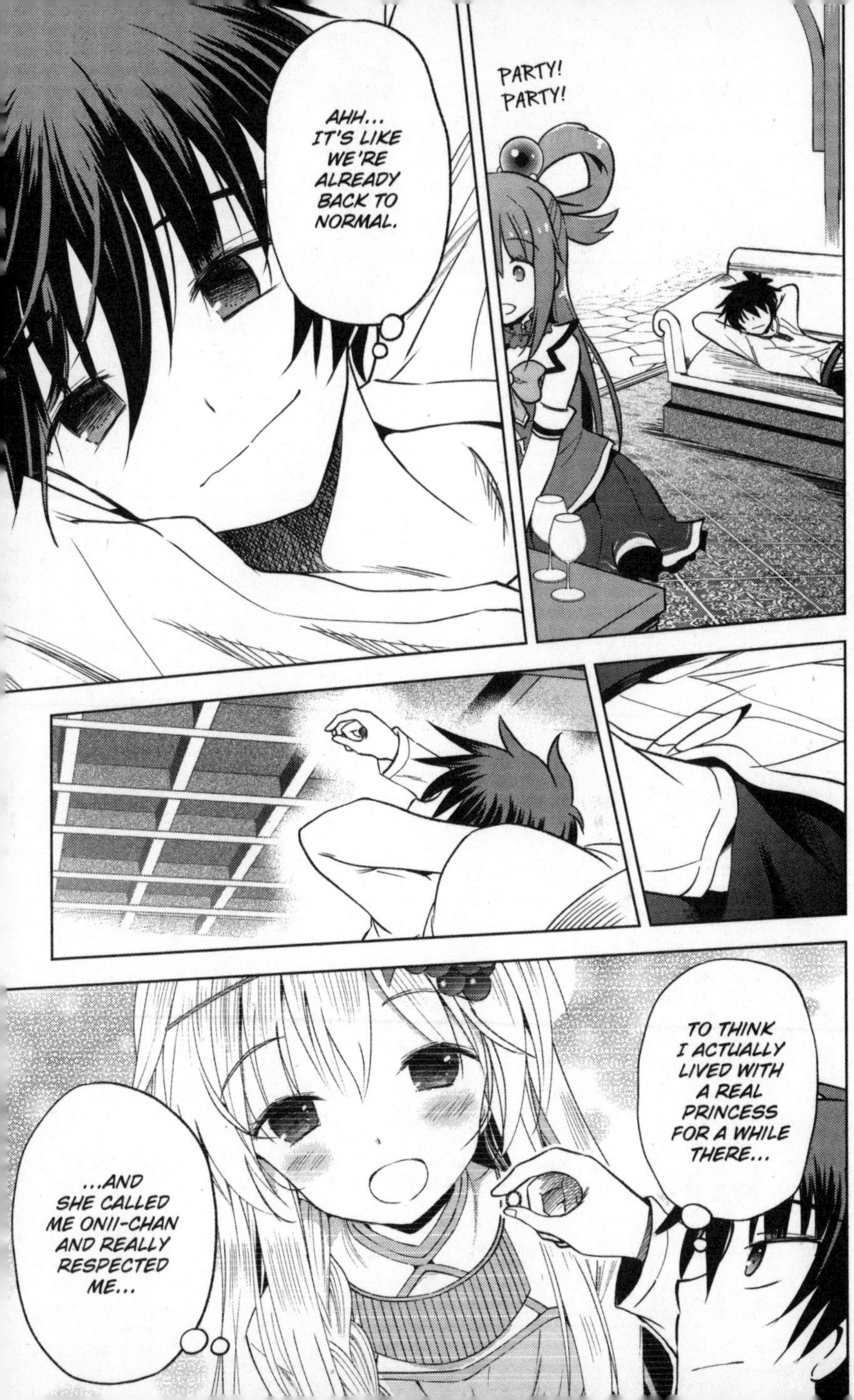
PARTY! PARTY!
AHH... IT'S LIKE WE'RE ALREADY BACK TO NORMAL.
TO THINK I ACTUALLY LIVED WITH A REAL PRINCESS FOR A WHILE THERE...
...AND SHE CALLED ME ONII-CHAN AND REALLY RESPECTED ME...

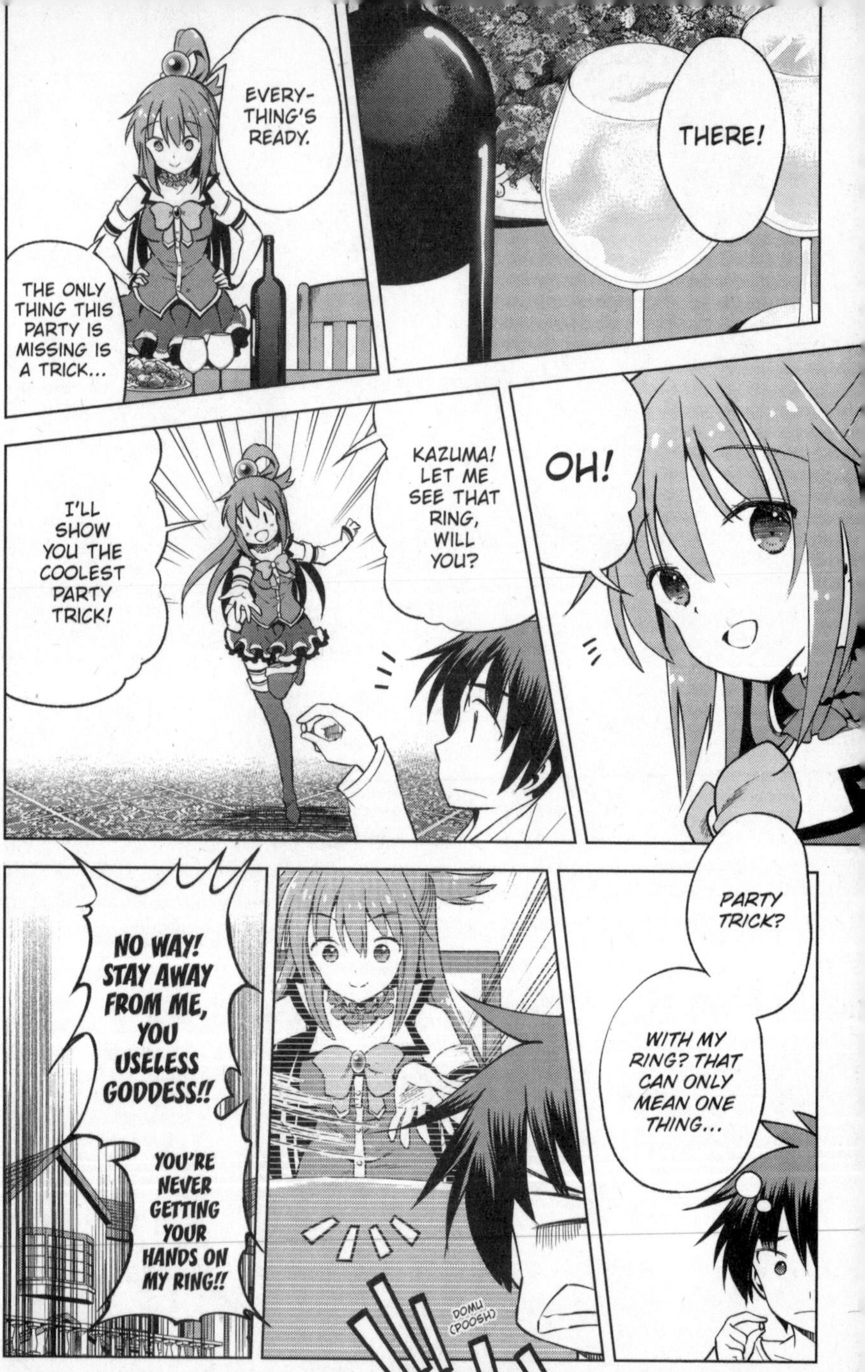
THERE!
EVERY-THING'S READY.
THE ONLY THING THIS PARTY IS MISSING IS A TRICK...
OH!
KAZUMA! LET ME SEE THAT RING, WILL YOU?
I'LL SHOW YOU THE COOLEST PARTY TRICK!
PARTY TRICK?
WITH MY RING? THAT CAN ONLY MEAN ONE THING...
DOMU (POOSH)
NO WAY! STAY AWAY FROM ME, YOU USELESS GODDESS!!
YOU'RE NEVER GETTING YOUR HANDS ON MY RING!!

GOD'S
BLESSING
ON THIS
WONDERFUL
WORLD!

11

GOD'S
BLESSING
ON THIS
WONDERFUL
WORLD!

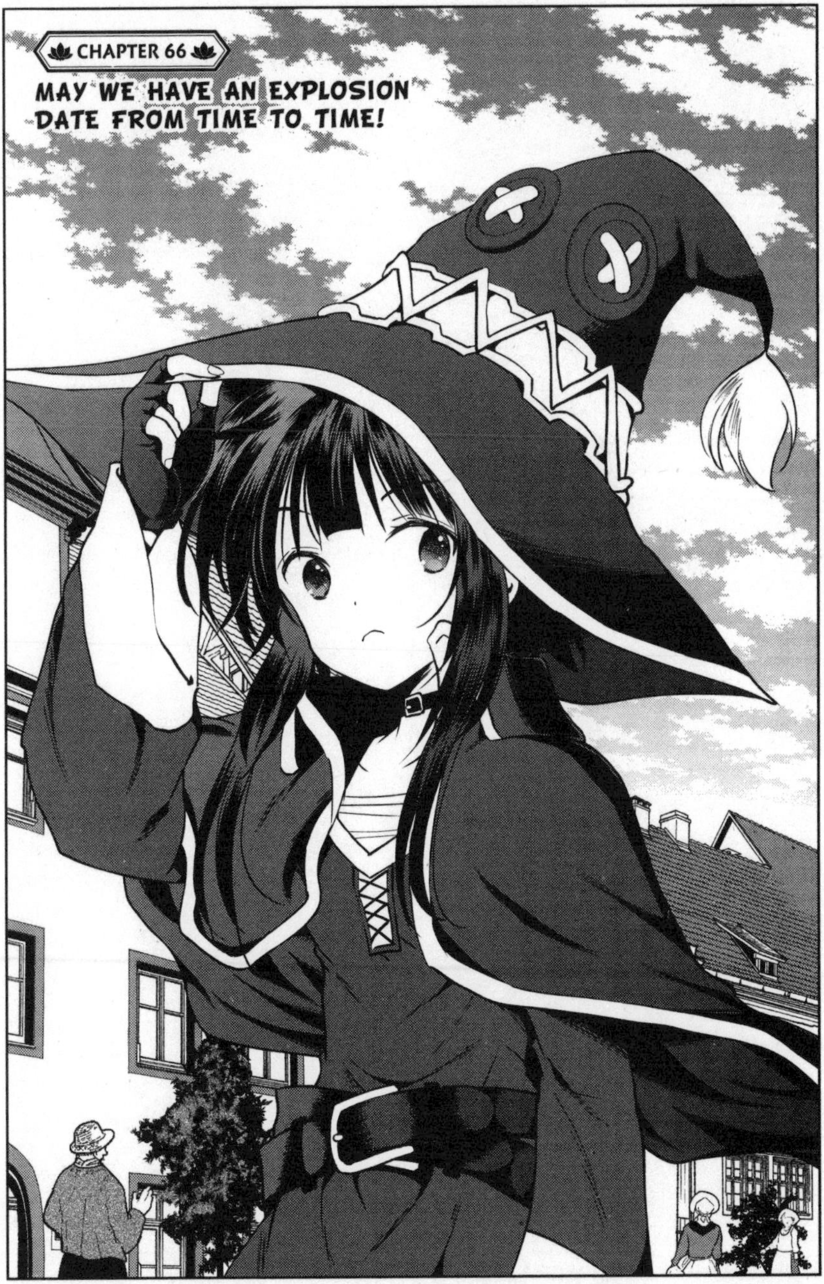
CHAPTER 66
MAY WE HAVE AN EXPLOSION DATE FROM TIME TO TIME!

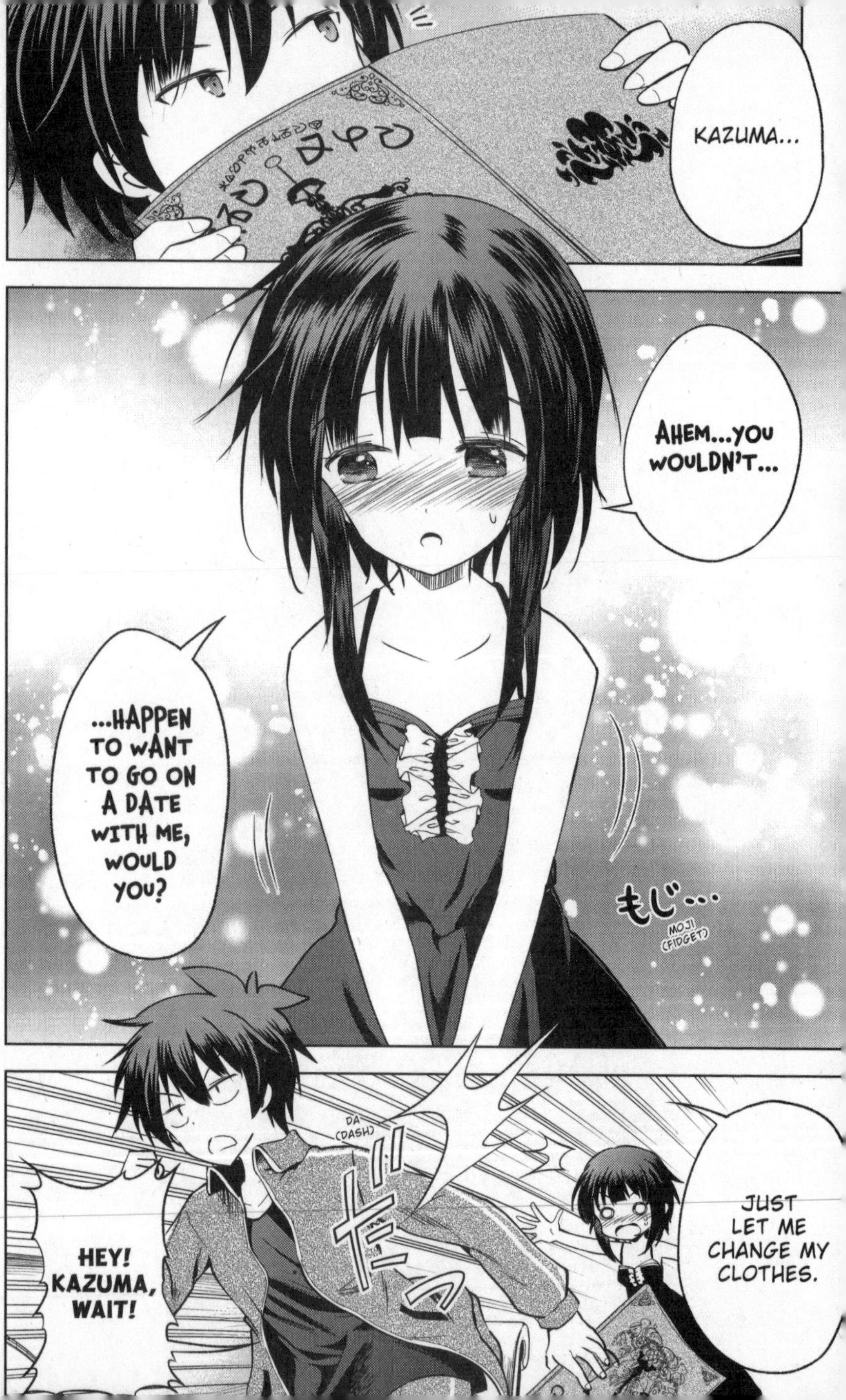
KAZUMA...
AHEM...YOU WOULDN'T...
...HAPPEN TO WANT TO GO ON A DATE WITH ME, WOULD YOU?
もじ…
MOJI (FIDGET)
JUST LET ME CHANGE MY CLOTHES.
ダーッ
DA (DASH)
HEY! KAZUMA, WAIT!

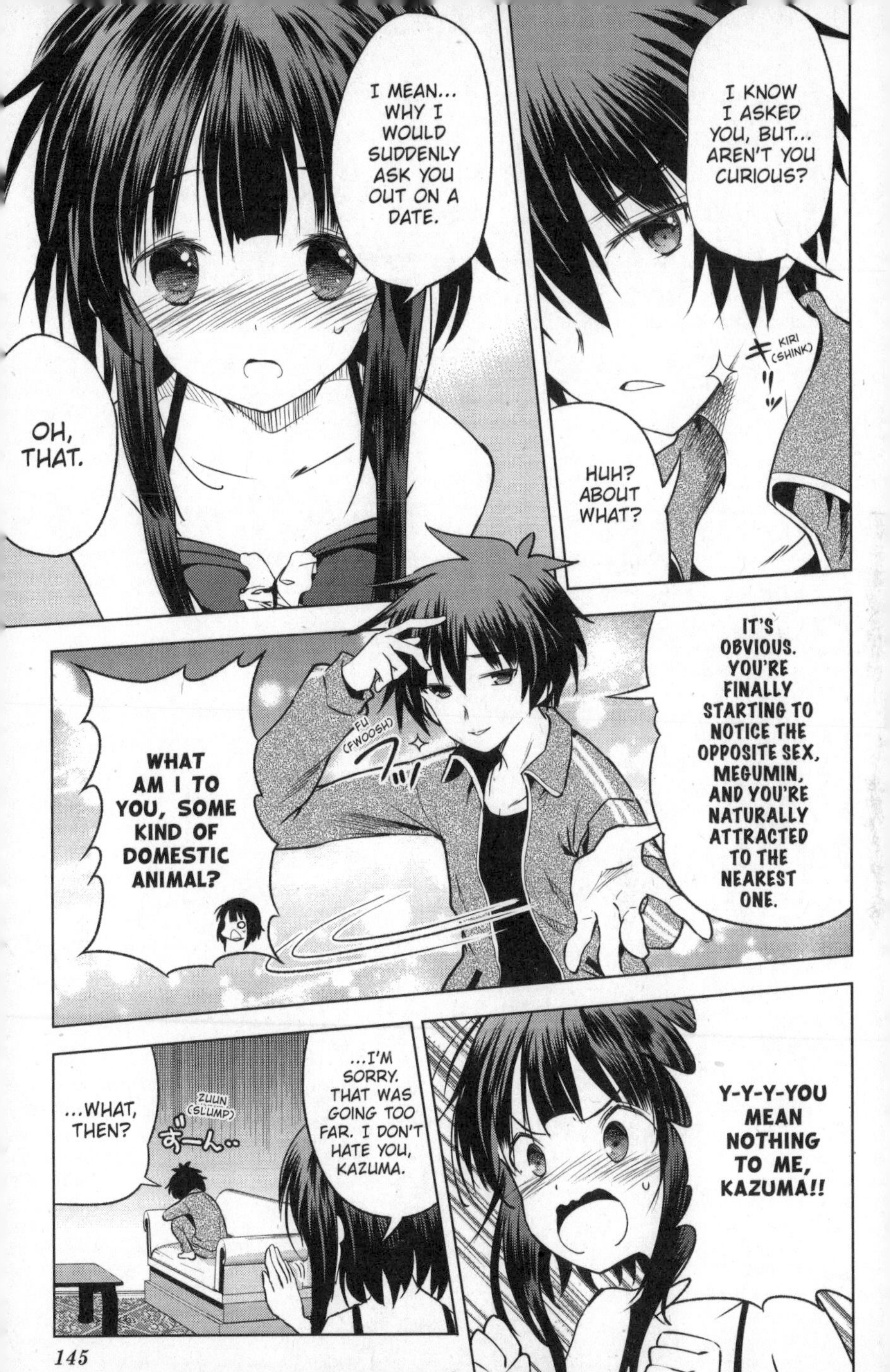
I KNOW I ASKED YOU, BUT... AREN'T YOU CURIOUS?
KIRI (SHINK)
HUH? ABOUT WHAT?
I MEAN... WHY I WOULD SUDDENLY ASK YOU OUT ON A DATE.
OH, THAT.
IT'S OBVIOUS. YOU'RE FINALLY STARTING TO NOTICE THE OPPOSITE SEX, MEGUMIN, AND YOU'RE NATURALLY ATTRACTED TO THE NEAREST ONE.
FU (FWOOSH)
WHAT AM I TO YOU, SOME KIND OF DOMESTIC ANIMAL?
Y-Y-Y-YOU MEAN NOTHING TO ME, KAZUMA!!
...I'M SORRY. THAT WAS GOING TOO FAR. I DON'T HATE YOU, KAZUMA.
ZUUN (SLUMP)
...WHAT, THEN?

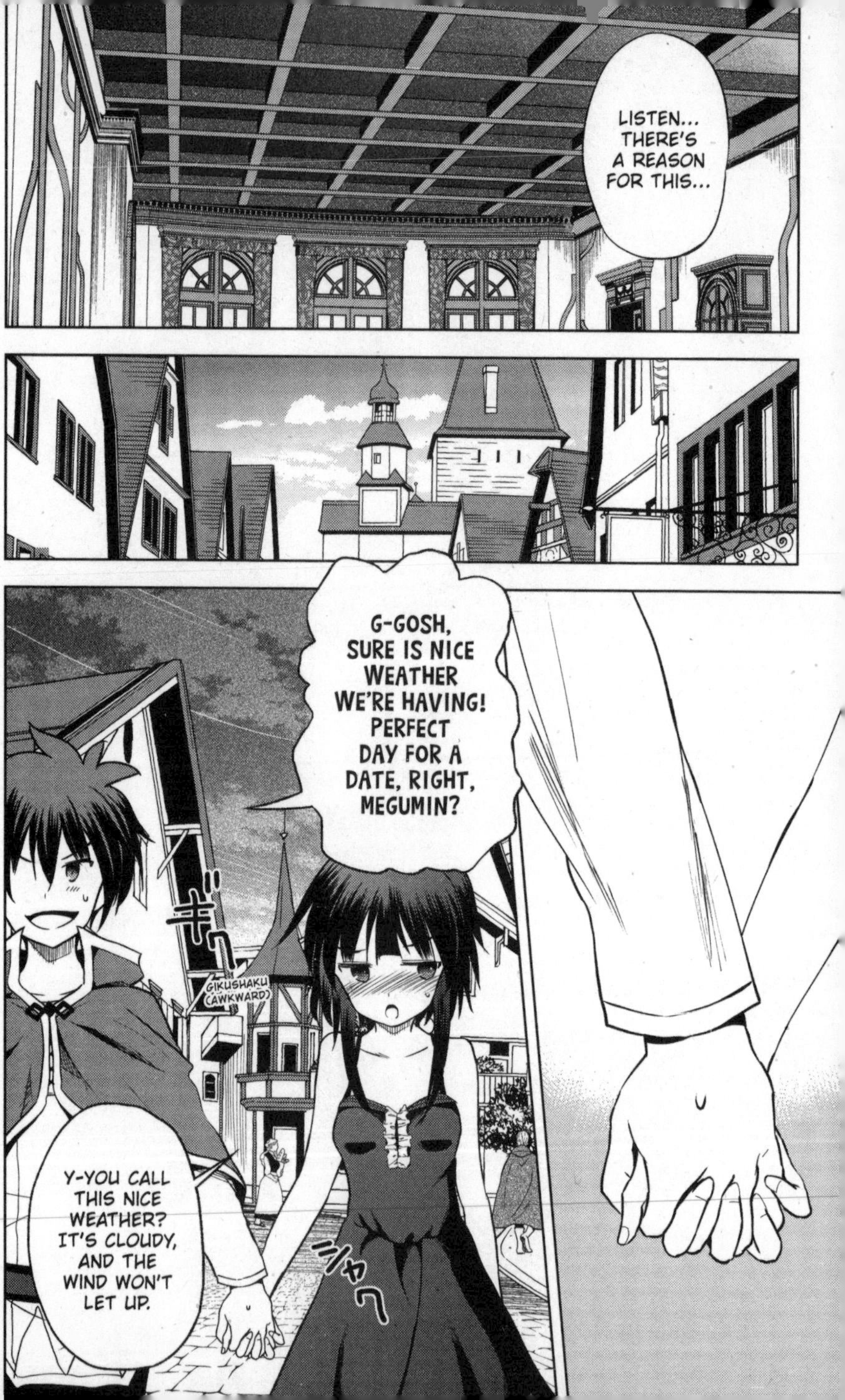
LISTEN... THERE'S A REASON FOR THIS...
G-GOSH, SURE IS NICE WEATHER WE'RE HAVING! PERFECT DAY FOR A DATE, RIGHT, MEGUMIN?
GIKUSHAKU (AWKWARD)
Y-YOU CALL THIS NICE WEATHER? IT'S CLOUDY, AND THE WIND WON'T LET UP.

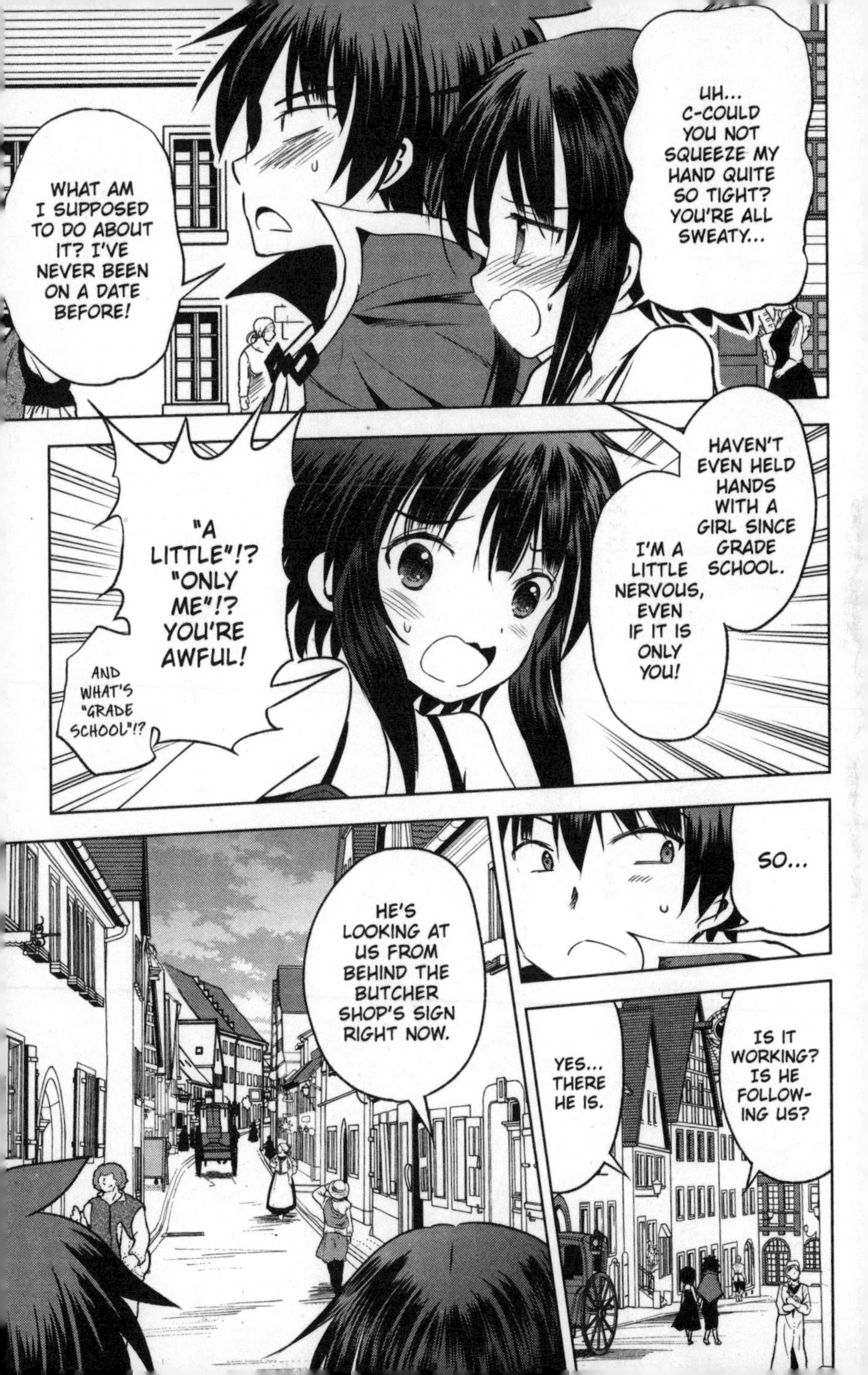
UH... C-COULD YOU NOT SQUEEZE MY HAND QUITE SO TIGHT? YOU'RE ALL SWEATY...
WHAT AM I SUPPOSED TO DO ABOUT IT? I'VE NEVER BEEN ON A DATE BEFORE!
HAVEN'T EVEN HELD HANDS WITH A GIRL SINCE GRADE SCHOOL.
I'M A LITTLE NERVOUS, EVEN IF IT IS ONLY YOU!
"A LITTLE"!? "ONLY ME"!? YOU'RE AWFUL!
AND WHAT'S "GRADE SCHOOL"!?
SO...
IS IT WORKING? IS HE FOLLOW-ING US?
YES... THERE HE IS.
HE'S LOOKING AT US FROM BEHIND THE BUTCHER SHOP'S SIGN RIGHT NOW.

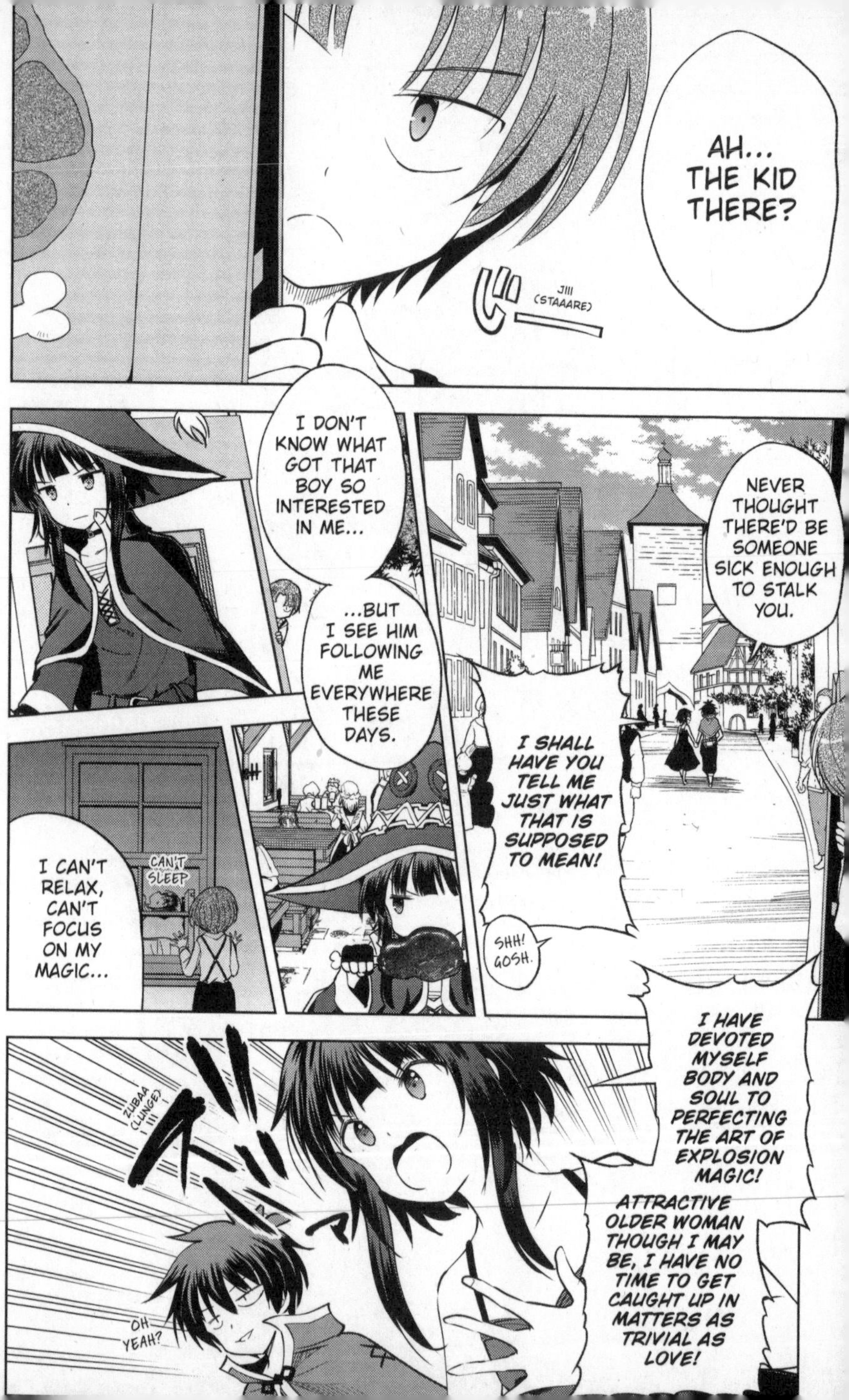
AH... THE KID THERE?
JIII (STAAARE)
NEVER THOUGHT THERE'D BE SOMEONE SICK ENOUGH TO STALK YOU.
I SHALL HAVE YOU TELL ME JUST WHAT THAT IS SUPPOSED TO MEAN!
SHH! GOSH.
I DON'T KNOW WHAT GOT THAT BOY SO INTERESTED IN ME...
...BUT I SEE HIM FOLLOWING ME EVERYWHERE THESE DAYS.
CAN'T SLEEP
I CAN'T RELAX, CAN'T FOCUS ON MY MAGIC...
I HAVE DEVOTED MYSELF BODY AND SOUL TO PERFECTING THE ART OF EXPLOSION MAGIC!
ATTRACTIVE OLDER WOMAN THOUGH I MAY BE, I HAVE NO TIME TO GET CAUGHT UP IN MATTERS AS TRIVIAL AS LOVE!
ZUBAA (LUNGE)
OH YEAH?

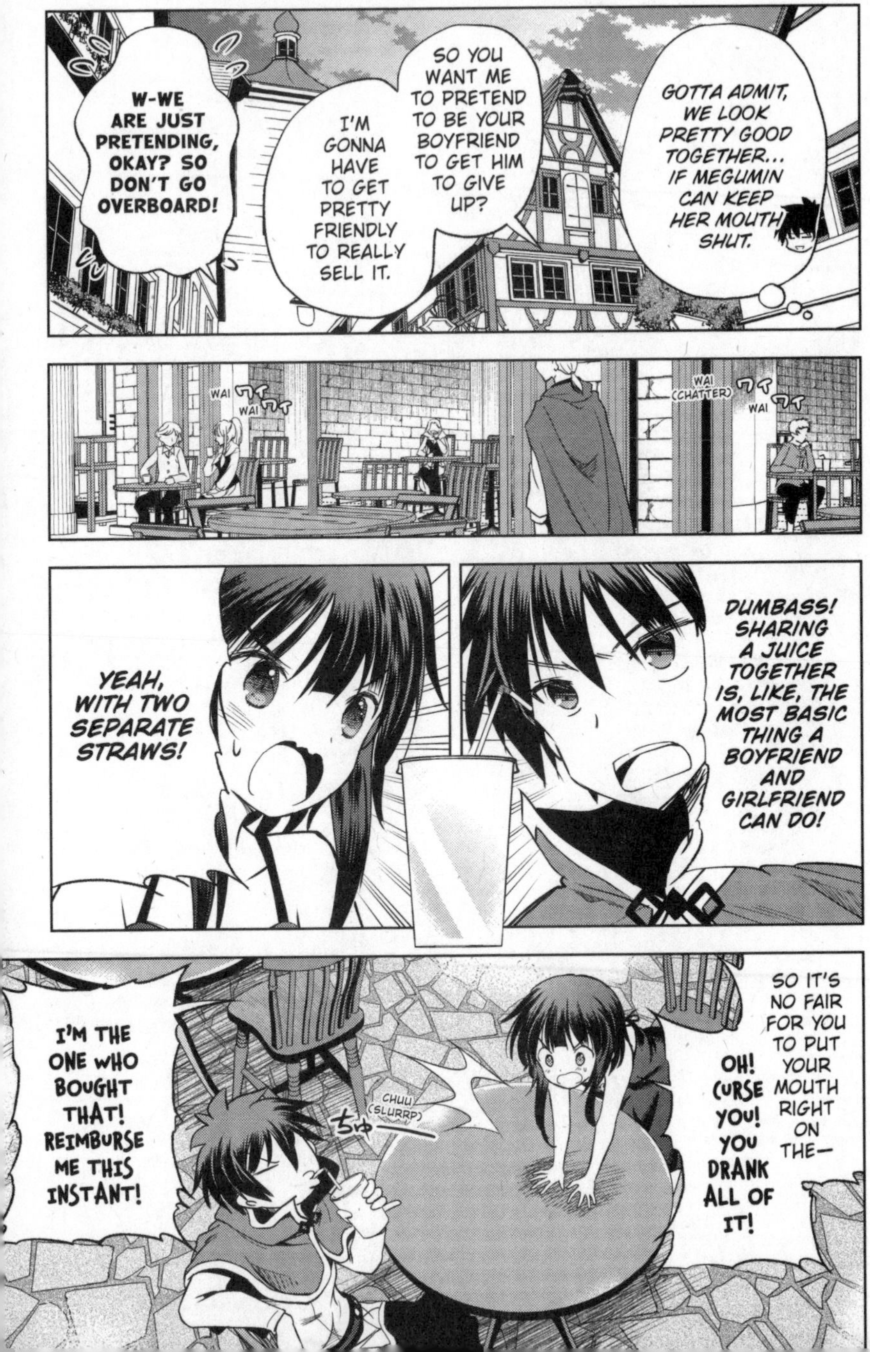
GOTTA ADMIT, WE LOOK PRETTY GOOD TOGETHER... IF MEGUMIN CAN KEEP HER MOUTH SHUT.
SO YOU WANT ME TO PRETEND TO BE YOUR BOYFRIEND TO GET HIM TO GIVE UP?
I'M GONNA HAVE TO GET PRETTY FRIENDLY TO REALLY SELL IT.
W-WE ARE JUST PRETENDING, OKAY? SO DON'T GO OVERBOARD!
WAI (CHATTER) WAI WAI
WAI WAI
DUMBASS! SHARING A JUICE TOGETHER IS, LIKE, THE MOST BASIC THING A BOYFRIEND AND GIRLFRIEND CAN DO!
YEAH, WITH TWO SEPARATE STRAWS!
SO IT'S NO FAIR FOR YOU TO PUT YOUR MOUTH RIGHT ON THE—
OH! CURSE YOU! YOU DRANK ALL OF IT!
CHUU (SLURRP)
I'M THE ONE WHO BOUGHT THAT! REIMBURSE ME THIS INSTANT!

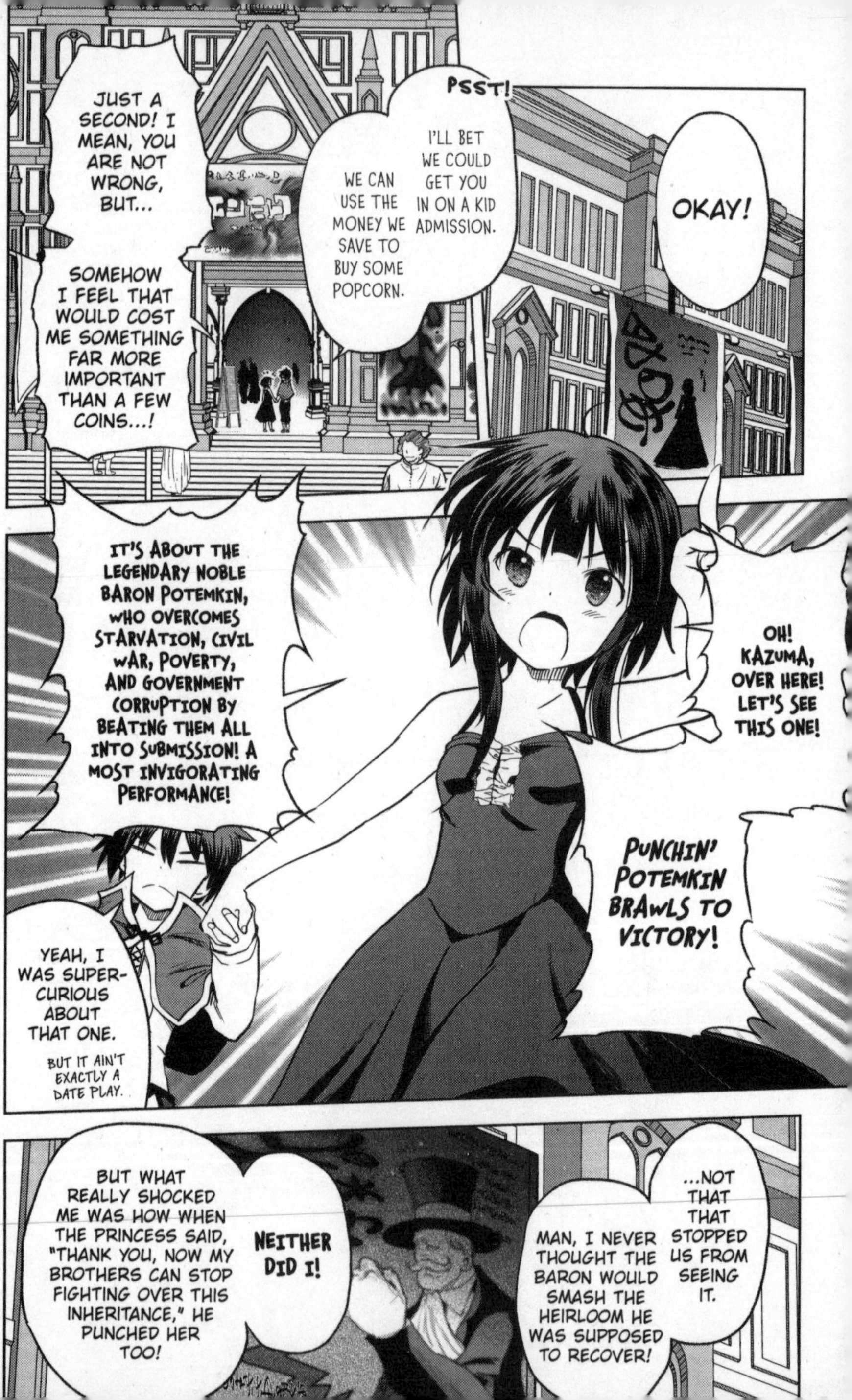
PSST!
I'LL BET WE COULD GET YOU IN ON A KID ADMISSION.
WE CAN USE THE MONEY WE SAVE TO BUY SOME POPCORN.
OKAY!
JUST A SECOND! I MEAN, YOU ARE NOT WRONG, BUT...
SOMEHOW I FEEL THAT WOULD COST ME SOMETHING FAR MORE IMPORTANT THAN A FEW COINS...!
OH! KAZUMA, OVER HERE! LET'S SEE THIS ONE!
PUNCHIN' POTEMKIN BRAWLS TO VICTORY!
IT'S ABOUT THE LEGENDARY NOBLE BARON POTEMKIN, WHO OVERCOMES STARVATION, CIVIL WAR, POVERTY, AND GOVERNMENT CORRUPTION BY BEATING THEM ALL INTO SUBMISSION! A MOST INVIGORATING PERFORMANCE!
YEAH, I WAS SUPER-CURIOUS ABOUT THAT ONE.
BUT IT AIN'T EXACTLY A DATE PLAY.
...NOT THAT THAT STOPPED US FROM SEEING IT.
MAN, I NEVER THOUGHT THE BARON WOULD SMASH THE HEIRLOOM HE WAS SUPPOSED TO RECOVER!
NEITHER DID I!
BUT WHAT REALLY SHOCKED ME WAS HOW WHEN THE PRINCESS SAID, "THANK YOU, NOW MY BROTHERS CAN STOP FIGHTING OVER THIS INHERITANCE," HE PUNCHED HER TOO!

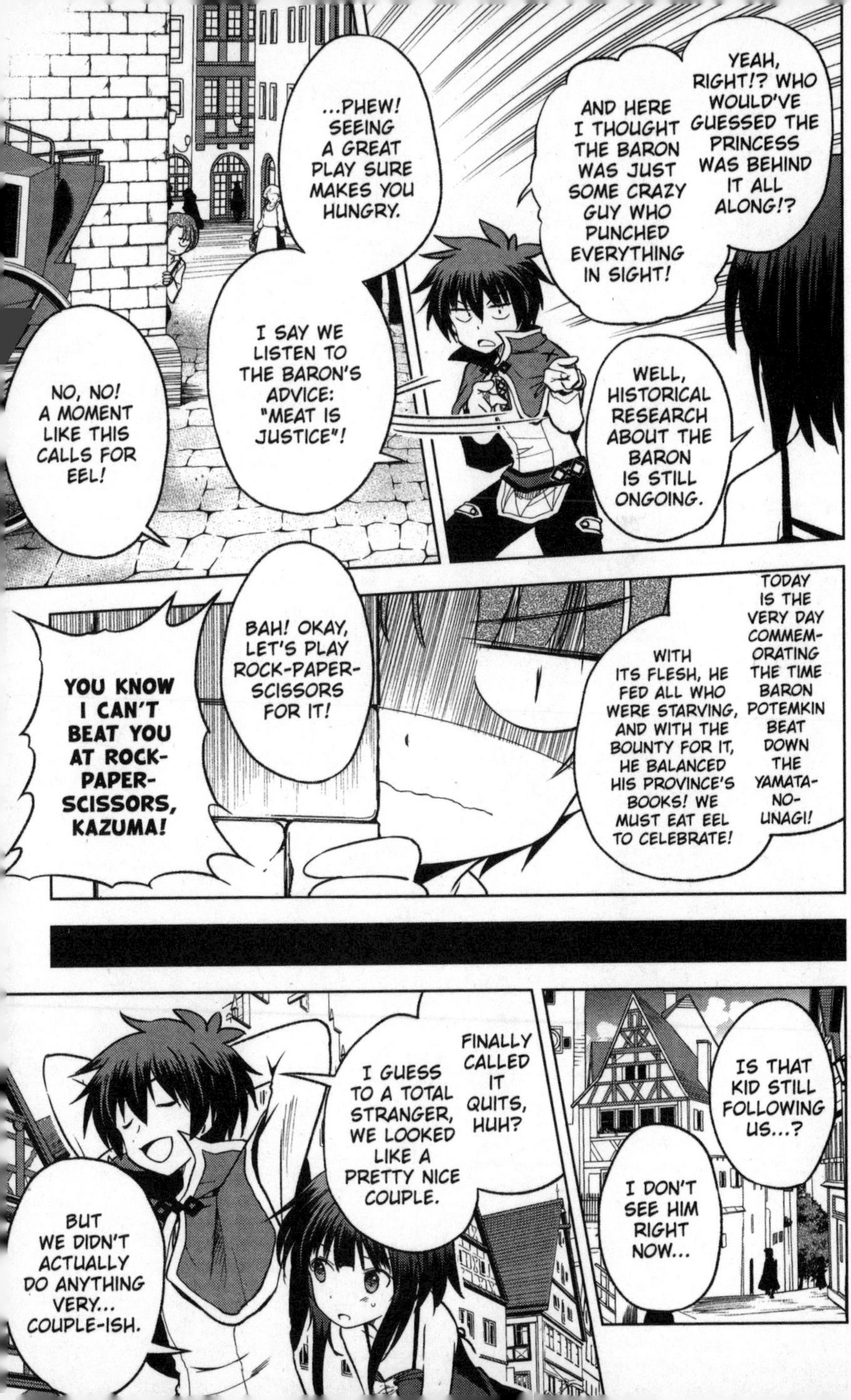
YEAH, RIGHT!? WHO WOULD'VE GUESSED THE PRINCESS WAS BEHIND IT ALL ALONG!?
AND HERE I THOUGHT THE BARON WAS JUST SOME CRAZY GUY WHO PUNCHED EVERYTHING IN SIGHT!
WELL, HISTORICAL RESEARCH ABOUT THE BARON IS STILL ONGOING.
...PHEW! SEEING A GREAT PLAY SURE MAKES YOU HUNGRY.
I SAY WE LISTEN TO THE BARON'S ADVICE: "MEAT IS JUSTICE"!
NO, NO! A MOMENT LIKE THIS CALLS FOR EEL!
TODAY IS THE VERY DAY COMMEM-ORATING THE TIME BARON POTEMKIN BEAT DOWN THE YAMATA-NO-UNAGI!
WITH ITS FLESH, HE FED ALL WHO WERE STARVING, AND WITH THE BOUNTY FOR IT, HE BALANCED HIS PROVINCE'S BOOKS! WE MUST EAT EEL TO CELEBRATE!
BAH! OKAY, LET'S PLAY ROCK-PAPER-SCISSORS FOR IT!
YOU KNOW I CAN'T BEAT YOU AT ROCK-PAPER-SCISSORS, KAZUMA!
IS THAT KID STILL FOLLOWING US...?
I DON'T SEE HIM RIGHT NOW...
FINALLY CALLED IT QUITS, HUH?
I GUESS TO A TOTAL STRANGER, WE LOOKED LIKE A PRETTY NICE COUPLE.
BUT WE DIDN'T ACTUALLY DO ANYTHING VERY... COUPLE-ISH.

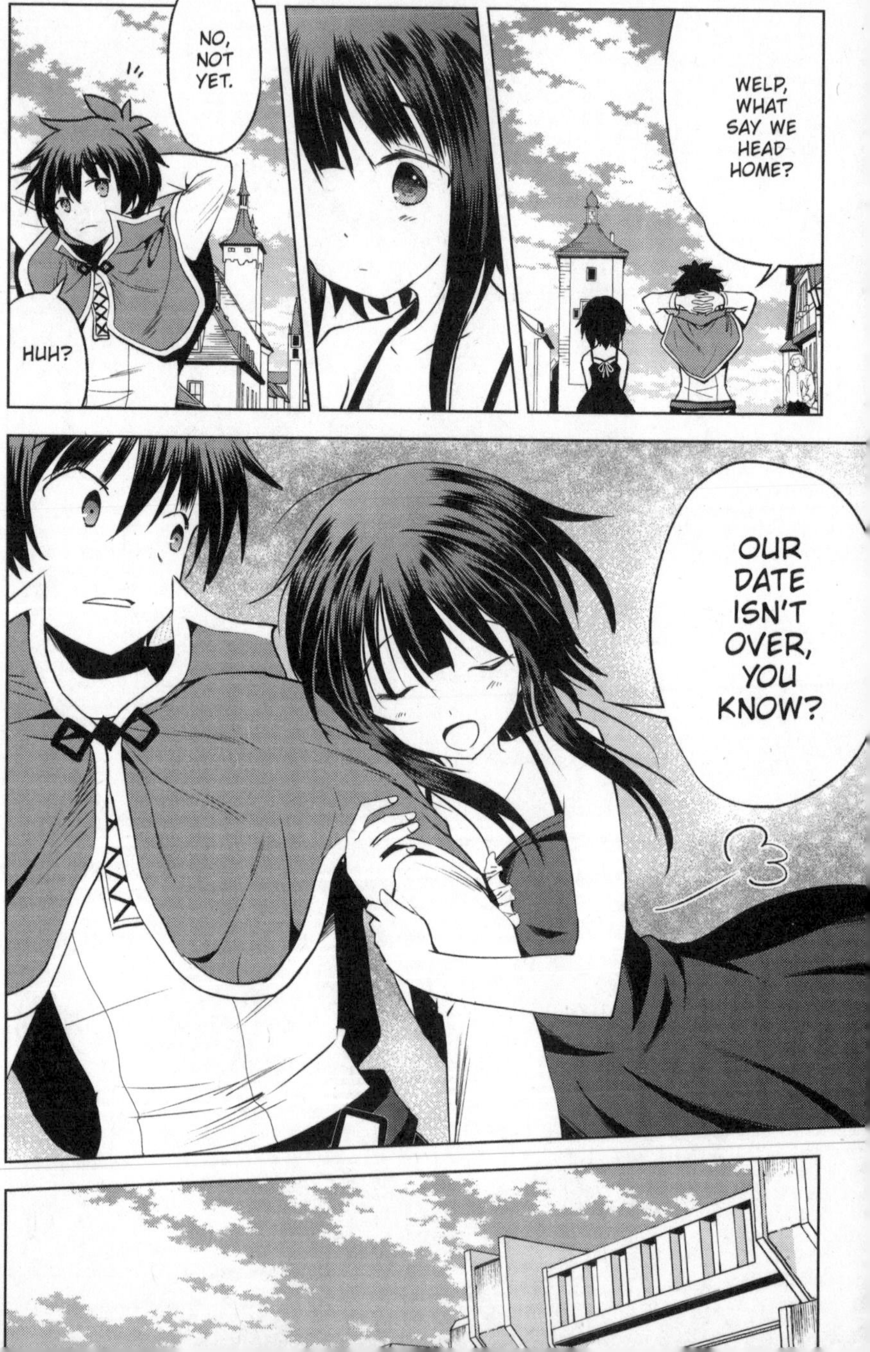
WELP, WHAT SAY WE HEAD HOME?
NO, NOT YET.
HUH?
OUR DATE ISN'T OVER, YOU KNOW?

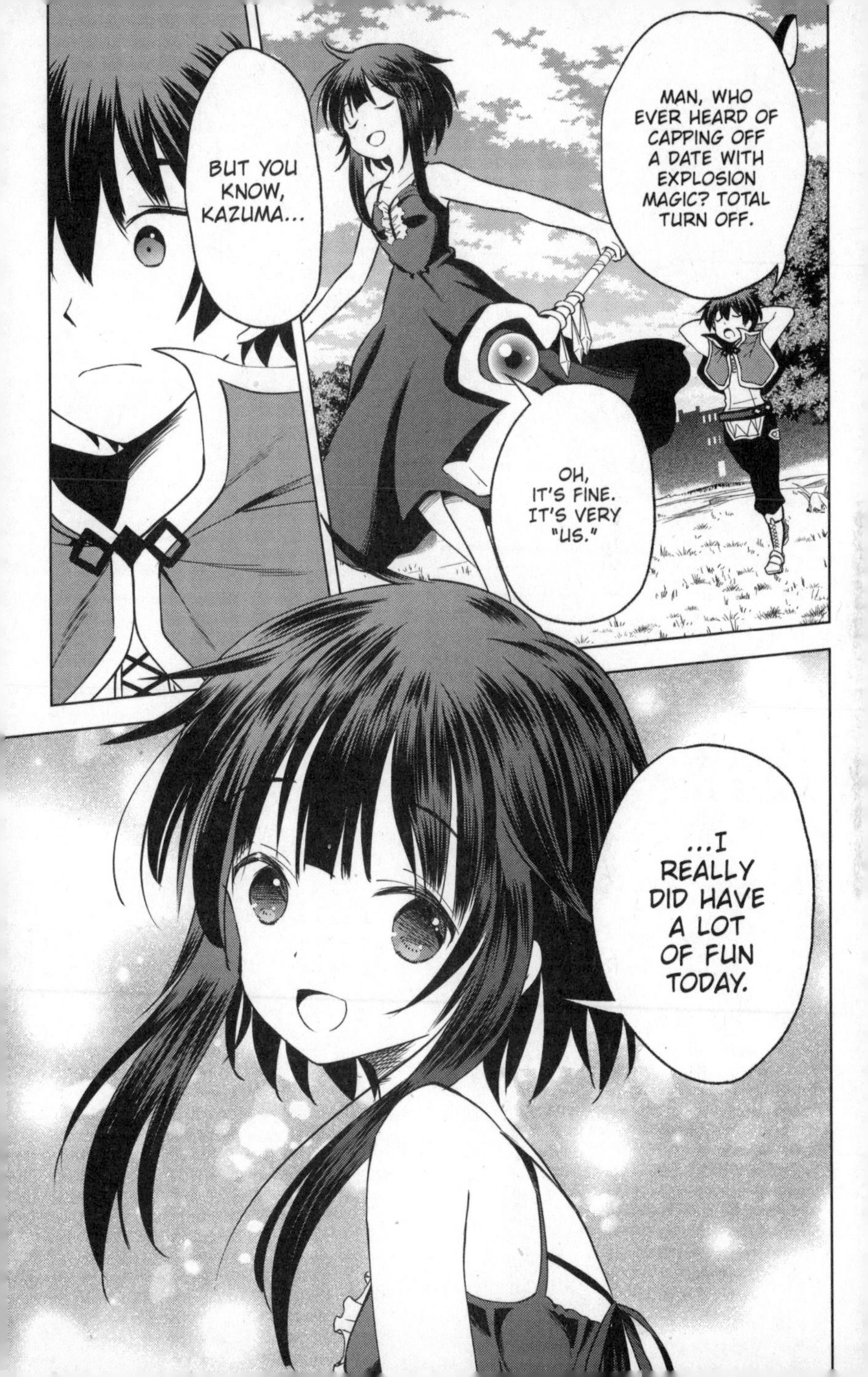
MAN, WHO EVER HEARD OF CAPPING OFF A DATE WITH EXPLOSION MAGIC? TOTAL TURN OFF.
OH, IT'S FINE. IT'S VERY "US."
BUT YOU KNOW, KAZUMA...
...I REALLY DID HAVE A LOT OF FUN TODAY.

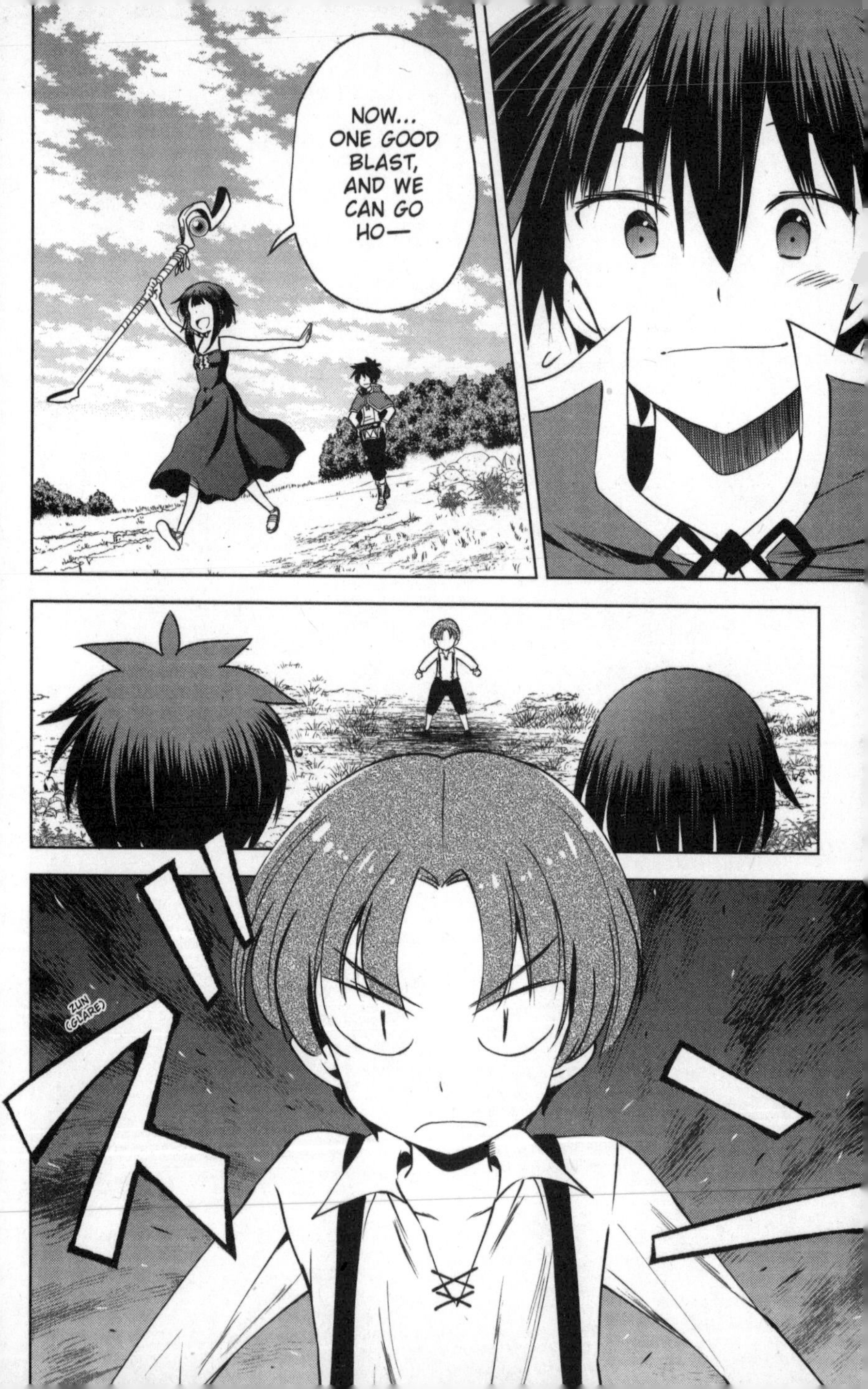
NOW... ONE GOOD BLAST, AND WE CAN GO HO—
ZUN (GLARE)

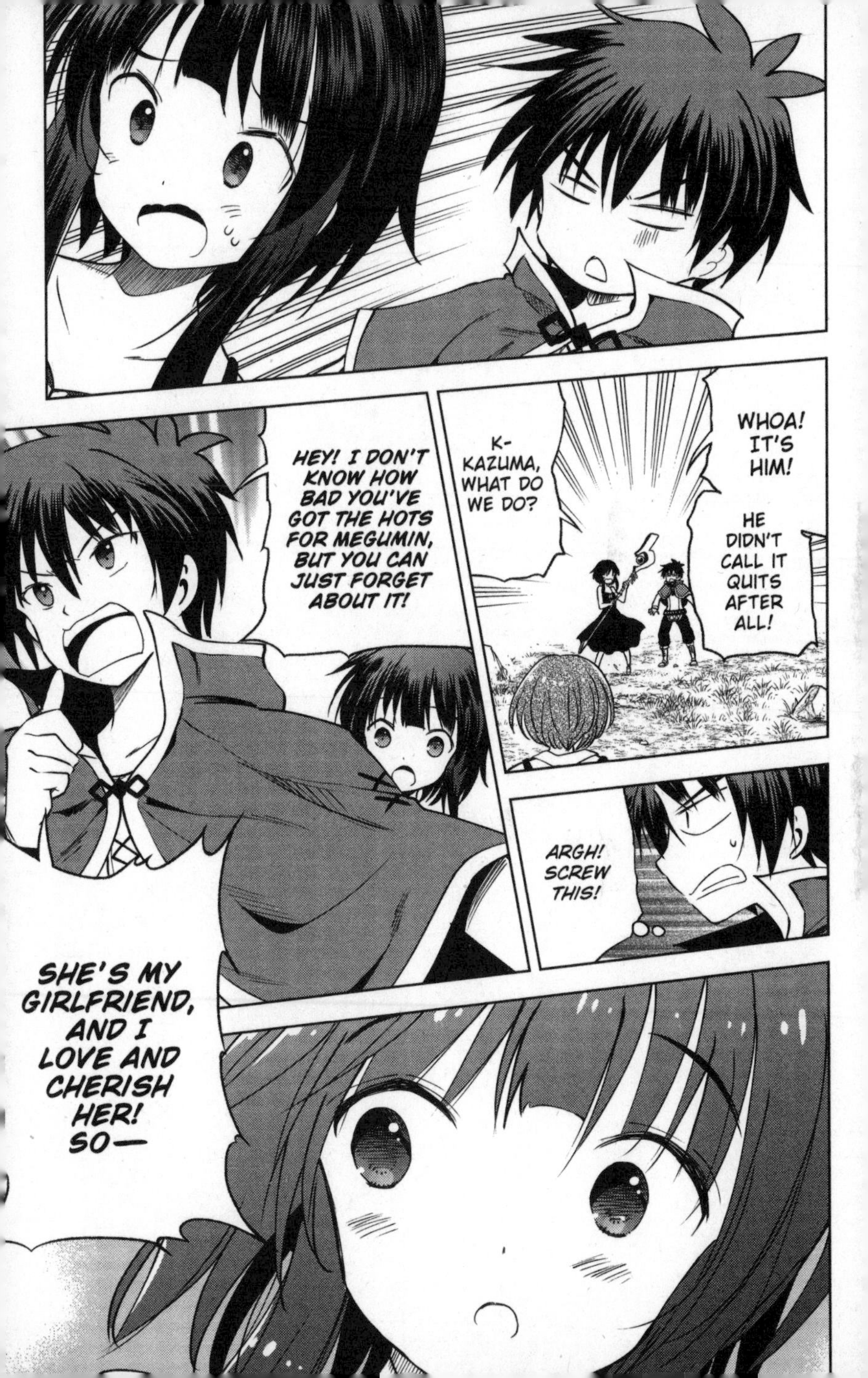
WHOA! IT'S HIM!
HE DIDN'T CALL IT QUITS AFTER ALL!
K-KAZUMA, WHAT DO WE DO?
ARGH! SCREW THIS!
HEY! I DON'T KNOW HOW BAD YOU'VE GOT THE HOTS FOR MEGUMIN, BUT YOU CAN JUST FORGET ABOUT IT!
SHE'S MY GIRLFRIEND, AND I LOVE AND CHERISH HER! SO—

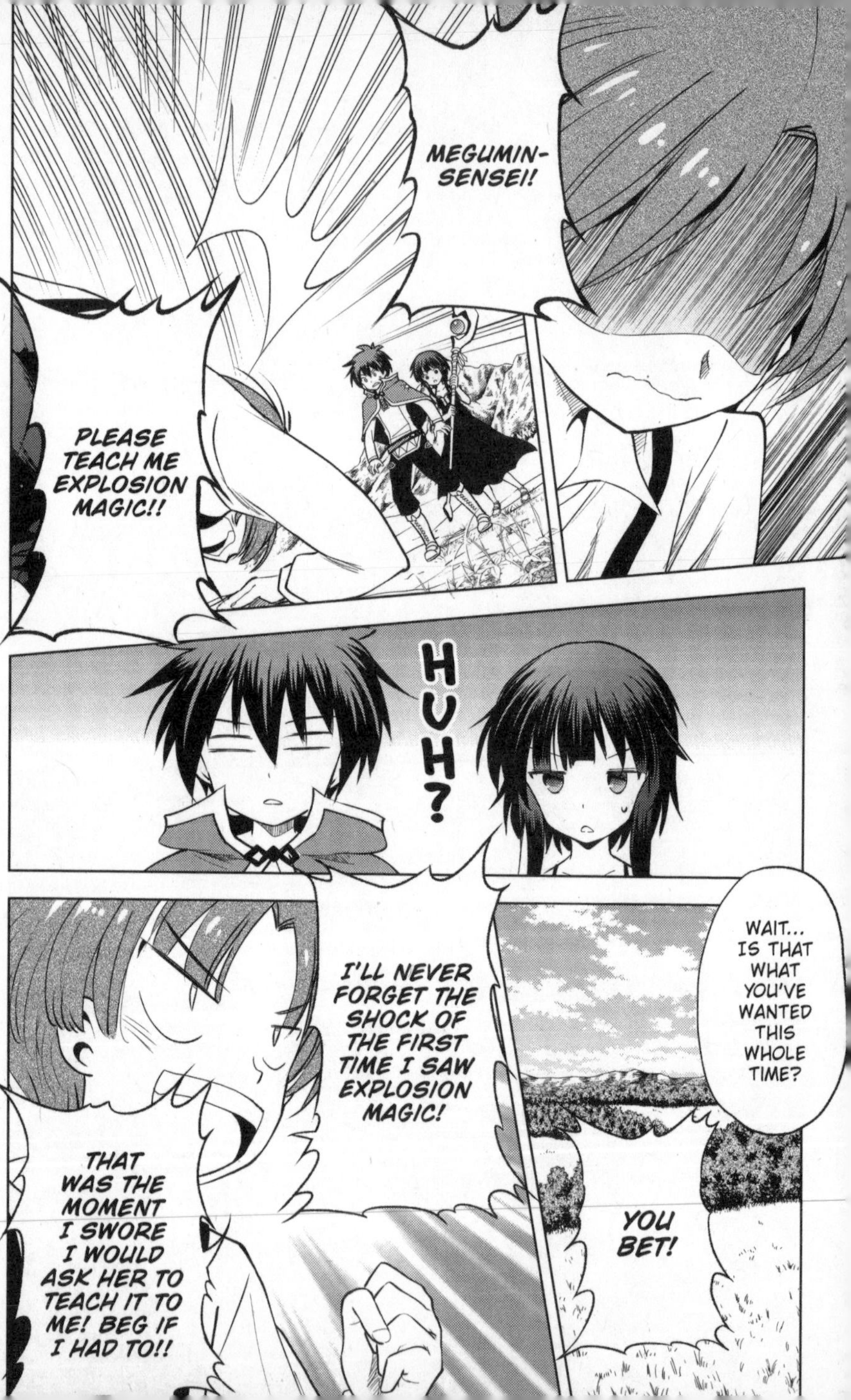
MEGUMIN-SENSEI!
PLEASE TEACH ME EXPLOSION MAGIC!!
HUH?
WAIT... IS THAT WHAT YOU'VE WANTED THIS WHOLE TIME?
YOU BET!
I'LL NEVER FORGET THE SHOCK OF THE FIRST TIME I SAW EXPLOSION MAGIC!
THAT WAS THE MOMENT I SWORE I WOULD ASK HER TO TEACH IT TO ME! BEG IF I HAD TO!!

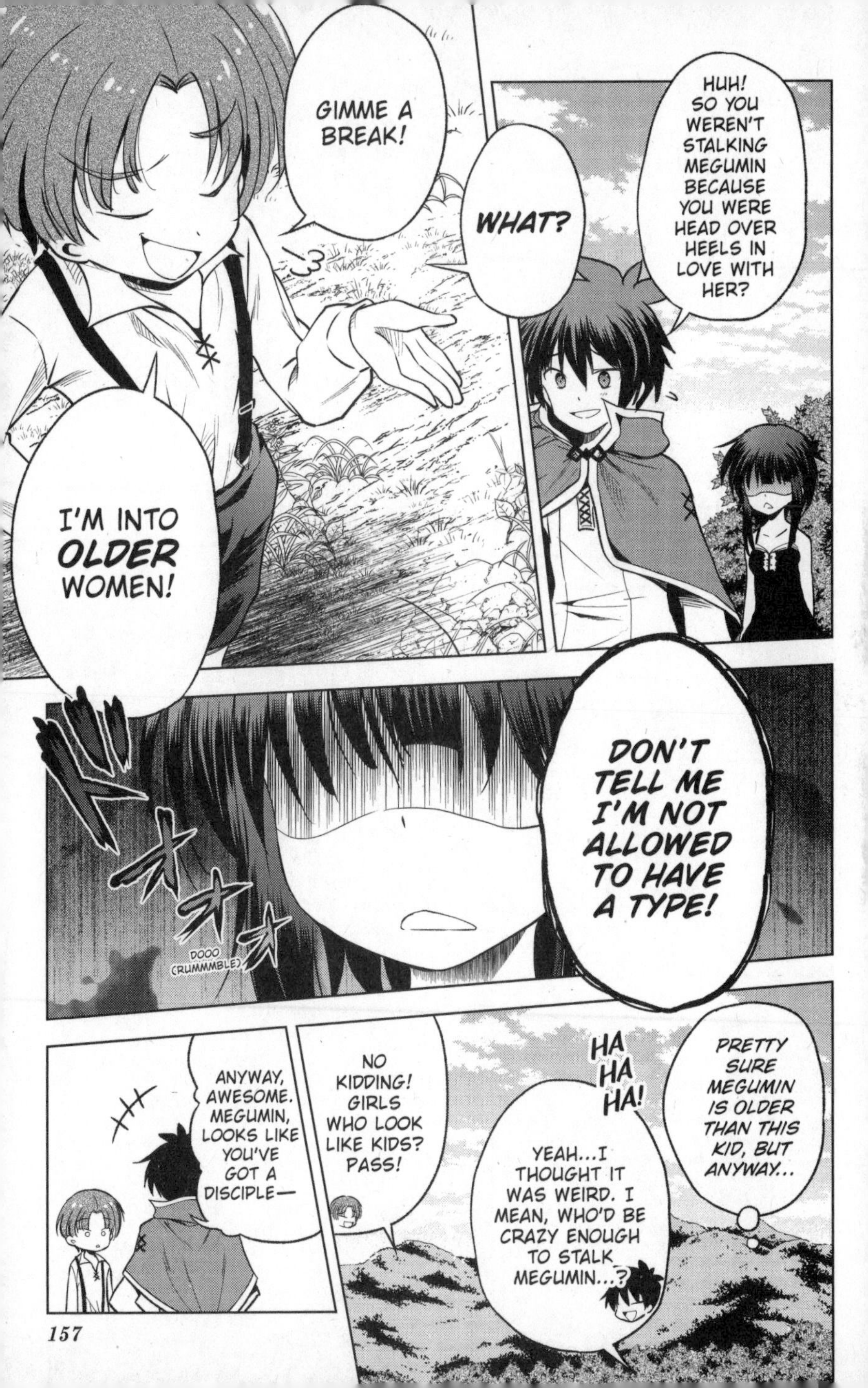
HUH! SO YOU WEREN'T STALKING MEGUMIN BECAUSE YOU WERE HEAD OVER HEELS IN LOVE WITH HER?
WHAT?
GIMME A BREAK!
I'M INTO OLDER WOMEN!
DON'T TELL ME I'M NOT ALLOWED TO HAVE A TYPE!
DOOO (RUMMMBLE)
PRETTY SURE MEGUMIN IS OLDER THAN THIS KID, BUT ANYWAY...
HA HA HA!
YEAH...I THOUGHT IT WAS WEIRD. I MEAN, WHO'D BE CRAZY ENOUGH TO STALK MEGUMIN...?
NO KIDDING! GIRLS WHO LOOK LIKE KIDS? PASS!
ANYWAY, AWESOME. MEGUMIN, LOOKS LIKE YOU'VE GOT A DISCIPLE—

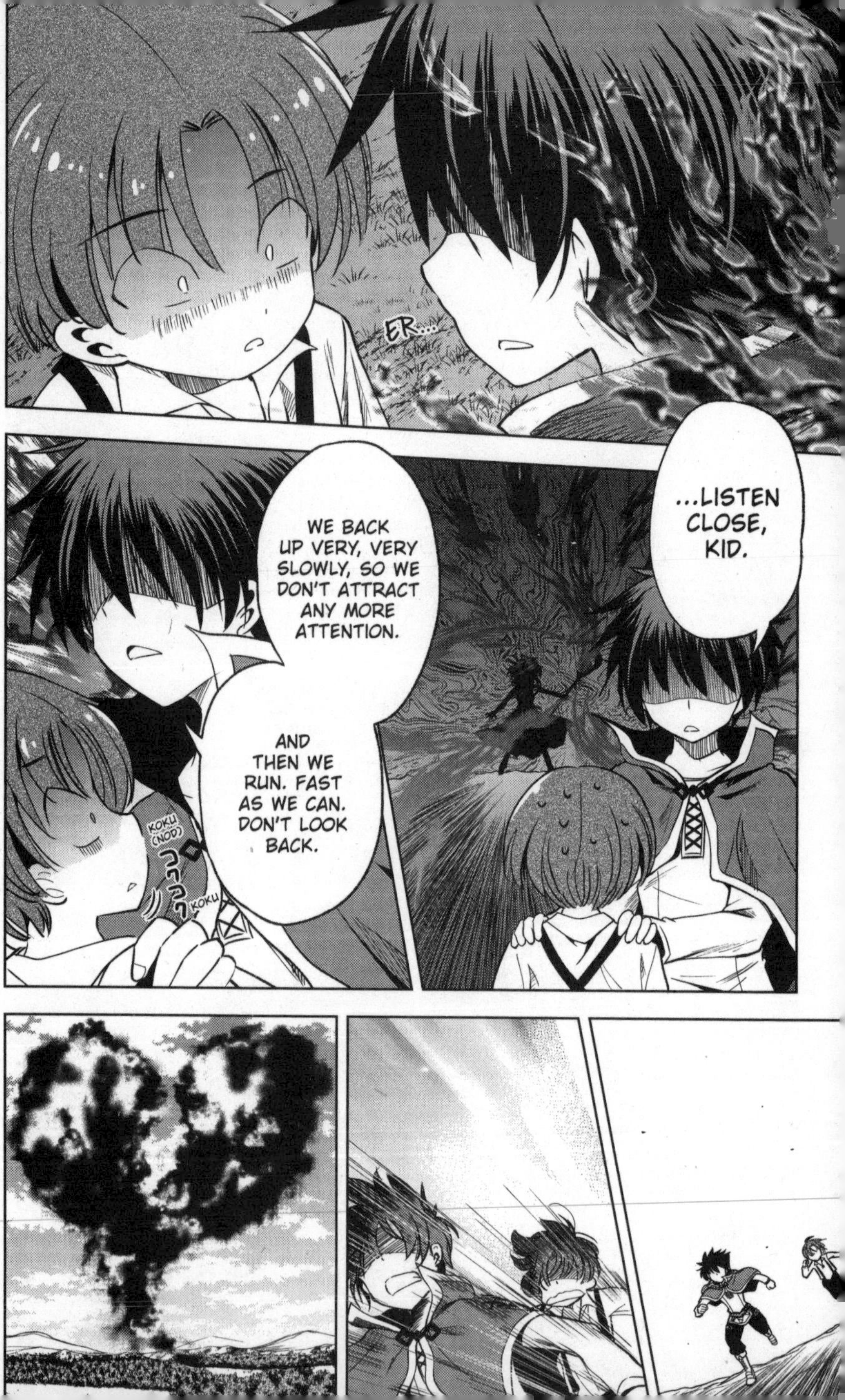
ER...
...LISTEN CLOSE, KID.
WE BACK UP VERY, VERY SLOWLY, SO WE DON'T ATTRACT ANY MORE ATTENTION.
AND THEN WE RUN. FAST AS WE CAN. DON'T LOOK BACK.
KOKU (NOD)
KOKU

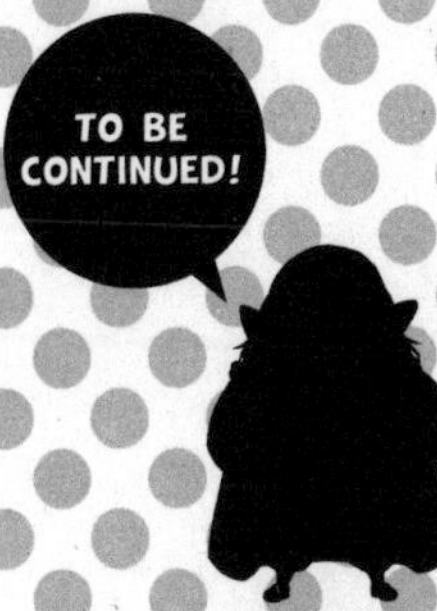
TO BE CONTINUED!

GOD'S BLESSING ON THIS WONDERFUL WORLD!

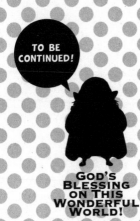

11

GOD'S
BLESSING
ON THIS
WONDERFUL
WORLD!

AFTERWORD

SO THE CAPITAL ARC COMES TO A CLOSE.
WE'LL HAVE TO SAY GOOD-BYE TO PRINCESS IRIS FOR A WHILE, BUT I'VE BEEN PLAYING THE JAPANESE *KONOFAN* GAME ON MY PHONE, WHERE SHE SHOWS UP—WITH VOICE! SO I'M NOT LONELY AT ALL. *KONOFAN* IS GREAT, BY THE WAY!
STARTING NEXT VOLUME, WE'LL SEE THE DISTANCE BETWEEN KAZUMA AND DARKNESS BEGIN TO SHRINK A LITTLE BIT.
HOPE TO SEE YOU IN VOLUME 12!

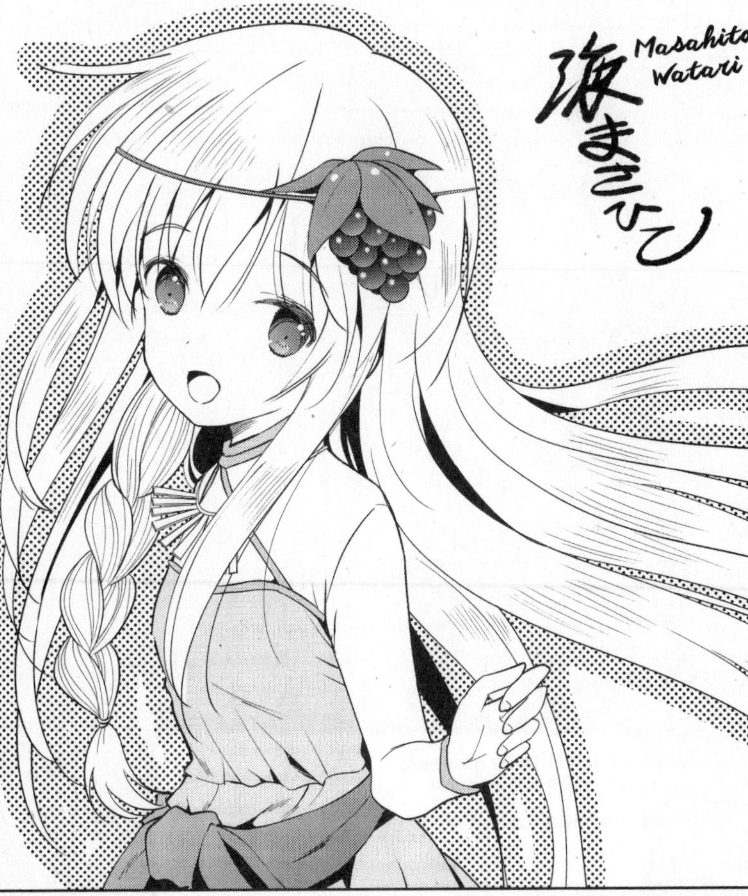
Masahito Watari

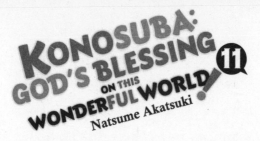

KONOSUBA: GOD'S BLESSING ON THIS WONDERFUL WORLD! 11

Natsume Akatsuki

TRANSLATION: Kevin Steinbach 💬 **LETTERING: Rochelle Gancio**

This book is a work of fiction. Names, characters, places, and incidents are the product of the author's imagination or are used fictitiously. Any resemblance to actual events, locales, or persons, living or dead, is coincidental.

KONO SUBARASHII SEKAI NI SYUKUFUKU WO! Volume 11
©Masahito Watari 2020
©Natsume Akatsuki, Kurone Mishima 2020
First published in Japan in 2020 by Kadokawa Corporation, Tokyo. English translation rights arranged with KADOKAWA Corporation, Tokyo through Tuttle-Mori Agency, Inc., Tokyo.

English translation © 2020 by Yen Press, LLC

Yen Press
150 West 30th Street, 19th Floor
New York, NY 10001

Visit us at yenpress.com
facebook.com/yenpress
twitter.com/yenpress
yenpress.tumblr.com
instagram.com/yenpress

First Yen Press Edition: December 2020

Yen Press is an imprint of Yen Press, LLC.
The Yen Press name and logo are trademarks of Yen Press, LLC.

The publisher is not responsible for websites (or their content) that are not owned by the publisher.

Library of Congress Control Number: 2016946112

ISBNs:

10 9 8

WOR

Printed